The Politics of Public–Private Partnerships in Western Europe

The Politics of Public–Private Partnerships in Western Europe

Comparative Perspectives

Thomas Krumm

Assistant Professor, Turkish-German University, Istanbul, Turkey

Edward Elgar PUBLISHING

Cheltenham, UK • Northampton, MA, USA

Published by
Edward Elgar Publishing Limited
The Lypiatts
15 Lansdown Road
Cheltenham
Glos GL50 2JA
UK

Edward Elgar Publishing, Inc.
William Pratt House
9 Dewey Court
Northampton
Massachusetts 01060
USA

A catalogue record for this book
is available from the British Library

Library of Congress Control Number: 2015954318

This book is available electronically in the **Elgar**online
Social and Political Science subject collection
DOI 10.4337/9781782549260

MIX
Paper from
responsible sources
FSC
www.fsc.org
FSC® C013056

ISBN 978 1 78254 925 3 (cased)
ISBN 978 1 78254 926 0 (eBook)

Typeset by Columns Design XML Ltd, Reading
Printed and bound in Great Britain by TJ International Ltd, Padstow

Contents

Preface vii
List of abbreviations ix

1 Introduction 1

2 PPP as a political issue 6
2.1 The politics of PPP 6
2.2 Many assumptions, less reliable knowledge 9
2.3 The impact of the 2008 global financial crisis 11
2.4 PPP at EU level and in Eastern Europe 15

3 PPP in Western Europe: challenges for comparative research 21
3.1 Research design 21
3.2 Dependent variable: PPP activity 23
3.3 Institutional variables 26
3.4 Socioeconomic agenda setters 31
3.5 Control variables 36
3.6 Comparative findings 42

4 The Nordic countries 53
4.1 Denmark 53
4.2 Finland 58
4.3 Sweden 61
4.4 Case comparison 65

5 United Kingdom and Ireland 67
5.1 United Kingdom 67
5.2 Ireland 81
5.3 Case comparison 92

6 Belgium and the Netherlands 96
6.1 Belgium 96
6.2 The Netherlands 105
6.3 Case comparison 111

7 Germany and Austria 114
7.1 Germany 114
7.2 Austria 133
7.3 Case comparison 140

8 France and Italy 144
8.1 France 144
8.2 Italy 157
8.3 Case comparison 168

9 The Iberian Peninsula and Greece 171
9.1 Portugal 171
9.2 Spain 180
9.3 Greece 189
9.4 Case comparison 199

10 Conclusion 206
10.1 Comparing socioeconomic factors 206
10.2 Comparing political and institutional factors 207
10.3 Comparing policy diffusion 212
10.4 Privatized Keynesianism? 214

References 221
Index 239

Preface

Despite the growing research output on public–private partnerships (PPPs), there is less systematic comparison of the PPP policies and politics of European governments. Edited volumes provide a collection of in depth case studies rather than a systematic comparison and scholarly articles mostly focus on details within one or two countries or cases. Against this background, the motivation for this book is to mitigate the gap in comparative research on PPP and to integrate the results of different branches of research on PPPs in Western Europe. Quite often, research on PPP is divided into different branches such as legal and institutional aspects, management, economic and financial dimensions and, last but not least, public policy analysis and politics research. Thus, there is a broad range of disciplines, such as economics, area studies and public policy, which often ignore the genuine political dimension of PPP as well as a comparative perspective.

Quite often, the strongest political support for PPP has been provided by individual politicians such as Gordon Brown in the United Kingdom (UK), Gerhard Schröder in Germany, Nikolas Sarkozy in France or Silvio Berlusconi in Italy. However, for a 'sustainable' institutionalization of PPP in a country it takes much more than the commitment of some leading politicians. Some of these factors of influence for the implementation of the PPP approach will be analysed in the course of this book. Due to the complexity of the matter, the focus of interest is on a selection of institutional, socioeconomic and political variables.

Focusing on the 'politics of PPP' in this book aims to raise awareness that PPP is not a 'naturally grown product' of politics but a result of political decision making based on public and private interests and facilitated or hampered by contextual conditions. Politics is about decision making, and political decisions often influence the 'performance' of public and private organizations and institutions. Political decision making has a distributive dimension, as politics influences 'who gets what, when and how' (Dye 1976). PPP supporters often argue that the sceptics simply ignore the benefits of public–private collaboration (such as efficiency gains), while PPP sceptics stress the negative impact on public sovereignty and social equality. Against such often normatively biased debates, the book aims to focus empirically on political drivers and stoppers of PPP in the context of institutional and socioeconomic factors. It does not try to answer questions of efficiency of PPP or even normative ones of the (un)desirability of PPP.

Instead, the book aims to systematically investigate factors explaining the different levels of PPP activity in Western Europe between 1990 and 2009, thereby building on qualitative and quantitative methods. In this macro-comparative approach country studies play an important role and cover aspects of the socioeconomic background, partisanship and institutional context as well as patterns of PPP politics at national and regional level. The book aims to bring together socioeconomic, regional, administrative and policy aspects under the encompassing title of 'The Politics of PPP'.

In a comparative perspective, we look in the first chapters for factors explaining the different intensities of PPP use in a sample of 14 Western European countries. We look for differences and similarities in political patterns concerning the use of PPP and investigate how these differences can be explained. Among others, we empirically test factors such as partisanship, veto players, structure of interest groups, and public finances. In the remaining chapters, comparative case studies are conducted in order to qualitatively test the results from the earlier quantitative chapter. Here, the comparison is based on a pairwise case selection, trying to put together cases with similar features in their test conditions such as unitary or federal structures. However, two groups encompass three cases: in the north of Europe, policies and politics of the Scandinavian states are often closely interconnected, and in the south, countries like Spain, Portugal and Greece often face similar challenges due to their location at the southern European 'periphery'. Surprisingly, the countries of the northern group are the least committed in terms of PPP policy support, while the southerners are among the most committed. The central European states are somewhere in between, with the UK forming an outlier in terms of PPP policy support. The book aims to contribute to the question: what are the factors that lead to this variation?

Finally, I would like to express my deep gratitude to the Fritz Thyssen Foundation (Cologne, Germany) and the Leverhulme Trust (London, UK). The Leverhulme Trust enabled me to spend a year at the University of Kent at Canterbury to study the PPP/PFI phenomenon in the UK, its European 'epicentre'. The Fritz Thyssen Foundation enabled further research at the Chemnitz University of Technology, Chair of European Government Systems in Comparison. Without their support (and that of many others), this book would have not been realized.

Abbreviations

AGIOn	Agentschap voor Infrastructuur in het Onderwijs (Belgium)
ANAS	Azienda Autonoma Nazionale delle Strade (Italy)
ASFINAG	Autobahnen- und Schnellstraßen-Finanzierungs-Aktiengesellschaft (the Autobahn and highway financing stock corporation) (Austria)
BAM	Beheersmaatschappij Antwerp Mobiel (Belgium)
BEA	Bail Emphytéotique Administratifs
BEH	Bail Emphytéotique Hospitalier (French hospital PPP)
BOO	Build, Own, Operate
BOT	Build, Own, Transfer
BZÖ	Bündnis Zukunft Österreich (Alliance Future Austria)
CDU	Christian Democratic Union (Germany)
CECOPP	Centro Español de Excelencia y Conocimiento de la Colaboración Público Privada (Spain)
CEF-O-PPP	Centre d'expertise français pour l'observation des partenariats public-privé (France)
CIF	Cellule d'Informations Financières (Belgium)
CIPE	Comitato interministeriale per la programmazione economica (Inter-Ministerial Committee for Economic Planning) (Italy)
CRESME	Centro Ricerche Economiche Sociali di Mercato per l'Edilizia e il Territorio (Italy)
CSF	Community Support Framework (Greece)
CSU	Christian Social Union (Germany)
DBFM	Design, Build, Finance, Maintain
DBFO	Design, Build, Finance, Operate
DBOT	Design, Build, Operate, Transfer
DKK	Danish Krona
ECB	European Central Bank
EIB	European Investment Bank
EP	Estradas de Portugal (Portugal)

EPEC	European PPP Expertise Centre at the EIB
EPPPR	European PPP Report of the European PPP Expertise Centre
EU	European Union
FAZ	Frankfurter Allgemeine Zeitung
FG	Fine Gael (Ireland)
FF	Fianna Fáil (Ireland)
FI	Forza Italia (Italy)
FPÖ	Freiheitliche Partei Österreichs (Freedom Party of Austria) (Austria)
GDP	Gross domestic product
GVA	Gross value added
ICT	Information and communication technologies
IGD	Institut de la gestion déléguée (France)
IMF	International Monetary Fund
IUK	Infrastructure UK (succeeded PUK)
LTIF	Long-term investment funds
MAPPP	Mission d'appui à la réalisation des partenariats public-privé (French PPP unit)
MURCEF	Portant mesures urgentes de réformes à caractère économique et financier (French law)
ND	Nea Dimokratia (Greece)
NDFA	National Development Finance Agency (Ireland)
NHS	National Health Service (UK)
NPD	Non-Profit Distributing (Scotland)
NPFO	National Project Financing Observatory (Italy)
NPM	New Public Management
NZZ	Neue Zürcher Zeitung
OECD	Organisation for Economic Co-operation and Development
OTF	Operational Task Force (UK)
ÖVP	Österreichische Volkspartei (Austrian People's Party)
PASOK	Panhellenic Socialist Movement (Greece)
PFI	Private Finance Initiative (UK)
PF2	Private Finance 2 (Revised PFI) (UK)
PP	Partido Popular (People's Party) (Spain)
PPP	Public–private partnership
PR	Proportional representation
PRG	Project Review Group (UK)
PSOE	Partido Socialista Obrero Español (Spanish Socialist Party) (Spain)
PUK	Partnerships UK (UK)

QCA	Qualitative Comparative Analysis
SCUT	Sem Custos para o Utilizador (without direct user costs) (Portugal)
SD	Standard Deviation
SEK	Swedish Krona
SEOPAN	Asociación de Empresas Constructoras de Ámbito Nacional (Spain)
SFT	Scottish Future Trust
SIOP	Sistema Informativo sulle Opportunità di PPP (Italy)
SNP	Scottish National Party (UK)
SOE	State-owned enterprise
SPD	Social Democratic Party (Germany)
SPÖ	Sozialdemokratische Partei Österreichs (Social Democratic Party of Austria) (Austria)
SPV	Special Purpose Vehicle
UK	United Kingdom
UMP	Union pour un Movement Populaire (Union for a Popular Movement) (France)
US	United States of America
UTFP	Unità Tecnica Finanza di Progetto (Italian PPP Task Force)
VAT	Value added tax
VfM	Value for Money
VIFG	Verkehrsinfrastrukturfinanzierungsgesellschaft mbH (Transport Infrastructure Financing Corporation) (Germany)

1. Introduction

If the saying 'there's life in the old dog yet' is true, then the Public–Private Partnership (PPP) approach to public procurement and service delivery still has its time. PPPs have received much scholarly attention from a broad spectrum of disciplines; and they have faced considerable scepticism in a lot of countries. In others, under certain governments, they have been pushed forwards and even sometimes regarded as 'the only game in town'. In terms of party politics, it is difficult to characterize them as more favoured by centre-right or centre-left governments. In the United Kingdom (UK), they were championed by the incoming New Labour government, commencing in 1997; Germany under the 'red–green' coalitions joined them soon thereafter. However, Italy under Berlusconi, France under Sarkozy, Spain under Aznar, Greece under Karamanlis and Austria under Schüssel are examples of centre-right governments strongly committed to the PPP approach, too. Even the UK under the conservative Major administration and later under the Cameron–Clegg coalition was supportive of PPP, or the Private Finance Initiative (PFI) as it was labelled in the early 1990s by the British government. Thus, one of the aims of this book is to analyse the partisan dimensions of support or obstruction of PPP across a sample of 14 states over the period 1990 to 2009. However, political parties are not the only actors who 'make politics'. As an economic policy tool favouring the involvement of private, commercially operating corporations instead of pure fulfilment by public administration, private sector corporations and lobbying groups can be expected to have an interest in supporting the PPP approach.

However, it would be too simple to focus only on their motivation of expanding their markets and accordingly raising their profits. Such motivations can be assumed to exist more or less in each market economy. But with regard to PPP, only in some countries during certain periods of time they appear to have been successful. This raises the question of further conditions that must be met in order to achieve a change of government policy. The early UK experiences under the Major government (abolishment of the Ryrie rules, see section 5.1.2) might be instructive for such a process. Other politico-economic factors are the level of public debt as well as deficit and the privatization activity exercised in a country (see section 3.5). More generally speaking, 'The Politics of PPP' aims to more deeply explore some of the factors that are supportive of a policy change in favour of PPP. Written by a political scientist, this book does not try to evaluate technical, financial or managerial aspects of single projects or even ask if they are really 'value for money' (VfM). Instead, it simply asks why did some countries' governments participate in this policy change (some sooner, some later), and others not? Therefore, it quantitatively and qualitatively tests a set of variables which in the literature are regarded to be responsible for such policy changes.

Initially, we have to introduce the basics of the PPP approach. In a general sense, PPPs can be described as 'forms of cooperation between public authorities and the world of business which aim to ensure the funding, construction, renovation, management or maintenance of an infrastructure or the provision of a service' (European Commission 2004: 3). The term PPP is also applied to forms of cooperation between public and private non-profit, civil society actors. However, in these cases the logic of action as well as organization deviates heavily from that of for-profit PPPs. This book is primarily focused on contract-based PPPs between public and commercial private actors.

PPP arrangements are characterized by a relatively long, fixed duration of contract time or permanent (organizational) models of the relationship between the public and the private partner (life-cycle approach), often complex funding arrangements with the private sector bearing the initial costs and long-time responsibility for operation and maintenance, whereas the public sector is in charge of the long-time refinancing of the private partner either by (regularly) fixed direct transfers or by (shadow) tolls or user fees. Most importantly, the public partner is in charge of selecting and determining objectives to be regarded as in the public interest, the quality of the respective services to be provided by private partners, and the pricing policy; and finally, the public partner takes responsibility for monitoring compliance with the objectives previously set (ibid.).

Furthermore, the distribution of risks between the partners has to be addressed sufficiently. This means, for instance, that for each phase of a PPP the kind of risk transferred (or shared) between the public and private partners has to be addressed during the negotiations and in the contract (Grimsey/Lewis 2005c). Regarding the operational phase, for instance, southern European concession models often preferred to transfer the demand risk to the private sector, while British PFI contracts tended to transfer the availability risk. Thus, besides the financial aspects, risk transfer is often a crucial point during contract negotiation.

Given the complex structures of PPP policies and projects, it cannot be the aim of this book to evaluate possible merits or shortcomings of the PPP approach in general or of individual projects (such as, for instance, the Transport for London contracts in the early 2000s). Rather, the book aims to comparatively analyse what governments do (in the field of PPP), why they do it and what differences it makes, in a similar way to how Thomas R. Dye (1976) concisely described the purpose of policy analysis. However, this perspective of policy analysis has to be complemented by elements of an institutional analysis. Both institutional and policy aspects can best be integrated into a comparative approach. The comparative perspective should help to broaden the still predominant focus of (idiosyncratic) within-country analysis to a between-country comparison. To avoid the shortcomings of classical methods of policy analysis, which were often designed for within-case analysis, wherever possible we try to introduce a comparative perspective.

Policy analysis often focuses on types of policies in terms of their (re)distributive effects, as addressed by Theodore Lowi (1964, 1972) in his classical contribution. Whereas distributive policies are not a zero-sum game, redistributive policies are. Clearly, redistributive policies raise more concerns and obstruction among the addressees of such policies. However, it has to be discussed in more detail whether PPP covers more aspects of a distributive or a redistributive policy. Shifting tasks and services partly from the public to the private sector suggests a redistributive aspect. From the perspective of its critics, the redistributive dimension is stressed (such as the transfer of jobs from the public to the private sector), whereas its supporters primarily point at the distributive aspects of, for instance, added value, efficiency gains and (at least in short term) positive effects on the public budget.

From a comparative perspective, such questions appear less relevant. Comparative politics has its own set of quantitative and qualitative instruments, often combined in a mixed methods approach. As the units of (comparative) analysis are countries, or states, the focus of interest shifts from individual projects to the overall politics and policies of PPP within a state in order to find out patterns and correlations between states in the use of such policies. If a government initiates PPP projects or laws, sets up PPP units or task forces, or outlines respective policy programmes, this indicates the commitment of the cabinet to PPP. Thus, in this book it can often only be reported what kind of project, at what time and with what volume a certain government has commissioned PPP. For a single country study this would be insufficient; for a macro-comparative approach this appears to be appropriate as this book is not the place to deliberate on all the internal complexity of the 14 countries and their projects.

In this context, tools of policy analysis will have their place alongside comparative instruments such as pairwise case comparison, veto player (or institutional) analysis and applying basic assumptions of the governance approach. Chapter 2 will help to set the research focus on the politics of PPP in Western Europe while Chapter 3 addresses methodological issues and conducts a quantitative comparison based on country data published by a European Investment Bank (EIB) report. The global financial crisis, commencing with the collapse of Lehman Brothers in September 2008, and its impact on the real economy also heavily affected the use of PPP across European public authorities. The European PPP Expertise Centre (EPEC) (2011b) estimates an average annual decline of 30 per cent in the immediate aftermath of the crisis. While the impact of the global financial crisis on PPP will also be discussed in the case studies, a special section in Chapter 2 provides a general introduction to the issue.

In the following chapters, the focus is on Western Europe's central and regional governments' PPP policies (chapters 4–9). In these chapters some general characteristics of the political system which influence policy making will initially be introduced – in some cases along with facts relating to the socioeconomic background. Then, patterns of adopting the PPP approach are reconstructed, before these patterns are compared between two (or three) countries with regional or institutional proximity. The aim is to identify patterns of adoption, first at the national level and then in pairwise case comparisons. Observing patterns of policy making has to take into consideration the political aspects of decision making. Comparing policies raises the question of political determinants of observed differences. Whereas PPP itself can be regarded as a policy tool, its different forms and extents of use are also a question of politics. Furthermore, relatively invariant aspects of polity such as legal traditions and frameworks also play a role in utilizing PPPs (see section 3.3).

Each of the chapters 4 to 9 include at least two countries as cases; two chapters include three cases for comparison. For the Nordic countries the comparison of Denmark, Finland and Sweden is very obvious. For the cases of the southern periphery, Greece appeared to be more adequately compared with the Iberian countries than with Italy, which, despite some economic troubles, exhibits more characteristics of the large central European countries than those of the southern periphery. Consequently, Italy is compared with France. Furthermore, comparing Ireland with the UK, Belgium with the Netherlands and Germany with Austria is again rather obvious. The grouping is done on a qualitative decision based on similarities between the selected cases. Thus, the logic of comparison equals the 'most similar case design' (see e.g. Berg-Schlosser/Cronqvist 2012). Selecting cases with similar characteristics in a group opens up the opportunity to look for the non-similar characteristics that help explain different outcomes in these cases.

Methodologically, the chapters combine a within- and a between-case analysis. For the within-case analysis, the following questions will be addressed:

- Institutional factors: what roles do federal or unitary structures, second chambers and veto players have? While most institutional factors are invariant, some can be changed by politics. This process is also known as institutionalization. The institutionalization of PPP results from politics and is a precondition for (further) PPP activities. Among institutional factors, the different legal traditions across Europe seem to play an important role. More flexible legal cultures such as the Anglo-Saxon common law seem to provide supportive conditions for PPP.
- Socioeconomic context: what roles do pluralism and corporatism, or more broadly the structure of organized interests, and lobbying have? Does the level of the gross domestic product (GDP) as an indicator of relative wealth has any influence on the level of PPP activity in a country?
- Political factors: what roles do parties, governments and bureaucracy have in the development and implementation of PPP? As the UK example illustrates, the emergence of a significant volume of PPP/PFI contracting is not a coincidence but the result of political decisions and massive support.
- Policy diffusion and path dependency: what role does the PPP policy in neighbouring or role model countries have for the (non-)adoption of PPP in a state and what role does previous experience with privatization, public–private collaboration and public sector reform have?

The final section of each chapter compares the two (or three) cases introduced before. In this section we focus on similarities and dissimilarities with regard to the outcome (level of PPP commitment and activity by public authorities), and to political structures and influential actors. The final chapter draws conclusions in terms of policy diffusion and comparative policy analysis and additionally addresses the idea of 'privatized Keynesianism' (Crouch 2011) as a more theoretically focused explanation for the success of PPP in at least the Anglo-Saxon countries.

2. PPP as a political issue

2.1 THE POLITICS OF PPP

Obviously, public–private collaboration is a multi-disciplinary topic. Scholarly interest in PPP is often focused on the economic and financial aspects of public–private collaboration (e.g. Grimsey/Lewis 2005a, Yescombe 2007), on legal and technical aspects, and also on the politics of PPP in certain countries such as the UK (e.g. Flinders 2005). Furthermore, also in the field of social and political sciences it is regarded as a contested issue; a considerable share of scientists have adopted a sceptical stance towards this policy (Hellowell 2012: 330), often in line with the rejection of the policy by the public sector unions. This rejection is often based on the classification of PPP as a 'neoliberal' policy with an empty, non-substantial rhetoric (Wettenhall 2003, Linder 1999). Other authors such as Colin Crouch (2011) stress the innovation of PPP as a blend of neoliberal policies with Keynesian elements such as the stimulation of (additional) demand without letting the public budget run immediately much deeper into debt. This policy of 'privatized Keynesianism' as it was labelled by Crouch evolved in the 1990s as a reaction to the flaws of classical Keynesianism (or what politicians made of it). In contrast, neoliberalism was elaborated by economists like Milton Friedman and transferred to Anglo-Saxon political systems by President Reagan in the United States (US) and Margaret Thatcher in the UK. In continental Europe, it also found supporters among politicians, although with less vigour than in the Anglo-Saxon world. There, it thoroughly transformed the logic and way of operation of public sector entities as well as state–market relations (Osborne/Gaebler 1992).

Against this background, the rise of the PPP approach in the 1990s is explained as the impact of the overall marketization of executive and administrative spheres of statehood in areas such as the procurement of health or prison services, where full or direct privatization would not (yet) be acceptable for a critical public sphere, especially in continental Europe. Thus, PPP is interpreted as a policy tool which transformed the 'neoliberal' agenda of the 1980s to a modernistic policy approach digestible even for moderate left-wingers such as those gathered under the label of 'New Labour' in the UK and 'Agenda 2010' in Germany under Chancellor Schröder in the early 2000s. According to its critics, what these broad marketing umbrellas have in common is that they attempt to legitimize the retreat of the state and foster a further release of market forces. Consequently, for those critics PPP appears to be decidedly a neoliberal policy (Crouch 2011, Ziekow 2011: 43).

Among others, the divide into sceptics (or critics) and proponents (or enthusiasts) of PPP may also result from different perceptions of what public policy decision makers (in a more general sense, states) are doing or ought to be doing. More generally speaking, they result from different perceptions of what 'public interest' is and how it should be realized. As already mentioned above, whereas PPP is seen by some as a non-political policy tool, its use is questioned by others as a matter of politics, more precisely as a piece in the overall attempt of 'rolling back' or 'hollowing out' the state. However, such theoretically derived concepts sometimes lack an empirical basis. In order to avoid simplifications, much more empirical work on the (political) factors driving PPP would have to be done. Owing to limited time and space, however, we have to focus on the 'usual suspects', some socioeconomic and institutional factors assumed to be facilitating or hampering policy changes.

Among the 'usual suspects' is the already mentioned problem of huge and even rising budget deficits in many states at central, regional and also local level. Thus, it is assumed that PPP appears for some policy makers interested in pre-financing and off-budget financing of projects as a welcome tool for bypassing financial calamities in the public sector. However, as we will see in the empirical testing, the level of average deficit seems to have only a moderate influence on governments' propensity to (not) use PPP. Despite a more pragmatic approach of governments to PPP over time, especially after the global financial crisis, the impact of politics on public authorities' willingness to use PPP as a means of procurement and service delivery is still regarded as high (Lenk/Röber 2011: 4).

The politics of PPP is not only about the driving factors behind the use of this policy: it is also, and in a more general sense, a question of political objectives to be achieved by means of PPP. In that sense public authorities are often limited by a sometimes quarrelsome political process in order to produce clear-cut and legitimate definitions of objectives which have to be realized or problems which have to be solved by means of public–private collaborations (ibid.: 2). Given the problem of incomplete contracts, with possible effects on costs, benefits and risks, a lively and critical democratic process is always on the edge of interfering with the policy or even the operational level of PPP. Especially after a change in government such as in the UK in 2010 and in Portugal in 2011 after the global financial crisis, politicians have used the emergency brake and stalled their predecessors' PPP programmes, and started a critical review process of the existing policy or initiated renegotiations of already operating project contracts.

As these examples illustrate, a comprehensive risk assessment is a crucial element of public–private collaboration, helping to avoid unwanted surprises for the public purse as well as for the taxpayers. Furthermore, review processes of the PPP policy as well as appropriate risk assessment also contribute to the legitimacy of this contested policy. The 'temptation' of PPP for policy makers is to transfer not only operational tasks to the private partner but also control and oversight mechanisms. Obligations of democratic control and legitimacy also raise the question of the nature and extent of political control with regard to PPP. From an institutional economics point of view, citizens act as principals of politicians, who then have to make decisions on public goods and services on behalf of the citizens. However, delegation and accountability are two sides of the same coin. While in a context of Weberian bureaucracy, the execution of such decisions might have been inefficient in an economical sense, in a democratic sense they gave less reason for 'political' concerns. Contrarily, in a New Public Management (NPM) or PPP context, fears might arise that the interests of the private sector 'become too dominant in PPPs, [and] citizens will be very critical about these arrangements […] because they fear that prices will rise and quality of service will decrease' (ibid.: 4).

PPP has also been discussed in the context of the NPM reforms in the 1990s. This reform debate was inspired by a political 'atmosphere' which transferred managerial ideas and practices from the private sector to the public sector bureaucracy (Schedler/Proeller 2011). Against the background of public sector expansion in the 1970s and 1980s in connection with aspects of increasing costs and inefficiency, NPM and PPP seemed to be promising answers to the most urgent problems of public sector bureaucracy: exploding costs and lack of efficiency. In the context of these debates, policy makers tried out a range of reform strategies and instruments, including decentralization of administrative and also executive structures, leading to 'agencification', contracting out and different forms of privatization. Such a spectrum of reform instruments cannot be pushed forward without legitimating overall ideas and grand strategies derived from them. Respective legitimating ideas came out clearly in the managerial spirit of the NPM reforms as expressed, for instance, in Osborne and Gaebler's reinvention of government (1992) but also in shifted images of the state, prescribing new roles such as 'public governance' and the active and enabling state. These reform debates in the 1980s and 1990s were much deeper rooted in the Anglo-Saxon countries than in central European states such as France, Germany, Austria and Italy. In Germany, for example, the prevalent style of public sector reform under the conservative Kohl cabinets until 1998 has been described as 'muddling through'. Privatization policies and NPM reforms even at cabinet level had to overcome much more resistance than, for example, in the UK under Margaret Thatcher and John Major.

As will be shown in Chapter 3, without strong policy support from national level, regional and local levels face severe difficulties in reaching higher degrees of PPP activity. For instance, in the UK a whole policy framework was put in place in order to foster the use of PFI across government departments, the National Health Service (NHS) and at local level. In the case of the London Underground PPPs, they were installed in the early 2000s by the Blair/Brown government even against the resistance of the then mayor Ken Livingston (Labour). One of the means for luring local governments into deeper PPP/PFI involvement has been the 'PFI credits' issued by Her Majesty's (HM) Treasury. The system of PFI credits was derived by then chancellor Gordon Brown from the idea of earned income tax credits as advocated by US president Bill Clinton to benefit low-income families. Similarly to that, the British PFI credits scheme was also targeted at low-performing local governments. Put simply, it was meant to inject some entrepreneurial spirit into the low-performing, often higher-indebted local communities. However, this system was completely revised under the coalition government in 2012 so that Whitehall sponsoring activities are no longer limited to the PFI route. Instead, local governments have been enabled to decide on their own which procurement procedure is most appropriate for a certain project. Ziekow (2011: 63) sees similar patterns for local governments in Germany, as PPP has been perceived as a policy tool to relieve strained budgets in order to cope with investment backlogs.

2.2 MANY ASSUMPTIONS, LESS RELIABLE KNOWLEDGE

As with many contested policies, intuitively generated 'theories' and implicit knowledge derived from world views also have considerable influence in the discussion about the usefulness and efficiency of the PPP approach. Methodologically, case studies about the benefits or damages, the motives and structures of PPP prevail. Comparative methods are hardly used, even less statistical methods. Attempting to answer why some governments like PPP/PFI more than others, in these social and political science studies a wide range of candidates have been debated. In this book, we will discuss some of them.

Among the most popular, the argument of bringing relief for strapped budgets is frequently used. This argument can be split into two: a) reducing or avoiding budget deficits and b) reducing or avoiding growth of the sovereign debt quota. Taking into consideration the political logic of competition and accountability, we expect the deficit to be the more urgent problem for a government. In the case of the debt quota it can be argued by the government that most of it had been piled up by its predecessors. However, this argument does not work in the case of rising deficits. Thus, we expect the deficit to be politically 'hotter' than the debt quota.

Value for money (VfM) is another 'top seller' among the arguments for PPP procurement. This argument broadly addresses the lack of efficiency in conventional public procurement and service delivery, while leaving enough room for interpretation of what exactly VfM means. Basic characteristics might include a 'whole of life' perspective, an assessment of quality levels and performance standards, and risk assessments, as well as pricing and cost aspects (Duffield 2010: 199).[1] According to HM Treasury (2006a: 7),

> VfM is defined as the optimum combination of whole-of-life costs and quality (or fitness for purpose) of the good or service to meet the user's requirement. VfM is not the choice of goods and services based on the lowest cost bid. To undertake a well-managed procurement, it is necessary to consider upfront, and at the earliest stage of procurement, what the key drivers of VfM in the procurement process will be.

HM Treasury added that the PFI route 'should only be pursued where it represents VfM in procurement' (ibid.).

Raising additional private investment is another argument in support of PPP. It addresses the multiplication effect of public investments in general and public–private collaboration specifically. In addition to this argument, the pre-financing argument is also often used. This argument stresses the possibility of carrying out investments via the PPP route which could not yet be financed and conducted by the public sector alone. However, the private 'pre-financing' enables the public authority to proceed with a (much needed) procurement or refurbishment or order a service for which it would have had to wait much longer if it had to be financed solely by the public purse.

From the (critical) perspective of political economy, the focus is on the influence of the private sector, especially the finance and construction sector, on public decision making. Among the main concerns from the perspective of political economy is the question of how economic processes and interests influence political decision making and vice versa. Historically, this can be analysed using the example of the early Labour government's PPP policy development after 1997, which drew in substantial private capital (Hare 2013).

2.3 THE IMPACT OF THE 2008 GLOBAL FINANCIAL CRISIS

As with crisis in general, the global financial crisis commencing after the collapse of Lehman Brothers in September 2008 came as a surprise and hit hard both the public and the private sectors of several countries. Public sectors were forced to spend billions of 'rescue money' in order to prevent a breakdown of the national banking systems owing to bad loans, but also to a lack of trust among the banks themselves. However, not all the Western countries were hit in a similar way, and not all of the public rescue money spent during the global financial crisis to stabilize banks (and governments) was lost money, as public entities such as banking rescue funds often acquired shares in the crisis banks in return, which in some cases were sold immediately (e.g. by the UK government) after the crisis, sometimes making large profits for the public purse.

Thus, the total approved or spent public money cannot be directly equated with losses for the public purse; rather it can be linked to the severance of affection for the banking sector resulting from the crisis. The more the sector got into trouble, the more 'rescue money' was actually needed. Until the end of 2011, the total sum of nationally used funds for the rescue of banks as a share of GDP was highest in Ireland, amounting to about 223 per cent of GDP in 2011 (or €350 billion from 2008 to 2011), followed by Denmark with 66 per cent and Greece with 32 per cent. The UK had the second largest sum of actually used funds, totalling about €300 billion up to the end of 2011, which, however, equated to only 17 per cent of its 2011 GDP. Portugal, another active PPP country, had only used €11 billion up to 2011 or 6.7 per cent of its 2011 GDP (FAZ 2013: 12).

These figures for funds retrieved by the banks are a heterogeneous category, as they encompass actually 'flown' money as well as state guarantees and similar measures of shielding risks. For example, within the €200 billion drawn by the German banking rescue fund 'Soffin', about €174 billion had been state guarantees. In total, direct capital injections to the German banking sector in the course of the crisis have been put at €63 billion according to the European Commission's Directorate-General for Competition. On average, across the European Union (EU) member states, the volume of approved funds for rescue measures sums up to 40.3 per cent of GDP and the volume of actually used funds to 12.8 per cent of GDP (ibid.).

With regard to the use of PPP, there is no clear correlation to the severity of crisis, as indicated by the public 'rescue measures'. For instance, while Ireland has been an intense user of PPP, Denmark was also severely hit by the global financial crisis but is the least active PPP country of our sample (Chapter 3). Also, Belgium had not at federal level shown a special commitment to PPP in the period up to 2009, but had to provide significant banking rescue funds. The UK, in terms of PPP/PFI commitment the number one in Europe, was only number five in terms of rescue money used as a share of 2011 GDP (17 per cent). At first sight these figures do not suggest a direct correlation of PPP activities and the severity of the global financial crisis in a country; however, a systematic investigation would need a more elaborated research design.

Basically, Cuttaree/Mandri-Perrott (2011) have distinguished three main impacts of the crisis on the politics and practice of PPP in Europe and Central Asia. Firstly, the private sector has become more conservative and risk averse, leading to fewer as well as smaller-sized projects. Secondly, securing financing has become more difficult, requiring more support from government both financially and politically. This makes 'off-balance-sheet arrangements' more difficult and thus less attractive for politicians. And finally, the now higher levels of risk challenge established modes of risk sharing between the public and the private sector.

However, while the PPP approach faced severe 'headwind' in the aftermath of the crisis, with few exceptions such as the UK, the approach has not significantly influenced macroeconomic figures. Furthermore, the emergence of the global financial crisis is mainly linked with the subprime mortgage crisis and its impact on the banking sector. Thus, it can be assumed that the politics of PPP was not among the drivers of the financial crisis. However, according to Crouch (2011), both the financial crisis and the PFI/PPP policy in the Anglo-Saxon countries can be seen as an effect of a policy regime labelled as 'privatized Keynesianism'. This question will be addressed separately (Chapter 10.4).

The question of how the global financial crisis has affected the PPP approach remains. How has states' PPP policy changed as a consequence of the crisis? It is widely acknowledged that the financial and economic crisis commencing in 2008 has worsened the political and financial conditions for PPP at least temporarily. Politics in several countries tried to compensate for at least some of the deteriorating conditions. On the other hand, some countries temporarily stopped their PPP policies and set up an overhaul. In the way PPP politics reacted to the crisis, different political strategies can be observed. Additionally, the financial and economic crisis led to a change in government in states where there was a subsequent election. Firstly, among the leading PPP countries, that is, the UK and Portugal, incoming conservative governments placed their respective policies under review. In the UK, the coalition government scrutinized already operational projects as well as those in tender for possible cost savings and renegotiations. Furthermore, it stopped the tendering of projects and started a policy review in which interest groups, experts and other policy makers were asked for their policy positions. Finally, in December 2012, the coalition 're-launched' its new PFI policy, now rebranded as 'PF2' (Private Finance 2, see section 5.1). Portugal's government chose a similar approach. It stalled all tendering and started a review of operational projects and policies. The similar reactions in the UK and Portugal also point to a close policy collaboration between these two countries in the field of PPP. Given the policy leadership of the UK, the direction of the policy transfer is not surprising.

After the slump in PPP activities due to the 'credit crunch' in 2008, the year 2010 saw the first substantial recovery taking place. According to a PPP market review of the EPEC, 112 projects with an aggregated value of more than €18 billion were signed in 2010. In terms of market values, these figures were at the level of the early 2000s, compared to the highest point in the last pre-crisis year, 2007, with over €30 billion of project volume. Among those who returned to using PPP in 2010, the first were the UK and Spain, with the former being top in terms of number of projects and the latter in terms of project volume. Among these post-crisis deals it has been observed that there were a higher number of projects considered as large scale, that is, with over €500 million of value and, often, a contract period of over 25 years (EPEC 2011c).

A year later, the EPEC (2012b) reported that in 2011 a total of 84 transactions reached financial close with an aggregate volume of €18 billion, nearly the same as in 2010. However, the drop in the number of deals from 112 to 84 confirmed the post-crisis trend to fewer, but larger, projects. The biggest deal signed in 2011 was the Tours–Bordeaux high-speed railway in France with a value of €5.4 billion. In 2012, the numbers and volumes of deals further dropped, partly due to the change in the French presidency. In May 2012, the UMP (Union pour un mouvement populaire or Union for a Popular Movement) member Nicolas Sarkozy was superseded by the socialist François Hollande. Especially during the second half of the Sarkozy presidency, France pushed PPPs heavily, among them some very large infrastructure projects. However, this changed under President Hollande.

Another mode of reaction across the countries at national level has been ministerial or governmental declarations of intent to further support the PPP approach through appropriate policy measures. Such measures include, for example, state guaranties for private lenders participating in a PPP in order to enable access to credit (EPEC 2011b). Given the erosion of trust during the 'credit crunch', which affected not only the interbank market, access to affordable money for private partners in a PPP was one of the main challenges. In general, the interest rates for (public and) private creditors in the money market worsened. Subsequently, interest rates reached a level where private project financing was hardly feasible anymore. Furthermore, credit givers preferred short-term deals at that time, while PPP partners were interested in long-term contracts.

This was especially the case in the troubled banking sectors of the southern periphery of Europe and in Ireland, where 'toxic papers' often formed large shares of the banks' core capital. In cases like Greece, only minor parts of such papers concerned private creditors, while the main problem was that these banks had taken on large amounts of government bonds. Thus, with the erosion of trust in the Greek government, the trustworthiness of Greek banks diminished too, and access to the interbank market was blocked. While the European Central Bank (ECB) had to fill this gap, the banks had to offer securities in exchange, which was not always easy (Fuster 2011a).

Politics sometimes responded with additional public 'kick-off financing', trying to mitigate the increasing gap in the private capital market. Market risks were compensated for by public guarantees, with the state acting as guarantor. However, these measures are not within the framework of the PPP's inherent logic, where risk transfer to the private sector initially was one of the main motivations (Ziekow 2011: 64). Due to the financial crisis, a rebalancing or renegotiating of risk transfer took place that often led to less risk transfer to the private sector. However, the Spanish government's reluctance to bail out troubled toll-road concessionaires is also an example of a 'tough stance' on the issue of public 'rescue money' and bailouts of troubled private corporations.

In terms of risk transfer, the private partners became more reluctant to bear a considerable share of the technological or financial risks in the context of PPPs. This is especially the case in road infrastructure concession models, in which the compensation of the private partner is linked to the volume of traffic. Before the crisis, such models were most popular in Spain, Portugal and France. After the crisis, private firms were quite unwilling to take any traffic volume risk. This reluctance was further driven by the response of the Spanish government to the troubled concessionaires of Spanish toll roads. As the traffic volumes slumped in the course of the crisis, several operators asked for government help. However, the Spanish government refused a bailout or even any relief, leading to several insolvencies. Consequently, firms were even more reluctant to accept long-term risks (e.g. traffic volumes) as part of the contract.

Another impact of the financial crisis was that public money was directed away from PPP towards more traditional economic stimulus programmes. This is somewhat surprising, as PPP is said to have a leverage effect on public and private investments. There are several reasons for this 'competition' between PPP and traditional stimulus programmes. Firstly, the PPP tendering process is relatively long, with an average of about one year from invitation to tender to contract closure, preparation of tendering not being included in this period. Thus, PPP is not the first choice for setting investment stimuli or as a countercyclical economic instrument (Ziekow 2011). For such purposes, traditional economic stimulus programmes can be set up much faster and are more easily managed. However, as a general trend, the capability of public entities to prepare and fulfil public services 'in-house' appears to be shrinking. Thus, the need to find appropriate forms of collaboration or sharing of tasks with private actors is likely to increase, despite its critics and its weaknesses, often exposed by, for instance, the national and regional audit offices (ibid.: 64f.).

2.4 PPP AT EU LEVEL AND IN EASTERN EUROPE

Although the focus of this book is on Western European governments' PPP policies, it is worth having a brief look at the European level and Eastern European countries, too. In doing so, the EU's policy towards PPP might be the most important political context factor of national (and regional) governments' PPP policy making. Furthermore, some remarks on the development of PPP policies by Eastern Europe's governments might be useful to complete the picture.

At EU level, the PPP approach has been adopted and adapted primarily by the European Commission. Here, a level of policy making or policy support and an operative level can be distinguished. The policy making towards PPP is mainly directed by the European Commission, which published in 2004 its famous 'Green Paper on Public–Private Partnerships and Community Law on Public Contracts and Concessions'. On the other hand we have the European Parliament. The European Parliament supported in a resolution adopted in October 2006 the Commission's initiative, but also called for further clarification and the application of public procurement law in the field of PPP (European Parliament resolution 2006/2043(INI)). The Commission responded to that with communication C(2007)6661 in February 2008, trying to clarify the Commission's understanding of the compatibility of EU provisions on public procurement and concessions with institutional PPPs. The 2008 communication 'does not create any new legislative rules. It reflects the Commission's understanding of the EC Treaty, the Public Procurement Directives and the relevant case-law of the European Court of Justice (ECJ)'.[2] At the end of 2011, a first proposal for a directive on the award of concession contracts was proposed; it was modified and adopted by the European Parliament in early 2014.[3] Within the European Commission, the Commissioner for Internal Market and Services is in charge of PPP and concessions. In a memo accompanying the new directive, Commissioner Barnier outlined their main objectives as simplification, flexibility and legal certainty in the field of public procurement via PPP and concessions. Public procurement, he argued, would sum up to 19 per cent of European GDP and thus be a main driver of economic growth.

With a simplification of procurement procedures and greater flexibility, the new directive should enhance the efficiency and strategic orientation of public procurement while 'respecting the principles of transparency and competition to the benefit of both public purchasers and economic operators. The rules on concessions will create a common framework for a major tool of public management in Europe, thus contributing to the conditions set for stimulating investment in major public services of the future'.[4]

At the level of EU policy making, after the global financial crisis several new instruments had been planned, such as 'long-term investment funds' (LTIFs), as a mean to encourage long-term infrastructure investments. Such funds should aim to provide funding for firms in need of long-term financial commitments, especially in the fields of infrastructure and transport, but also in property and sustainable-energy projects.

> These asset classes are typically too illiquid to be held by retail-focused Ucits[5] funds, which must allow redemption at least twice a month [...] Retail demand for the new long-term funds is uncertain, but the commission says that between €1.5tn and €2tn will be needed to finance infrastructure projects in Europe up to 2020, indicating a need for large-scale financing. (Marriage 2013: 9)

In the LTIF project, an investment is tied until the fixed end date of ten years or more. As compensation, investors will receive a regular stream of income 'produced by the investment asset and possibly collect an illiquidity premium' (ibid.).

At the operative level, the role of the EIB as a lender for developmental infrastructure projects has to be mentioned. The EIB has a major function in financing PPP projects across Europe, which has become even more important after the global credit crisis. The EIB raises its capital mainly via bonds from the private capital market and finances projects (mainly) of the member states in four (strategic) areas: skills and innovation, financial access for smaller businesses, climate action and strategic infrastructure (www.eib.org). Furthermore, under the auspice of the EIB, the EPEC was set up in 2011 as a European PPP task force by the EIB and the European Commission and has currently 41 institutional members all from the public sector (www.eib.org/epec/).

Table 2.1 summarizes the lending activities of the EIB for PPP projects between 1990 and 2013. Focusing only on PPP activities financed by the EIB in terms of project volume, the UK ranks first, followed by Spain, Portugal, France and Greece. For the UK and Spain, a continual flow of EIB credits can be observed, with a peak in the UK in 2002 and in Spain in 2010. For Portugal and France, different patterns can be observed. Portugal has had several periods of no credit flow from the EIB, with the longest one from 2011 to 2013. In France, the EIB credit flow started only recently, in 2007, with a peak in 2011, and in Greece the first period of PPP in Europe until the year 2000 saw EIB money being drawn most intensely, with a second period following from 2006 to 2009. At the lower end of the table, Finland got EIB credits for two medium-sized projects (in 2005 and 2011), while Denmark drew no money from the EIB for PPP.

Interestingly, the EIB document lists two Danish large-scale bridges as PPPs, whereas on the holding company website they are listed as completely owned by the Danish state. To sum up, the EIB can be characterized as a major PPP supporting force in Europe. Its support encompasses not only the provision of technical and managerial expertise, but also the provision of credit within the context of the EIB's mission. While both the EPEC and the EIB might be characterized as primarily focused on the operational level, their role in European-level policy making should not be underestimated. Formally, PPP policy making at European level is concentrated in the European Commission, more precisely in the Internal Markets and Services Directorate-General. EU policy making towards PPP has shifted from a more enabling stance at the beginning to a broader, competition focused policy more recently. With this focus, PPP has lost prominence, being only one competition strengthening tool among others. However, this might also indicate a more general acceptance of it.

Table 2.1 PPP financing of the EIB (in € million), 1990–2013

	1990–1999	2000	2001	2002	2003	2004	2005	2006	2007	2008	2009	2010	2011	2012	2013	2000–2013	No. of projects 1990–2013	Volume 1990–2013	Rank
UK	1 148	196	212	1 420	1 189	738	499	1 325	886	79	1 181	287	129	291	884	9 316	52	10 464	1
Spain	0	162	278	295	785	403	54	397	306	211	130	1 063	258	328	561	5 231	30	5 231	2
Portugal	1 036	514	600	300	0	264	0	0	285	839	290	345	0	0	0	3 437	18	4 473	3
France	0	0	0	0	0	0	0	0	143	411	0	280	861	306	155	2 156	10	2 156	4
Greece	1 222	370	0	0	0	0	0	152	150	200	9	0	0	0	0	881	7	2 103	5
Netherlands	400	0	400	0	125	25	0	0	0	194	0	214	0	0	256	1 214	8	1 614	6
Italy	0	0	0	0	0	44	70	0	0	353	0	0	0	0	800	1 267	6	1 267	7
Germany	371	0	80	105	0	0	0	0	89	0	225	0	209	0	49	757	9	1 128	8
Ireland	0	0	0	0	170	130	0	173	306	0	0	45	0	50	72	946	13	946	9
Sweden	122	0	0	0	0	0	0	0	0	0	0	699	0	0	0	699	2	821	10
Austria	0	0	0	0	40	48	0	350	0	0	0	0	0	0	0	438	3	438	11
Belgium	0	0	0	0	0	0	0	96	0	313	0	0	0	0	0	409	2	409	12
Finland	0	0	0	0	0	0	153	0	0	0	0	0	134	0	0	287	2	287	13
Denmark	0*	0	0	0	0	0	0	0	0	0	0	0	0	0	0	0	0	0	14
Total	4 299	1 242	1 570	2 120	2 309	1 652	776	2 493	2 165	2 600	1 835	2 933	1 591	975	2 777	27 038		31 337	

Note: * Whereas the EIB has labelled the Great Belt Links and the Oeresund Links as PPPs, the respective webpage of the holding company Sund & Baelt Holding A/S indicate a 100 per cent public ownership by the Danish state, see http://www.storebaelt.dk/english/about.

Source: Adapted from EPEC 2014.

Similar to Western Europe, Eastern Europe shows a heterogeneous picture with regard to PPP. Similar to the UK and Portugal in the west, Hungary has been a forerunner in terms of PPP in the east, using them not only for economic reasons but also 'as a means through which both to restructure the provision of public services to meet social needs and to develop a civil society in the aftermath of the communist regimes' (Osborne 2007: 1). However, in 2010, the Hungarian (and also the Slovakian) government developed a sceptical position towards PPP, after years of intense use. At first sight, this change might seem similar to the revision of PPP in the UK and Portugal after changes in government and with regard to the impact of the global financial crisis. However, in Hungary, and also in Slovakia, the policy change was more fundamental.

Under the previous Hungarian cabinets of Ferenc Gyurcsány (2004–2009) and Gordon Bajnai (2009–2010), PPP was more popular, but also burdened with some legal and regulatory problems, which particularly scared off local governments. The new Hungarian government in 2010 (the cabinet of Orban II) was especially suspicious of the influence of foreign private companies via PPP in Hungarian domestic politics and economics. Again, similarly to Portugal and the UK, already closed contracts and operational projects had been criticized by the government as too expensive, thereby also criticizing the previous, contract signing governments. As in the UK and Portugal, investigations of existing contracts were started; however, no legal action was initiated. Instead, the government decided in the first half of 2011 to suspend current tenders and buy itself out of existing PPP contracts. With this aim, the Hungarian National Development Ministry started a review of existing schemes, in order to identify potential savings. 'Currently, financing the PPP projects costs the government €449m (HUF120bn) every year, which increases to €11.2bn when calculated over the duration of a 15 to 30-year contract' (www.pppbulletin.com/news/view/17661).

Also in 2010, Slovakia took a critical stance towards its PPP programme. It scrapped a large-scale motorway project with a value of about €3.3 billion following concerns over 'value for money' and delays in the negotiation process. The government's position was made clearer in a remark of the transport minister, who 'insisted the government has enough money to undertake infrastructure projects without needing private investment. He added the government would focus on delivering projects in a more transparent way' (www.pppbulletin.com/news/view/15756). Overall, the picture for Eastern Europe seems to be similar heterogeneous than in Western Europe, with some governments withdrawing from the PPP approach or not even starting it.

NOTES

1. For the VfM discussion see also Burger/Hawkesworth (2011) and http://wbi.worldbank.org/wbi/news/2013/11/04/value-money-public-private-infrastructure-projects [10 August 2014].
2. http://ec.europa.eu/internal_market/publicprocurement/partnerships/public-private/index_en.htm [11 February 2014].
3. http://ec.europa.eu/internal_market/publicprocurement/partnerships/concessions/index_en.htm [11 February 2014].
4. http://europa.eu/rapid/press-release_MEMO-14-18_en.htm?locale=en [11 February 2014].
5. Undertakings for Collective Investments in Transferable Securities.

3. PPP in Western Europe: challenges for comparative research

This chapter focuses on the methods and empirical results of a qualitative and quantitative comparison of PPP activities across Western European states. It introduces and tests variables which could correlate with the level of PPP activity in a country. Therefore, using EIB data, a quantitative assessment of the number and volume of PPP projects between 1990 and 2009 is correlated with a range of variables which are assumed to promote (or hinder) PPP activity. The independent variables are grouped as institutional, socioeconomic and control variables. Methods applied are bivariate correlations and a Qualitative Comparative Analysis (QCA).

3.1 RESEARCH DESIGN

The selection of cases and variables is one of the most crucial steps in developing a research design. In order to minimize selection bias, this study focuses on the politics of PPP in the EU 15 minus Luxembourg, that is Austria (AT), Belgium (BE), Germany (DE), Denmark (DK), Greece (EL), Spain (ES), Finland (FI), France (FR), Ireland (IE), Italy (IT), the Netherlands (NL), Portugal (PT), Sweden (SE) and the United Kingdom (UK).While this chapter applies simple quantitative methods and a QCA, chapters 4 to 9 focus on qualitative case comparisons. There, the 14 states are grouped into four pairs and two groups of three for the purposes of qualitative comparison. These case groupings combine the possibilities of in-depth case studies with pairwise or small-N case comparisons. Furthermore, the concluding chapter provides a qualitative comparative assessment of all 14 cases, in order to further condense the generalized results. Despite the predominantly qualitative approach, to a certain degree, a selective use of information is unavoidable. Large-scale projects such as the London Underground PPP and the German Toll Collect system cannot be analysed in detail. However, such projects provide evidence of the large-scale commitment of the contract-signing governments.

When performing empirical social research on PPP, data problems do often arise. In some countries, PPP units such as Partnerships UK (PUK), the MAPPP (Mission d'appui à la réalisation des partenariats public-privé) in France, ÖPP Deutschland AG in Germany, and the construction industry's SEOPAN (Asociación de Empresas Constructoras de Ámbito Nacional) in Spain provide useful quantitative and qualitative project information and to a certain degree also policy information. However, not all countries have such units, and even if they do, their databases often do not encompass all the projects signed in a given period (e.g. due to voluntary reporting of contractors such as in Germany) or are missing details due to the private sector's right to 'commercial in confidence'. This illustrates not only the selectivity of documentation at the national level, but also the interplay between public and private actors in the field of documentation and data management. In particular, quantitative international comparisons are still dependent on figures provided by PPP lobbying organizations or interested actors in the field such as the EIB. Such information is often very detailed and seems to offer valuable insights into a state's or region's PPP activity and policy. In order to maximize transparency, we indicate the data sources in as much detail as possible.

At European level, the EPEC within the EIB publishes (bi)annual figures that help estimate cross-national PPP activity. For example, the first half of 2011 was very busy for the French PPP market, totalling nearly 60 per cent of Europe's overall PPP market value. For this period the EPEC counted 47 PPPs across just eight countries, with a total value of €9.7 billion. This trend towards fewer but larger projects in a limited number of countries during the recovery from the global financial crisis was especially driven by the UK and France, with the biggest deals located in France (e.g. the Tours–Bordeaux high-speed railway at €3 billion, the A63 highway at €1 billion, and the Balard defence headquarters at €800 million). In Italy, the biggest project in 2011, the A24 Strada dei Parchi motorway, totalled only €600 million. With regard to France, an important factor in the political context was the approaching presidential election of May 2012. Thus, in the French case study (see section 8.1) it has to be asked if PPP was used by the incumbent president (Sarkozy) as a political means of combining deficit reduction with investment in public infrastructure in the run-up to the election. With regard to the politics of PPP, the trend towards fewer but bigger projects in terms of transaction size (from an average of €90 million in 2009 to over €200 million in 2011) can also be interpreted as a reaction to the global financial crisis. While smaller projects without political support at the highest level might have not been able to proceed because banks shied away from the risk, larger projects with political support were still able to attract private money.

After case selection, the variables have to be chosen. Most importantly, the dependent variable has to be based on sound data. The variable was selected using data from Kappeler/Nemoz (2010), who provide, so far, the most accurate comparative quantification of European states' PPP activities (see section 3.2). As a contested policy, there has been much debate about the factors influencing a jurisdiction's propensity to use PPP as a means of public procurement and service delivery. Consequently, there are many socioeconomic, political and institutional variables that could be linked with a high (low) PPP activity in a given state. Thus, the next sections introduce some of them and illustrate how they can be contributing to a higher (lower) PPP activity. The independent variables are divided in three groups: institutional and political variables (section 3.3), socioeconomic agenda-setter variables (section 3.4) and (socio-economic) control variables (section 3.5).

3.2 DEPENDENT VARIABLE: PPP ACTIVITY

Attempts to quantify PPP activities in an international comparative perspective are rare so far. To a certain degree, Hammami et al. (2006) is an exception; however, it is not focused on European states. The best quantification of PPP activities at a European cross-country level so far is provided by Blanc-Brude et al. (2007) and Kappeler/Nemoz (2010). However, to get country-specific volumes the percentage shares of countries in the European PPP market from Kappeler/Nemoz (2010) have to be recalculated as project volume as a percentage of total project volume. In doing so, the total value of all the 1340 projects above €5 million detected by Kappeler/Nemoz (2010: 7) between 1990 and 2009 of €253 744.9 million has to be split according to the documented percentage shares of the countries. From this, we get the aggregated project volume for each country of those projects above the €5 million threshold for the period between 1990 and 2009 (Table 3.1).

As time series data are not available, quantitative developments within a country cannot be analysed in this part of the study. This situation also limits the possibility of proceeding to a cross-sectional comparison. Longitudinal developments such as increasing or decreasing project numbers or volumes within a country or the sample in general cannot be considered.

In a next step, the resulting investment volumes of each state have to be set in relation to a country-specific indicator such as the population

Table 3.1 Country shares in the PPP market, 14 European states, 1990–2009 aggregated

	Number of projects (percentage share)	Project volume (percentage share)	Breakdown of project volume 1990–2009 (€ m)
Austria (AT)	0.2	0.5	1 268.72
Belgium (BE)	0.9	1.3	3 298.68
Germany (DE)	4.9	4.1	10 403.54
Denmark (DK)	0.1	0.0	0.00
Greece (EL)	1.0	5.5	13 955.97
Spain (ES)	10.1	11.4	28 926.92
Finland (FI)	0.1	0.2	507.49
France (FR)	5.4	5.3	13 448.48
Ireland (IE)	1.3	1.6	4 059.92
Italy (IT)	2.4	3.3	8 373.58
Netherlands (NL)	1.2	1.8	4 567.41
Portugal (PT)	3.1	7.0	17 762.14
Sweden (SE)	0.1	0.2	507.49
UK (UK)	67.1	52.5	133 216.07

Source: Adapted from Kappeler/Nemoz 2010.

size, the GDP or the level of public investment. Furthermore, the period for each of these three possible indicators has to be clarified. Under ideal circumstances, the mean for the period 1990 to 2009 would be used. However, for some indicators and some countries, Eurostat does not provide figures for the early and, sometimes even, the mid-1990s. Thus, the period means are calculated starting from the year in which a complete data series begins. In most of the incomplete data cases, this is given at least from the second half of the 1990s.

Having to choose among the population size, the GDP and the level of public investment in order to relativize the PPP volume figures, the last appears to be most appropriate (Table 3.2). The population size is too

Table 3.2 Country-specific indicators of PPP activity

	Project volume per capita in 2000 in €	Rank	Project volume as a share of GDP (1996–2009)	Rank	Mean public investment in € m (1995–2009)	Ratio of project volume to mean public investment	Rank
AT	158.54 (8 002 186)	10	0.561 (226 064.4)	10	3 289.4	38.57	7
BE	322.16 (10 239 085)	7	1.202 (274 265.7)	6	4765.2	69.22	6
DE	126.62 (82 163 475)	11	0.484 (2 147 773.69)	11	35 837.7	29.029	9
DK	0 (5 330 020)	14	0 (185 198.2)	14	3 370.7	0	14
EL	1 279.92 (10 903 757)	4	7.400 (188 581.5)	3	5 437.4	256.66	3
ES	722.27 (40 049 708)	6	3.843 (752 549.4)	4	27 348.5	105.77	4
FI	98.13 (5 171 302)	12	0.355 (142 652.4)	12	3 760.3	13.49	12
FR	222.12 (60 545 022)	9	0.865 (1554547.5)	8	49 187.1	27.34	11
IE	1 074.68 (3 777 763)	5	3.199 (126 887.0)	5	4 841.5	83.85	5
IT	1 471.03 (56 923 524)	3	0.661 (1 265 471.6)	9	29 047.2	28.82	10
NL	287.91 (15 863 950)	8	1.001 (456 068.2)	7	15 139.6	30.16	8
PT	1 742.23 (10 195 014)	2	13.141 (135 160.8)	1	4 378.8	405.63	2
SE	57.26 (8 861 426)	13	0.185 (273 773.1)	13	8 400.2	6.04	13
UK	2 266.14 (58 785 246)	1	8.459 (1 574 673.8)	2	25 303.9	526.46	1

Notes:
The mean of the seventh column is 115.78; the standard deviation is 163.59.
Figures in parentheses in second column = population; figures in parentheses in fourth column = GDP.

Sources: Krumm 2014: 452, based on Kappeler/Nemoz 2010 and Eurostat data.

general a figure and even the GDP encompasses private sector activity which is not relevant for estimating a public authority's PPP commitment. However, these figures are also reported in Table 3.2, with the population as of 1 January 2000 according to Eurostat. The means of the GDP in market values from 1996 to 2009 (Greece 2001–2009) were calculated from Eurostat data (nama_gdp_k). As for 5 of the 14 countries data for the first years were not available, the starting point has been set to the year 1996. For Greece, the available longitudinal data only started in 2001. In the fourth column, in the second line of each case, the period means in millions of Euros are documented in parenthesis.

The most specific ratio can be derived by using the sum of public investment in a national economy.[1] Data about public investment (gross investments) from 1995 to 2009 can be retrieved from Eurostat (COFOG, gov_a_exp). The means have been calculated for all countries from 1995 to 2009, because of a lack of data before 1995 for some of the cases.

In the national accounts, the public investments are only a minor share of the GDP; the major shares are forms of private consumption. Consumptive public expenditure, private investments and net exports are further components of the GDP, which, however, are not directly relevant for the public use of PPP. Thus, the level of public investment is the most appropriate indicator that is available, even better than the GDP. Comparing the country rankings for each of the three variants, it is however surprising that there are no big differences, the exception being Italy which is ranked 3 according to population (in the year 2000), and 10 according to public investment. A value of nil for Denmark does not indicate that there is no activity since only larger projects above the threshold of €5 million in investment volume have been registered.

3.3 INSTITUTIONAL VARIABLES

3.3.1 Legal Traditions and State Guarantees

The selected sample of 14 Western European countries, from Finland in the north to Greece in the south, encompasses a variety of legal traditions that might facilitate or impede a policy change towards higher levels of PPP. Thus, the following section focuses on legal 'families' or traditions across the sample and tries to point to possible implications for the politics of PPP. As such legal traditions are quantitatively difficult to operationalize, the coding of Table 3.3 is only included in the bivariate correlation and not in the QCA. Even for the correlations, it is the only 'qualitative', nominal variable. Despite this limitation of nominal coding, it is the only available variable to statistically test the influence of different legal traditions on a country's level of PPP activity. Thus, the variable might provide important background information on why PPP has been much more successful in the Anglo-Saxon than in the Nordic countries. According to the literature on legal traditions, the sample can be divided into two main groups: common law and civil law countries.

Common law tradition can be assumed to be more 'PPP friendly' than civil law tradition, as can be illustrated by some Anglo-Saxon countries. According to this assumption, the UK and Ireland are candidates for the most supportive legal environment for an active PPP policy. In general, common law jurisdictions have a less prescriptive approach to the structuring of PPPs than civil law jurisdictions. Common law and civil law jurisdictions have distinct approaches to many issues relevant to PPP. However, differences also exist among civil law countries, as illustrated in Table 3.3. In civil law tradition, Roman-French, Roman-German and Roman-Scandinavian branches have developed, which tend towards increasing degrees of codification.

In many civil law countries, several rights implied by law are relevant to the PPP approach. For example, a public authority may be unable to renounce a right conferred to it by the administrative laws and subsequent regulations. This can have a severe impact on the right of contracting (EPEC 2011a: 51). These rights may, for instance, enable authorities to prematurely withdraw from a contract or entitle operators to additional compensation in the event of an unexpected rise of operation costs. Also, authorities may be entitled to unilaterally change a contract if this is in the public interest. Furthermore, civil and common law jurisdictions also provide different approaches towards security and insolvency. Whereas common law jurisdictions emphasize in insolvency situations the aspect of rescue and reorganization, civil law jurisdictions focus in such situations on the winding up of companies (ibid.: 21). In common law jurisdictions case law and precedents form the basis of commercial transactions and principles underpinning the allocation of risk (ibid.: 51).

In contrast, almost all legal systems in continental Europe are based on the civil law tradition of written and codified law (civil code). Furthermore, an elaborated administrative law stipulates basic norms with no options of derogation or overriding by the contracting parties. Thus, it provides a comparatively inflexible framework for the negotiation of PPP contracts. Quite often in countries with civil law tradition, concession law is one frequently used means to define the details of services that can be procured via PPP. Such laws have been introduced, for example, in Belgium, Italy, Poland, Portugal and Spain. They often focus on specific

Table 3.3 Legal traditions in the selected cases

Type	Anglo-Saxon	Roman-French	Roman-German	Roman-Scandinavian
Case	Ireland (IE) United Kingdom (UK)	Belgium (BE) Greece (EL) Spain (ES) France (FR) Italy (IT) The Netherlands (NL) Portugal (PT)	Austria (AT) Germany (DE)	Denmark (DK) Finland (FI) Sweden (SE)
Code	1	2	3	4

Source: Adapted from Haensch/Holtmann 2008: 614.

sectors such as motorways and are sometimes across-sector arrangements. 'When a country enacts a PPP law, it normally requires changes and references to other binding legislation and regulations' (EPEC 2011a: 52). A legal tradition in concession law (such as in the Roman-French legal tradition) may be helpful in enabling authorities 'to enter into PPP contracts within the scope of their powers, particularly in the case of authorities which are not departments of State (that is, part of central government)' (ibid.).

In addition to such overarching legal traditions, other legal and regulatory PPP frameworks at national level have to be taken into consideration, too. Such frameworks may include provisions to facilitate investments in PPPs, reducing transaction costs, ensuring an appropriate regulatory control, and enabling legal and economic dispute resolution mechanisms to be built into the contracts. According to EPEC (2011a: 51) a PPP legal framework should of course include legal rights to establish PPPs, along with regulations on the transfer of public assets to private entities and the competencies of PPP companies in choosing subcontractors as well as on enabling governments to provide financing. Furthermore, a (legal) PPP framework may also encompass policy documents, guidance notes and elements about the design of a PPP contract itself (ibid.).

The debate about state guarantees for PPPs somehow echoes the debate about public 'bailouts' of public and private entities, including private banks attributed systemic relevance in the context of the bailouts in the southern European financial crisis states. Similar to public (e.g.

ECB) guarantees to crisis banks and states, the purpose of state guarantees is to restore trust in credit and to provide and facilitate access to credit (EPEC 2011b). For EPEC (2011b: 5) state guarantees can help incentivize private actors such as banks, capital market investors, equity providers and sponsors to join in PPP programmes or projects. They are not limited to certain forms, actors or programmes, and were already known before the onset of the global financial crisis in 2008, however, they are used very differently across European countries.

According to EPEC, state guarantees can help to build up confidence and emphasize the government's commitment, accelerate implementation of investments and safeguard the credibility of PPP programmes (ibid.: 7). State guarantees may comprise both the leverage of additional financial resources and the tapping of new sources of funds from the private sector, the reduction of costs of capital and improving value for money, reducing instability in the financial sector and avoiding upfront public sector spending (ibid.: 8). However, similar to state guarantees in the private banking sector, those in the field of PPP raise concerns about one of the core concepts of PPPs, namely the transfer of risks to the private sector. Consequently, the use of state guarantees across Western European states in PPP schemes is limited. EPEC (2011b: 33) mentions only a few examples, mostly in the Roman-French legal tradition. In France, for instance, loan and refinancing guarantees have been used since the authorities introduced a state guarantee scheme for high-level PPP projects as a response to the global financial crisis in early 2009, in combination with a large PPP pipeline. Thus, the government 'authorised a EUR 10 billion guarantee facility to be utilised on projects approved by an inter-ministerial committee and which were scheduled to reach financial close prior to the end of 2010. The scheme is managed by MAPPP, the French PPP unit' (ibid.).

In Italy, there are no formal state guarantees. However, similar instruments such as revenue or usage guarantees have been applied for individual projects, such as the 'Milan Metro Line 5' project in 2007 (€505 million). Furthermore, for strategic infrastructure projects, loan guarantees which also covered PPPs were provided by the Italian export credit agency (SACE SpA) of the Italian Ministry of the Economy and Finance. In Flanders (Belgium), the government introduced a refinancing guarantee scheme in April 2009 to mitigate the impact of the financial crisis. This scheme was available for projects to be tendered by April 2011 and conducted as Design, Build, Finance, Maintain (DBFM) contracts with the region-owned company in charge of public transportation in the area (De Lijn).[2] State guarantees have been used for the 'Flemish PPP schools' project (closed in 2010) which covered up to 211 schools. In Germany, the 'Forfaitierungsmodell' extensively used at local-level comprises a limitation of risk transfer to the private sector. However, it is not a model specially invented for the use of PPPs or in the context of the credit crunch. Rather, it has been criticized by PPP opponents as shielding too much risk from the private partners, undermining the idea of risk sharing in a PPP (Rügemer 2008).

In Portugal, as a reaction to the global financial crisis, the government passed legislation in early 2009 'allowing it to extend guarantees for up to EUR 6 billion in favour of projects, including PPPs' and covering a wide range of state support mechanisms (EPEC 2011b: 35). In Spain, the Council of Ministers in November 2009 adopted a draft law which allowed state guarantees for commercial bank debt for future PPPs. 'This would make the concept of "Responsibilidad Patrimonial" (or "State Responsibility") more explicit and quantifiable in PPP contracts. This concept has been interpreted as meaning that lenders will recover their debt outstanding in the case of termination caused by a PPP company default' (ibid.). In Greece, plans to 'include a guarantee from the Greek Ministry of Finance for the sub-sovereign payment obligations' are under preparation (ibid.: 36). In the UK, the European homeland of PPP/PFI, 'there is no SG [state guarantee] scheme as such' (ibid.: 34).

3.3.2 Veto Players

As a contested policy instrument, PPP is opposed by actors who are trying to stop or slow down a deeper tendency for the public sector to carry out more PPP projects. If these actors are 'veto players', they might successfully prevent a more intense use of PPP. An appropriate approach to analyse the chances of PPP opponents preventing a more intense use of PPP is the veto player approach by George Tsebelis (2002). In this approach, veto players are defined as individuals or institutions whose agreement is necessary for a change of the policy status quo. It assumes that the number of veto players and their ideological distances are good predictors for the chances of a policy change. More precisely, with an increase in the number of veto players or their ideological distances, 'policy stability' should also increase. However, as ideological distances are more difficult to operationalize, studies often focus on the number of veto players. Furthermore, in this study we limit the scope of veto players to the number of governing parties, thus, on partisan veto players at governmental level. Other kinds of veto players might encompass heads of state, second parliamentary chambers, and constitutional courts.

Owing to the necessary consensus required among coalition partners, each single coalition party has the power to exercise a veto with regard to

PPP. According to Tsebelis (2002), it's the veto players, not the agenda setters, that decide the success or failure of policy changes. In other words, veto players limit the room for manoeuvre of a government, so that their favoured policies cannot be realized without concession to and compromise with other parties in a (coalition) government. Thus, the tested variable includes only the number of parties in government whose approval for introducing PPPs or supporting legislation at national level in a country is a necessary condition. The variable is also based on the assumption that the central level of the political system plays a crucial role in the implementation of the PPP approach across all levels. While PPPs are also performed at the local and regional levels of a political system, it can be assumed that without the support of the central level at these lower levels no extensive activity comes about.

Thus, according to the theory, a small number of partisan veto players in the central government is conducive to the implementation of PPP in a country, because the existence of many veto players forces a government to compromise, which in turn reduces the likelihood of policy change. Furthermore, a low number of partisan veto players in government can also lead to a shift from party influence to executive power.

For the purpose of this study, the operationalization of this variable was done by calculating the average number of government parties per year for the period 1990–2009, with data obtained from the World Bank's Database of Political Institutions (DPI 2009). The number of parties in government in Italy was derived from figures provided in Pasquino (2008). For Germany, since the number of the cooperating parties CDU (Christian Democratic Union) and CSU (Christian Social Union) was not uniform, they were each counted as a single partisan veto player (Table 3.4). This means that despite the change of government in 1998 and 2005, in the investigation period two partisan veto players are counted for the whole period (see also Saalfeld 2005: 54).

3.4 SOCIOECONOMIC AGENDA SETTERS

3.4.1 The Construction Sector

In terms of 'agenda setters', not all sectors of the economy have similar levels of interest in PPP arrangements. Among those sectors most deeply involved are construction and financial services. While the construction sector provides the 'hardware' for infrastructure and facility projects, the financial sector provides the crucial 'software' for the private partners across different sectors of the economy. With regard to the construction sector, PPP is frequently used most intensely for infrastructure projects such as planning, building and maintaining or enhancing streets, bridges or tunnels. Furthermore, in the building sector a broad range of services are offered, from planning and constructing of new facilities and refurbishments of existing ones to complex facility management agreements. Not infrequently, land development and ownership issues are also included in such deals.

At the macro level, a large construction sector in a national economy often plays an active role in lobbying the public and local, regional and national governments (as well as at EU level) for PPP. While the construction sector may be interested in making (long-term guaranteed) sales and profits, from the point of view of governments there are several reasons to take PPP into consideration in such a context. For example, large-scale projects can be seen as a kind of support for the regional or national construction sector to prevent short-time working, further reduction of staff, or foreign takeovers of domestic firms. In Germany, for example, an intense commitment from the federation of the construction industry (HDB) and the then social democratic chancellor in 2002 in high-level talks was observed (Sack 2009: 197). These talks happened in the context of a decline in construction activity after a peak period – induced by the German reunification – and the bankruptcy of a large construction company (Holzmann) in the same year. Despite this decline, ten years later the core construction sector still consisted of over 750 000 employees. Also, the development of the PPP Acceleration Law in 2005 was lobbied for by the sector's main association (Hauptverband der Deutschen Bauindustrie, HDB, see Sack 2009: 207). Spain is another example of a country with a large construction sector (real estate boom up until 2007) with a strong emphasis on PPP (Rügemer 2008: 52).

To empirically test this variable, we use the sector share of gross value added (GVA) according to the national accounts (Eurostat). The GVA includes services provided in a given country in a given period of economic performance of the economy as a whole or of individual sectors. It is calculated by deducting the value of intermediate consumption from the value of all goods and services produced.

Owing to the lack of data for some countries up to 1994, we limit the observation period to 1995–2009. Within this period, in the already mentioned case of Germany the size of the construction sector shrank from 6.9 per cent of GVA in 1995 to 4.1 per cent in 2006. However, not all cases show such a declining trend for their construction activity. Ireland and Spain experienced significantly increasing sector trends up to 2006, as did the UK, although the growth was somewhat weaker. Spain's construction sector represented 14.2 per cent of GVA in 2006 according to Eurostat. Table 3.4 summarizes the indicators for the construction sector for the selected sample and time period.

3.4.2 The Financial Sector

Besides the construction sector, the provision of financial services also has an important role in the PPP approach, independently from the field of public–private collaboration. Only in a limited number of cases might the EIB replace or supplement the high initial investment costs of a project which are not borne by the public purse. Thus it is necessary for private banks and financial organizations to lend to the private partners in a PPP. Despite the involvement of sometimes large companies as the private partner in the contract, they frequently depend on external financing (Yescombe 2007). This leads to significant capital requirements, which are mostly covered by the national banking and financial sector. In addition to the banking sector, a certain amount of external funding is provided by the EIB. This is especially the case for 'peripheral' or 'lagged' economies within the EU, as the lending policy of the EIB is bound to structural and developmental objectives. Given the importance of the financial sector participation in a PPP, the 'financial close' of a project is always very important, especially in the period after the global credit crunch in 2008 (see section 2.3).

Given these requirements for external financing, the financial sector could be very interested in the PPP approach, as it transfers these initial requirements from the public to the private purse, enabling the financial sector additional long-term deals and profits. Furthermore, banks or creditors may charge higher interest rates for private borrowers than public ones, given the (usually) lower risk of public borrowers. In Germany, during the introduction of PPP, the active role of the association of public banks (VÖB – Bundesverband Öffentlicher Banken Deutschlands) has been observed (Sack 2009: 207). For the UK, Rügemer (2008) has emphasized the role of the City of London, as the financial centre of the country, for introducing and promoting PFI in the UK. Italy is another example of a country with links between a large financial sector and the promotion of the PPP approach via the Ministry of Finance. Thus, it is very likely that representatives of this sector could act as the 'agenda setter' for the public and the governments to lobby for PPP and thereby create additional demand for external, public or private capital from the banking sector. The larger this sector is, the more influence or 'pressure' it might generate and the more politicians might be inclined to back the PPP approach.

To empirically test this theoretically plausible correlation, we compare the share of the GVA from the financial sector to the total value added in a given economy per year. Due to missing values in the data from Eurostat (nama_nace38_c), the period of observation was limited to the years 1995–2009 again. According to this criterion, Ireland, the UK and the Netherlands should be the most intensive PPP users (Table 3.4).

3.4.3 Interest Group Arrangements

The structure of interest group arrangements has long been neglected as a possible factor of influence on the level of PPP activity. This may be due to the fact that empirical international comparisons of systems of interest group arrangements are rather rare. Up to date of writing, the works of Siaroff (1999) and Lijphart (1999) have set the benchmarks (with the latter mainly based on the former). Such empirical approaches usually take pluralism and corporatism as different poles of the dimension that characterizes the structure of interest group arrangements in a country. The leading role of the UK in introducing the PPP/PFI policy in Europe (Hellowell 2012) leads to the assumption that this pluralistic institutional feature of the UK might also have contributed to the spread of PPP/PFI across the country itself.

Pluralistic systems of interest group organization are characterized by a variety of rather small interest groups, weak peak or umbrella organizations, and weak tripartite structures. Under such institutional conditions, it can be assumed that organizations such as labour unions cannot build great resistance against planned PPP activities in their respective jurisdictions. In contrast, in more corporatist dominated systems, top unions, entrepreneurial organizations and other 'promotional groups' can indeed promote or resist ideas or policies at the political level. As a contested policy, it can be assumed that, for example, labour unions might use their political influence at macrostructural level to prevent or slow down a policy change towards PPP. In other words, corporatist interest group arrangements might function as 'opportunity structures' for PPP opponents such as labour unions and other public sector specific 'protective groups' (Hague/Harrop 2010: 230), enabling them to exercise resistance that must be overcome by proponents in order to proceed.

Katzenstein (1985) has placed the development of corporatist structures in the context of small, open economies (e.g. Switzerland, the Netherlands). In his view, corporatism has developed as a protective mechanism against unwelcome influences of the global economy. Thus, corporatism would be a socioeconomic compensation or defence strategy in open, but not adversarial dominated, institutional orders. In contrast, in

Table 3.4 Institutional and agenda-setter variables at a glance

	LEGTRAD	PVP			FSEC			CSEC			INTG_A		INTG_B	
	Legal traditions in the sample	Partisan veto players at government level, 1990–2009			GVA financial sector, 1995–2009 (%)			GVA construction sector, 1995–2009 (%)			Siaroff 1999		Lijphart 1999	
	Code	SD	Mean	Rank	SD	Mean	Rank	SD	Mean	Rank	Mid-1990s	Rank	1971–1996	Rank
AT	3	0.00	2.00	5	0.21	5.41	6	0.47	7.53	3	4.625	13	0.62	13
BE	2	1.20	4.55	13	0.30	6.01	5	0.24	5.30	12	3.750	8	1.25	9
DE	3	0.00	2.00	5	0.42	4.68	11	0.91	5.03	13	4.125	10	1.38	8
DK	4	0.85	2.85	10	0.51	5.29	7	0.33	5.33	11	4.250	11	1.12	11
EL	2	0.35	1.15	2	0.40	4.71	10	0.81	6.89	5	2.000	1	3.50	1
ES	2	1.20	1.60	4	0.36	4.93	8	1.82	11.53	1	2.000	1	3.25	3
FI	4	1.05	4.30	12	0.61	3.32	14	0.67	6.24	7	4.375	12	1.00	12
FR	2	1.53	3.05	11	0.22	4.19	13	0.55	5.46	10	2.250	4	3.00	4
IE	1	0.43	2.25	7	1.50	8.79	1	1.92	7.45	4	2.625	6	2.88	7
IT	2	1.45	4.95	14	0.33	4.79	9	0.50	5.69	8	3.000	7	3.00	4
NL	2	0.43	2.75	8	0.61	6.53	3	0.17	5.64	9	4.000	9	1.25	9
PT	2	0.35	1.15	2	0.72	6.26	4	0.45	7.57	2	2.375	5	3.00	4
SE	4	1.07	2.80	9	0.47	4.50	12	0.33	4.68	14	4.625	13	0.50	14
UK	1	0.00	1.00	1	1.34	7.58	2	0.50	6.35	6	2.000	1	3.50	1

Notes:
CSEC at current basic prices and exchange rates; national accounts at current prices. Code nama_nace38_c.
SD = empirical standard deviation.

Sources: PVP: DPI 2009 and own amendment for Germany (Niedermayer 2006) and Italy (Pasquino 2008). FSEC and CSEC: www.eurostat.eu. Mean, standard deviation (SD) and rank own calculation. See also Krumm 2014: 455.

pluralistic notions of democracy, a superior authority who wants to help the 'common good' or common interest prevail by means of regulation and integration of the organizational influence is not necessary. In these views, the immediate political solutions arise through the interaction of individual (groups of) interests – and can be implemented by the government without major resistance.

The rise of the PPP approach since the 1990s could therefore correspond with the 'decline' of corporatism in traditionally strong corporatist countries. Thus, it can be expected that a high degree of interest group pluralism can facilitate a high level of PPP activity.

As indicators, the integration score formulated by Siaroff (1999) for the mid-1990s (INTG_A) and the corporatism index of Lijphart (1999, INTG_B), which is based on Siaroff (1999) but covers a larger period, are used. The differences between the ranks in Siaroff (mid-1990s) and Lijphart's period of 1971–1996 are biggest in the cases of the UK, the Netherlands, Italy and Finland. According to Siaroff's ranking for the mid-1990s, which comes closest to monitoring the situation in the early phase of our investigation period, the UK, Greece and Spain should depict the highest PPP activity, if the structure of the interest group system has any significance (Table 3.4).

3.5 CONTROL VARIABLES

3.5.1 Deficit

As governments usually like to spend in order to keep their people happy, a certain level of fiscal pressure is an almost permanent issue for most of the countries. However, in the European context, the public and political support for 'austerity policy' varies across different regions, with a much tighter deficit policy in the north and a more relaxed policy in the south (especially in Greece). Thus, the achievement of budget surpluses on the one hand or deeply running the budget into deficit on the other could have an influence on the openness of government towards the PPP approach. As a budget deficit has to be justified, opposition parties can attack governments, both in parliament, especially during the annual parliamentary budget debate, and in the general public, and they can criticize the governments for their unsound and undisciplined budgetary policy. Against this background, there could be an incentive to increase the use of PPP as an alternative form of financing and a means to reducing the strain on the current budget.

PPP as an alternative to immediate full public financing might be particularly attractive to governments with high deficits, as the necessary credits for a project are made from the private sector and are not (fully) included in the public accounts at the beginning of a project. By using PPP, a government can refer to benefits, without the cost of it leading to an immediate rise in the current and next budgets. Despite such bypassing opportunities being limited due to a change of rules by the International Accounting Standards Board in April 2009, it can be hypothesized that states with high annual deficits have bigger incentives to avoid fiscal stress and therefore make greater use of PPP. While in theory this link between higher PPP activity and higher budget deficits appears to be convincing, empirical proof remains rare.

In order to empirically test such a correlation, the deficit variable has to be operationalized. Due to the research design introduced earlier, we have to calculate average (mean) percentages of annual funding gaps for the investigation period. However, as data for the early 1990s are not available at Eurostat, we have had to limit the deficit period, which runs until 2009, by starting with the year 1995. The data were retrieved from Eurostat in November 2011. Table 3.5 documents the values for the first and last year of the period as well as some in between (2000 and 2005). Furthermore, the standard deviation as well as the mean is calculated. The ranks in the last column are based on the mean. The largest average deficits are assigned to the highest ranking values in the scale; countries with an average budgetary surplus were ranked with low values to express the expected correlation. The countries with the largest average deficits are Greece, Portugal and Italy. The Nordic countries can boast having the only surplus budgets on average over the investigation period, most obviously in the case of Finland with an average surplus of 1.8 per cent.

3.5.2 Sovereign Debt

If a high budget deficit can be regarded as ‘acute stress’ in the field of financial policy, a high sovereign debt ratio can be said to be triggering ‘chronic stress’ in that regard. In contrast to the annual budget deficit, the level of sovereign debt accumulated in a country triggers different kinds of ‘stress’ on a government, as can be illustrated with the case of Greece after the global financial crisis. In terms of accountability, governments can argue that the bulk of the debt has been accumulated by previous governments. However, a government may be held to have done nothing towards its reduction. In addition, the Euro convergence criteria according to the Maastricht Treaty allow only a total debt of 60 per cent of

Table 3.5 Fiscal balance of government in per cent of GDP, 1995–2009

	1995	2000	2005	2009	Standard deviation	Period mean	Rank
AT	–5.8	–1.7	–1.7	–4.1	1.6	–2.3	6
BE	–4.5	0.0	–2.7	–5.8	1.9	–1.5	9
DE		1.3	–3.3	–3.2	1.6	–2.2	7
DK	–2.9	2.3	5.2	–2.7	2.6	1.2	13
EL		–3.7	–5.2	–15.8	3.4	–6.9	1
ES	–6.5	–1.0	1.0	–11.2	3.4	–2.2	7
FI	–6.2	6.8	2.7	–2.5	3.5	1.8	14
FR	–5.5	–1.5	–2.9	–7.5	1.5	–3.3	4
IE	–2.1	4.7	1.6	–14.2	4.5	–0.4	11
IT	–7.4	–0.8	–4.3	–5.4	1.8	–3.5	3
NL		2.0	–0.3	–5.6	1.8	–1.0	10
PT	–5.0	–2.9	–5.9	–10.1	1.8	–4.2	2
SE	–7.4	3.6	2.2	–0.7	2.8	0.2	12
UK	–5.9	3.6	–3.4	–11.5	3.3	–2.8	5

Notes:
Missing values for Germany and the Netherlands in 1995, Greece until 1999.
The values of the recent years reported to Eurostat may be subject to change.

Sources: Eurostat [tsieb080] and own calculation. Date of access: 9 November 2011.

GDP. Apparently, the highly indebted countries in the EU, also labelled as the 'PIGS group' (Portugal, Italy, Greece, Spain), are more likely to belong to the medium- to high-level PPP countries. On the other hand, Belgium, France and Germany too did accumulate higher debt ratios without pioneering for PPP. Also the UK (rank 12) is not under the top scorer in this variable.

Thus, we can expect that the overall debt level might trigger less stress on a government's fiscal policy than the annual deficit. However, the total level of debt (as a share of GDP) can also be assumed to trigger financial stress for a government. The degree of influence the debt level has on the level of PPP activity in a state should be empirically tested, as with increasing debt level the ability of a government to act decreases. Thus, highly indebted governments may be tempted in such a situation of chronic stress to use the PPP approach in order to improve their ability to act without in the short-term running further into debt. Governments could, for example, modernize and expand a country's infrastructure and thereby increase their popularity, without increasing the national debt level by leaps and bounds. Thus, it can be expected that governments with a high debt quota are more inclined to use PPP than those with lower indebtedness or even surpluses to improve their capabilities for acting.

Table 3.6 Sovereign debt ratios of public entities in per cent of GDP, 1995–2009

	1995	2000	2005	2009	Standard deviation	Period mean	Rank
AT	68.3	66.5	64.6	69.5	2.3	65.7	4
BE	130.4	107.9	92.1	95.9	14.3	104.8	2
DE	55.6	59.7	68.0	74.4	4.7	63.0	5
DK	72.6	52.4	37.8	41.8	13.2	49.6	11
EL	97.0	103.4	100.0	129.3	8.6	102.8	3
ES	63.3	59.3	43.0	53.8	10.1	53.2	10
FI	56.6	43.8	41.7	43.3	6.5	44.8	14
FR	55.5	57.3	66.4	79.0	5.7	62.2	6
IE	82.0	37.8	27.4	65.2	18.0	45.0	13
IT	121.5	109.2	105.9	115.5	6.1	110.5	1
NL	76.1	53.8	51.8	60.8	9.2	57.9	8
PT	59.2	48.5	62.8	83.0	9.1	59.2	7
SE	72.8	53.9	50.4	42.7	11.5	55.4	9
UK	51.2	41.0	42.5	69.6	8.0	46.2	12

Note: The values of the recent years reported to Eurostat by national statistic offices may be subject to change.

Source: Eurostat. Date of access: 9 November 2011.

As can be seen in Table 3.6, a leading group comprising Italy, Greece and Belgium stands out, with Belgium being the country where debt has been reduced most strongly within this group (–34.5 per cent). The bottom group, with a relatively low average level of sovereign debt of below 50 per cent of GDP, is formed by Finland, Ireland, the UK and Denmark. With Ireland and the UK being among the 'model students' of the northern periphery, the results of this variable differ a little from the familiar pattern of the Nordic countries. Sweden's average debt is even higher than that of Spain. In this longitudinal study, from 2005 a split of the countries into an upper group formed by Germany, France, Portugal and Austria, and a lower group formed by the Netherlands, the UK, Sweden, Finland, Spain, Denmark and Ireland becomes clearer. In Ireland, and somewhat more weakly in the UK, a sharp increase in the debt ratio from 2007 is noticeable. With regard to this variable, we would expect Italy, Belgium and Greece to be the top PPP users.

3.5.3 GDP

As another control variable, we also have to test for the influence of the GDP per capita. The GDP is widely regarded as an indicator of a country's annual economic activities or output. It is usually defined as the aggregated value of consumption, investment, government spending and net exports in a given country and period. It is sometimes also regarded as an indicator for the standard of living in a country or the country's economic well-being. However, such interpretations of the GDP have also been criticized, as for standard of living and economic well-being other factors not included in the GDP might be relevant. As inflation does not contribute to the real GDP, it appears more appropriate for comparative use than the inflation driven nominal GDP.

In the context of the PPP approach, it can be expected that well-performing economies might have a lower incentive to use the PPP policy. Better performing economies might have already found their ways and means to produce added value and thus might have lower incentives to undertake reforms and use contested policy tools such as PPP in the public sector. They might have alternative ways such as differentiated tax increases as measures for public finance. In contrast, for low-performing economies the incentives to use new, probably more efficient and cost saving but also contested policy instruments such as PPP, might be higher. Thus, we expect a high GDP per capita to reduce countries' willingness to use PPP, whereas a low GDP per capita can contribute to a more risk-tolerant policy towards PPP. The details of operationalization of this variable are outlined in Table 3.7.

3.5.4 Privatization Proceeds

In political science, PPP is often analysed in the context of ('neoliberal') privatization policies. Thus, it is widely regarded as a special form of privatization, more precisely as functional privatization (Krumm 2013b). Whereas privatization usually means full (material) privatization or formal (judicial) privatization, a PPP can appear under both public and private law and comprise more or less substantive tasks. The specific difference of a contractual PPP to full or formal privatization is the limited durability of the cooperation. Whereas traditional privatization usually is hard to reverse (despite some cases of renationalization), contractual PPPs raise, according to the life-cycle approach, at the end of the contract period questions of how to fulfil the specific tasks in the future. However, these aspects mainly concern formal differences between privatization and PPP. In the context of politics, in several cases in our sample an intensive phase of material privatization preceded the adoption of the PPP approach. In the UK, as the archetypal case, the 1980s were marked by an intensive policy of privatization under the Thatcher government, while in the 1990s, when the PFI and later the PPP policies took off, privatization was already over its peak.

A similar pattern can be observed for Portugal. In contrast to, for example, Greece, Portugal started, soon after a democratic transformation, a large-scale privatization programme of the huge state-owned sector. As a precondition, they even had to change the constitution and abolish certain norms that prohibited privatization. After an intense phase of privatization in the 1980s, Portugal turned to the PPP approach in the 1990s. Compared to the UK and Portugal, Greece is at the other end of the spectrum. In Greece there has been (and still is) an oversized and ineffective public sector. Even in the course of the economic crisis commencing with the global financial crisis, Greek politicians and officials were highly reluctant to privatize state-owned assets and enterprises. Coerced by the 'troika', consisting of the European Commission, the International Monetary Fund (IMF) and the ECB, to open up protected industries and privatize public enterprises, the result was more sobering. In 2008 the only large privatization was the sale of Olympic Airways for about €200 million. Even in this case the state had to reduce staff by half, using compensation payments and early retirement schemes to increase its attractiveness for private investors. In the following years, privatization proceeds were even lower; despite the crisis, privatization of the large public state-owned enterprises (SOEs) remained highly unpopular among public and politicians.

Whereas Greece was on the one hand highly reluctant to privatize, they were on the other hand quite enthusiastic about the PPP approach. They passed a PPP law in 2005 (the same year as in Germany), which among others things set up the Special Secretariat for PPP and regulated the political decision-making process for PPP projects (see section 9.3). Despite the lack of efficiency in the first years of the Special Secretariat, Greece soon produced a considerable level of activity under the Karamanlis government.

In France, the support for privatization and PPP rose relatively late compared to the UK or even Germany. However, similar to Spain and

Portugal, there is a long tradition of concessions that could be utilized for the PPP approach. As will be shown in section 8.1 in more detail, the 'statist' understanding of the role of the state in the economy has long been prevalent. Radical unions and public opinion also successfully obstructed privatization and liberalization for a long time. However, between 2004 and 2008 privatization proceeded in France at a relatively high rate. This period of intense privatization coincided also with an intense adoption of the PPP approach.

The Nordic countries again pursued a different approach to privatization and PPP. Given the Nordic welfare state model, the potential for privatization and PPP could have been expected to be relatively high. In fact, it was not. Some countries like Finland had already pursued a more intense privatization approach in the 1980s; however, their general level of privatization as well as PPP activity remained low. This can be explained by the political consensus and political culture on the one hand and the relatively effective public sector organization on the other. In other words, with relatively effective SOEs the 'temptation' of privatization and PPP is less intense (Köthenbürger 2006: xviii).

Differences between privatization and PPP are also sector specific. Onset by the EU, privatization in the late 1980s first occurred in such sectors as electricity and telecommunication. Those sectors where the EU has set early legislation for liberalization and privatization, like telecommunication, have especially experienced huge transformations.

In contrast to these sectors, PPPs were first applied to the roads, rail and light-rail infrastructure, and later were transferred to sectors such as education, health and prisons. In these sectors, the EU has set different priorities, focusing less on privatization and liberalization. With, for instance, the Trans European Network (TEN) programme, they focused more on supporting infrastructure for the free flow of goods and persons as a foundation of the single European market. Table 3.7 summarizes the data of the socioeconomic variables.

3.6 COMPARATIVE FINDINGS

3.6.1 Bivariate Correlations

In a first step, quantitative correlations between the PPP investment level and the possible factors of influence introduced above were tested by an ordinal correlation (Spearman's rho, Table 3.8). A Pearson correlation gives outliers such as the UK or Denmark too much weight in the results, given the relatively small size of the sample. However, it is documented

Table 3.7 Control variables in comparison

	PRIV_A (1990–2000)			PRIV_B (1990–2009)		DEFI (1995–2009)			GDP per capita (1995–2009)		
	Privatization proceeds (US$ m)	% of GDP	Rank	Mean	Rank	Std. dev.	Mean	Rank	Std. dev.	Mean	Rank
AT	1 439	5.87	9	0.402	10	1.6	–2.3	6	2 349	28 440	5
BE	9 611	4.44	11	0.157	14	1.9	–1.5	9	1 959	27 513	8
DE	21 711	1.22	14	0.255	12	1.6	–2.2	7	1 556	26 500	9
DK	6 048	4.64	10	0.240	13	2.6	1.2	13	2 180	36 487	1
EL	12 329	8.50	6	0.756	3	3.4	–6.9	1	2 094	15 753	13
ES	37 660	5.93	8	0.415	9	3.4	–2.2	7	1 854	19 473	12
FI	11 000	10.00	2	0.980	2	3.5	1.8	14	3 502	27 527	7
FR	75 488	6.14	7	0.497	6	1.5	–3.3	4	1 546	26 133	10
IE	7 613	9.22	3	0.434	8	4.5	–0.4	11	5 777	34 113	2
IT	108 642	9.03	4	0.643	5	1.8	–3.5	3	1 025	23 787	11
NL	13 641	4.19	12	0.456	7	1.8	–1.0	10	2 505	30 227	4
PT	25 292	18.24	1	1.482	1	1.8	–4.2	2	917	14 087	14
SE	17 295	8.81	5	0.687	4	2.8	0.2	12	3 317	30 247	3
UK	42 808	3.92	13	0.359	11	3.3	–2.8	5	2 887	27 933	6

Note: Missing values for Germany and the Netherlands 1995, Greece till 1999.

Sources: INTG: Siaroff 1999, S. 198; Lijphart 1999, S. 177. PRIV_A: Zohlnhöfer et al. 2008, S. 99. PRIV_B: Privatization Barometer 2011; per cent share of privatization proceeds by partial or total privatization of public enterprises. Available online at www.privatizationbarometer.net/index.php [16 February 2013]. DEFI: Eurostat [tsieb080]. Means and rank own calculation.

in Table 3.9. Furthermore, as coefficients according to Pearson are often lower than those of a rank correlation, care was taken that variables were not excluded too early for the further steps. However, in contrast to multiple regression models, bivariate correlations can only test 'gross models'. Thus, for example, mediation and suppression effects between the independent variables cannot be made visible. On the other hand, besides the bivariate effects on the PPP activity level, correlations between the independent variables can be reported and give hints on the possible decrease of variable effects in a multivariate model. The effect of such cross correlated variables in bivariate models often becomes much weaker in multiple regression models.

The results of the rank correlations (as well as of Pearson's r) indicate a highly significant influence of the partisan veto players on the level of PPP activity. This variable shows the highest coefficient (–.766) as well as the highest level of significance (.001) among the tested variables in Table 3.8. However, a significant correlation of the veto player variable with the construction sector variable might reduce the effect in a multiple regression setting. The second strongest effect is indicated for the interest group variable according to Siaroff (1999). Again, a significant correlation with another independent variable has to be reported (with deficit and GDP), which is likely to lower the effect in a multiple regression setting.

Among the agenda-setter variables, the size of the construction sector comes next (correlated with the PVP variable) and then, with a slight distance in the coefficient, the size of the financial sector. The financial sector variable is only at a 5 per cent significance level and shows no correlation with the other independent variables. Furthermore, the level of deficit reached a 5 per cent significance level and a coefficient of -.585. Its negative sign posts in the 'right' direction of the estimated correlation of higher deficit (lower, negative value in Table 3.7) and higher PPP activity. However, it is also cross correlated with two control variables, the GDP and debt, and the structure of interest groups. In contrast to the average deficit level, the average debt level is far from any significance for a higher or lower PPP activity. This confirms our expectation that among the two public finance variables, the deficit is much more relevant for the level of PPP activity.

Surprisingly, the level of privatization proceeds has no effect for both tested indicators on the level of PPP activity. As a consequence, this supports the assumption that PPP should not be interpreted as a kind of 'privatization light'. Instead, the non-correlation strongly suggests that PPP is applied independently from privatization policies; its application follows its own logic. For the GDP variable, the sign of the coefficient

Table 3.8 *Bivariate rank correlation (Spearman's rho)*

		PPP	PVP	FSEC	CSEC	INTG_A	INTG_B	PRIV_A	PRIV_B	DEFI	DEBT	GDP	LEGTRAD
PPP	coefficient	1	–.766**	.613*	.675**	.692**	–.709**	–.046	.011	–.585*	.073	–.455	–.759**
	sig.		.001	.020	.008	.006	.004	.876	.970	.028	.805	.102	.002
PVP	coefficient	–.766**	1	–.433	–.616*	–.486	.473	.101	–.068	.407	.213	.198	.388
	sig.	.001		.122	.019	.078	.087	.731	.817	.148	.464	.497	.170
FSEC	coefficient	.613*	–.433	1	.385	.206	–.259	–.204	–.345	–.066	–.138	.262	–.646*
	sig.	.020	.122		.175	.480	.372	.483	.227	.823	.637	.366	.013
CSEC	coefficient	.675**	–.616*	.385	1	.458	–.477	.385	.292	–.394	–.169	–.371	–.442
	sig.	.008	.019	.175		.100	.084	.175	.311	.164	.563	.191	.113
INTG_A	coefficient	.692**	–.486	.206	.458	1	–.968**	–.011	.111	–.724**	.124	–.646*	–.751**
	sig.	.006	.078	.480	.100		.000	.970	.707	.003	.673	.013	.002
INTG_B	coefficient	–.709**	.473	–.259	–.477	–.968**	1	–.020	–.095	.635*	–.040	.590*	.798**
	sig.	.004	.087	.372	.084	.000		.946	.747	.015	.893	.026	.001
PRIV_A	coefficient	–.046	.101	–.204	.385	–.011	–.020	1	.802**	–.064	–.152	–.244	.033
	sig.	.876	.731	.483	.175	.970	.946		.001	.828	.605	.401	.911
PRIV_B	coefficient	.011	–.068	–.345	.292	.111	–.095	.802**	1	–.255	–.059	–.407	.052
	sig.	.970	.817	.227	.311	.707	.747	.001		.379	.840	.149	.860
DEFI	coefficient	–.585*	.407	–.066	–.394	–.724**	.635*	–.064	–.255	1	–.620*	.770**	.494
	sig.	.028	.148	.823	.164	.003	.015	.828	.379		.018	.001	.073
DEBT	coefficient	.073	.213	–.138	–.169	.124	–.040	–.152	–.059	–.620*	1	–.495	–.040
	sig.	.805	.464	.637	.563	.673	.893	.605	.840	.018		.072	.891
GDP	coefficient	–.455	.198	.262	–.371	–.646*	.590*	-.244	–.407	.770**	–.495	1	.253
	sig.	.102	.497	.366	.191	.013	.026	.401	.149	.001	.072		.383
LEGTRAD	coefficient	–.759**	.388	–.646*	–.442	–.751**	.798**	.033	.052	.494	–.040	.253	1
	sig.	.002	.170	.013	.113	.002	.001	.911	.860	.073	.891	.383	

Note: Sig. = significance; * $p<0.05$, ** $p<0.01$; two-tailed, N = 14.

Source: Own calculation.

Table 3.9 Bivariate correlation (Pearson)

		PPP	PVP	FSEC	CSEC	INTG_A	INTG_B	PRIV_A	PRIV_B	DEFI	DEBT	GDP	LEGTRAD
PPP	coefficient	1	–.665**	.448	.250	–.646*	.626*	.319	.356	–.524	–.067	–.492	–.554*
	sig.		.009	.108	.389	.013	.017	.267	.211	.054	.820	.074	.040
PVP	coefficient	–.665**	1	–.377	–.482	.472	–.413	–.132	–.173	.431	.382	.343	.323
	sig.	.009		.184	.081	.088	.142	.653	.553	.124	.177	.230	.260
FSEC	coefficient	.448	–.377	1	.143	–.304	.290	.018	–.186	–.024	–.210	.181	–.690**
	sig.	.108	.184		.626	.291	.315	.952	.523	.936	.470	.556	.006
CSEC	coefficient	.250	–.482	.143	1	–.499	.453	.224	.144	–.219	–.189	–.277	–.331
	sig.	.389	.081	.626		.069	.104	.442	.622	.451	.517	.337	.248
INTG_A	coefficient	–.646*	.472	–.304	–.499	1	–.981**	–.253	–.196	.669**	–.121	–.549*	.782**
	sig.	.013	.088	.291	.069		.000	.384	.502	.009	.681	.035	.001
INTG_B	coefficient	.626*	–.413	.290	.453	–.981**	1	.263	.214	–.678**	.164	–.561*	–.769**
	sig.	.017	.142	.315	.104	.000		.364	.463	.008	.575	.037	.001
Priv_A	coefficient	.319	–.132	.018	.224	–.253	.263	1	.921**	–.189	–.002	–.506	–.038
	sig.	.267	.653	.952	.442	.384	.364		.000	.518	.996	.065	.896
Priv_B	coefficient	.356	–.173	–.186	.144	–.196	.214	.921**	1	–.233	–.053	–.610*	.077
	sig.	.211	.553	.523	.622	.502	.463	.000		.422	.856	.020	.795
DEFI	coefficient	–.524	.431	–.024	–.219	.669**	–.678**	–.189	–.233	1	–.573*	.777**	.558*
	sig.	.054	.124	.936	.451	.009	.008	.518	.422		.032	.001	.038
DEBT	coefficient	–.067	.382	–.210	–.189	–.121	.164	–.002	–.053	–.573*	1	–.397	–.190
	sig.	.820	.177	.470	.517	.681	.575	.996	.856	.032		.160	.516
GDP	coefficient	–.492	.343	.181	–.277	–.549*	–.561*	–.506	–.610*	.777**	–.397	1	.283
	sig.	.074	.230	.556	.337	.035	.037	.065	.020	.001	.160		.327
LEGTRAD	coefficient	–.554*	.323	–.690**	–.331	.782**	–.769**	–.038	.077	.558*	–.190	.283	1
	sig.	.040	.260	.006	.248	.001	.001	.896	.795	.038	.516	.327	

Note: Sig. = significance; * $p<0.05$, ** $p<0.01$; two-tailed, N = 14.

Source: Own calculation.

posts in the 'right' direction of the estimated negative effect between 'wealth' and PPP activity; however, it does not even reach a 10 per cent significance level.

Finally, it turns out that the legal tradition strongly correlates with the level of PPP activity. The strength of the coefficient and the significance level are similar to those of the partisan veto player variable. This result corroborates our assumption expressed in Table 3.3. The two main groups (common and civil law countries), and their four respective legal traditions, do significantly correlate with the level of PPP activity among the tested 14 cases. Anglo-Saxon case law, followed by Roman-French, Roman-German and Roman-Scandinavian civil law, seems to strongly influence the propensity of the selected cases to achieve higher levels of PPP activity. However, as this variable was coded only qualitatively (nominal values), further exploration of this finding would be needed. Due to its nominal coding, we exclude it from further calculations.

As a result it can be noted that the partisan veto player variable seem to have the strongest effect on the level of PPP activity, followed by the structure of interest groups (pluralism) and then the size of the construction sector. All three are significant at the strong level of 1 per cent; however, all three are also correlated with at least one more independent variable.

The size of the financial sector and the level of the budget deficit can be distinguished as a second group. Among all tested variables, only the size of the financial sector is not confounded with other variables. As the deficit is significantly correlated with the structure of interest groups, it can be expected that the influence of these variables might be reduced in a multiple regression model. A third group of variables encompasses the non-significant variables of the GDP and the level of privatization proceeds. Between these, due to its medium–strong coefficient, the GDP should remain 'under observation' (Krumm 2014: 461).

In Table 3.9 we have applied a more challenging interval correlation (Pearson). The PVP variable is a bit weaker than in the rank correlation but still 'leading the pack'. Both the construction and the financial sector have lost their significance. The two interest group variables remain significant and come close to the PVP variable. Also, deficit has failed to reach the 5 per cent significance level, however, comes very close to it with a significance of .054. Legal tradition (as a nominal variable) also remains significant in this correlation. To sum up, the more sophisticated Pearson correlation guides our focus of attention to the number of partisan veto players and the structure of interest groups (as well as the legal tradition) among our selection of variables.

3.6.2 Qualitative Comparative Analysis (QCA)

In a solely quantitative setting, the next step would be a multiple regression analysis. However, for small and medium-sized samples, mixed methods have to be applied in order to enhance the reliability of results. Thus, as a next step a QCA (see e.g. Berg-Schlosser 2005, Berg-Schlosser/Cronqvist 2012) is an appropriate means to further test the results of the previous section. QCA is available in several variants: a more contrast-focused crisp-set version with dichotomous coding of the variables (conditions, see Ragin 1987), a multivalue variant with a dichotomous coding of the dependent variables (outcome) and a multi-value coding on the independent variables (conditions, see Cronqvist 2007). Furthermore, the most advanced version is the fuzzy-set variant with the possibility of a continuous coding of the outcome and the conditions (Ragin 2000). With continuously coded conditions and outcome, fuzzy-set QCA (fsQCA) offers the lowest loss of information; on the other hand, a coding in small steps can lead to a significant loss of clarity in the results. Thus, finding an appropriate measure for the 'reduction of complexity' is best done by trial and error. In our study, multivalue QCA (mvQCA) with dichotomous outcome and trivalent conditions seems to offer an appropriate level of reduction of complexity without simplifying too much. The loss of information is still smaller as in the crisp-set variant, without losing too much of the contrast-sharpening function of a QCA.

The selection of variables is limited to those with significant coefficients in the previous section plus the GDP. The structure of interest groups is included only with the better results of the Siaroff indicator (INTG_A), as this one showed the higher significance level. Non-significant variables are excluded in order to keep the number of conditions small (Schneider/Wagemann 2007).

Technically, in a first round using the Tosmana software (tool for small-N analysis, see www.compasss.org/software.htm), the outcome 1 was set to 'explain' and the outcome 0 to 'exclude'; in a second round vice versa. In both rounds the same conditions (PVP, INTG_A, CSEC, FSEC, DEFI and GDP) as well as logical remainders were included for analysis. Missing outcomes and contradictions (not existing in the sample) were not included for analysis. Truth tables and thresholds were identical in both rounds. Thresholds were set with the cluster function of Tosmana and visually tested with the built-in threshold setter. The outcome was corrected manually by coding the number four ranked Spain into the group of active states in order to avoid a contradicting configuration. Table 3.10 shows the mvQCA coding. An identical configuration is only given for the cases of Germany and the Netherlands.

Table 3.10 Configuration of conditions and outcome with mvQCA

	PVP	CSEC	FSEC	INTG_A	DEFI	GDP	PPP (outcome)
Threshold	1.8; 3.7	6; 9.5	3.7; 7	2.5; 3.4	–5.6; –0.7	21 630; 32 180	100
AT	1 (2)	1 (7.53)	1 (5.41)	2 (4.625)	1 (–2.3)	1 (28 440)	0 (38.57)
BE	2 (4.55)	0 (5.3)	1 (6.01)	2 (3.75)	1 (–1.5)	1 (27 513)	0 (69.22)
DE	1 (2.6)	0 (5.03)	1 (4.68)	2 (4.125)	1 (–2.2)	1 (26 500)	0 (29.029)
DK	1 (2.85)	0 (5.33)	1 (5.29)	2 (4.25)	2 (1.2)	2 (36 487)	0 (0)
EL	0 (1.15)	1 (6.89)	1 (4.71)	0 (2)	0 (–6.9)	0 (15 753)	1 (256.66)
ES	0 (1.6)	2 (11.53)	1 (4.93)	0 (2)	1 (–2.2)	0 (19 473)	1 (105.77)
FI	2 (4.3)	1 (6.24)	0 (3.32)	2 (4.375)	2 (1.8)	1 (27 527)	0 (13.49)
FR	1 (3.05)	0 (5.46)	1 (4.19)	0 (2.25)	1 (–3.3)	1 (26 133)	0 (27.34)
IE	1 (2.25)	1 (7.45)	2 (8.79)	1 (2.625)	2 (–0.4)	2 (34 113)	0 (83.85)
IT	2 (4.95)	0 (5.69)	1 (4.79)	1 (3)	1 (–3.5)	1 (23 787)	0 (28.82)
NL	1 (2.75)	0 (5.64)	1 (6.53)	2 (4)	1 (-1)	1 (30 227)	0 (30.16)
PT	0 (1.15)	1 (7.57)	1 (6.26)	0 (2.375)	1 (–4.2)	0 (14 087)	1 (405.63)
SE	1 (2.8)	0 (4.68)	1 (4.5)	2 (4.625)	2 (0.2)	1 (30 247)	0 (6.04)
UK	0 (1)	1 (6.35)	2 (7.58)	0 (2)	1 (–2.8)	1 (27 933)	1 (526.46)

Sources: Krumm 2014: 462; own calculation with Tosmana, v. 1.3.0.1 (index values in parentheses).

The first round result of the reduction with Tosmana (minimizing value 1, including logical remainders) is:

PVP {0} (EL+ES+PT+UK) → Outcome PPP {1}

Subsequently, the result of the reduction for the cases with the outcome 0 (including logical remainders) is:

PVP {1, 2} (AT+BE+DE+NL+DK+FI+FR+IE+IT+SE) → Outcome PPP {0}

These results of the mvQCA corroborate the relevance of the veto player variable, was already clear from the correlation analysis above. A low number of partisan veto players (PVP 0) is the only necessary and sufficient condition (main implicant) for all the cases in the sample with a high PPP activity (outcome 1) among the tested variables. Vice versa, a low and medium number of partisan veto players (PVP 1, 2) is necessary and sufficient for explaining a low PPP activity (outcome 0) for all included cases. In order to look out for potential further implicants (e.g. under a slightly different case selection), Table 3.11 depicts a cross-tabulation of the outcomes and the tested conditions.

As shown in Table 3.10, the condition of a low number of veto players (PVP 0) is on its own sufficient to distinguish the different PPP outcomes. All cases with the outcome 1 (high PPP activity) show the condition of a low number of veto players (PVP 0) (necessary condition), which additionally is not represented by cases with the outcome 0, making it a sufficient condition. Thus, the consistency of the necessary condition and the coverage of the sufficient conditions are both 'one'. The sufficient condition PVP completely covers the explanatory high PPP activity (see Ragin 2006 for details of necessary and sufficient conditions as well as coverage).

In the remainder of this section, some more implicants are discussed which might explain the outcome for a limited number of cases. For example, an attempt could be made to get a similar constellation for the interest group arrangements (INTG_A) as for the PVP variable by coding France as more corporatist. However, by decreasing the lower threshold, first Portugal and then France would be transferred to the 'middle class' of medium active states. Thus, the desired effect would not show up, unless Portugal was excluded from the sample. This also illustrates the sensitivity of the results to slight changes in the selection of cases. However, in the given sample of 14, this condition is closest to becoming a necessary and sufficient condition for all included cases.

Table 3.11 Cross-tabulation of outcome, conditions and cases

		Partisan Veto Players (PVP)		
		0	1	2
Outcome (PPP)	0	–	AT, DE, DK, FR, IE, NL, SE	BE, FI, IT
	1	EL, ES, PT, UK	–	–
		Size of Construction Sector (CSEC)		
		0	1	2
Outcome (PPP)	0	BE, DE, DK, FR, IT, NL, SE	AT, FI, IE	–
	1	–	EL, PT, UK	ES
		Size of financial sector (FSEC)		
		0	1	2
Outcome (PPP)	0	FI	AT, BE, DE, DK, FR, IT, NL, SE	IE
	1	–	EL,ES, PT	UK
		Structure of interest groups (INTG_A)		
		0	1	2
Outcome (PPP)	0	FR	IE, IT	AT, BE, DE, DK, FI, NL, SE
	1	EL, ES, PT, UK	–	–
		Deficit (DEFI)		
		0	1	2
Outcome (PPP)	0	–	AT, BE, DE, NL, IT, FR	DK, SE, IE, FI
	1	EL	ES, UK, PT,	–
		GDP per capita		
		0	1	2
Outcome (PPP)	0	–	AT, BE, BE, FI, FR, IT, NL, SE	DK, IE
	1	EL, ES, PT	UK	–

Source: Krumm 2014: 464.

Surprisingly, a low GDP explains three out of the four cases with a positive outcome (EL, ES, PT). However, the fourth case (UK) is on rank 6 in the upper midfield of the average GDP values. Raising the lower threshold in order to include the UK into the group of low GDP countries would first regroup five other countries before reaching the UK. Thus, we would have to exclude five states from the sample in order to produce the desired effect.

In addition, a large construction sector (CSEC 2) only explains a high PPP activity for Spain and DEFI {0} explains PPP {1} only for Greece. The outcome PPP {1} for the UK is explained by the constellation FSEC {2}•GDP {1}, FSEC {2}•INTG {0} as well as FSEC {2}• DEFI {1}. In all three alternative constellations, the financial sector variable is included. This stresses the role of the financial sector in PPP development in the UK. However, if the outcome PPP {1} for the UK, Portugal and Greece is to be explained, the constellation is CSEC {1}•INTG {0} – without any role for the financial sector. Similar sector-specific conditions as with the financial sector for the UK can be expected with the high budget deficit for Greece and the role of the construction sector for Spain. However, these are only some case-specific highlights that cannot be generalized for other cases with positive outcomes. To sum up, with mvQCA the smallest common denominator for all four positive cases is the partisan veto player (PVP) variable. This result confirms the rank from the correlation analysis above, in which the number of partisan veto players showed the strongest effect on a policy change in favour of the PPP approach, followed by the structure of interest groups (Krumm 2014).

NOTES

1. See also Kappeler/Nemoz (2010: 15) for this procedure: 'To better understand their relevance, it is useful to compare the value of PPPs to total government investment because this is the best comparator that is available.'
2. The Flemish scheme was used to set up guarantees to lenders under the conditions that '(i) the debt refinancing obligation of the PPP company falls between year 5 and year 10 of the DBFM contract life; and (ii) the PPP company is not able to refinance the debt at prevailing market conditions. In the event of a call under the guarantee, the Flemish government would repay the senior lenders and would substitute the original loan facility with a new one on identical terms albeit with a 25 bps pricing increase. As a quid pro quo for providing the guarantee, the scheme requires that, if the refinancing is successfully implemented on the banking market, 75% of the financial benefits from the refinancing are passed through to the public sector' (EPEC 2011b: 35).

4. The Nordic countries

The overall approach of the Nordic countries towards PPP can be described as quite sceptical. There are some publicly funded pilot projects at national level and some local activities, but PPP politics never 'lifted off' in these countries. Surprisingly, there is a lot of research literature on PPP in the Scandinavian countries, contrarily to the level of PPP commitment there. Taking the size of the GDP and public investment into account, the ranking according to Table 3.2 is: Finland, Sweden and Denmark. Institutional variables such as a corporatist style of policy making require discussion when explaining the comparatively low level of activity in these countries. Furthermore, privatization policies primarily focused on assets in the field of 'natural monopolies' or 'network industries' such as roads and railways, ports, airlines, power generation and distribution, water and sewage, and telecommunications (Köthenbürger 2006: xvi). Thus, the following chapter aims to explore similarities and differences within this group of rather reluctant PPP users.

4.1 DENMARK

While a consensus orientation is a common feature of Nordic party systems, it is stronger in Danish politics than in Finland and Sweden, leading to a high degree of institutional stability and continuity. Similar to Sweden, minority governments occur quite often in Denmark. The weak parliamentary basis of coalition governments as well as the high parliamentary fragmentation makes quick policy changes less likely. They also contribute to a strong legislature (or weak executive) in terms of Lijphart's (1999) legislative–executive dimension. At cabinet level, collective responsibility is highly valued in theory, while in practice each minister tries to act as autonomously as possible, sometimes raising questions of inter-ministerial coordination. Contrarily to most other cases, cabinet decisions are non-binding and the prime minister has no right to instruct his or her ministers as, for example, the German chancellor has. Inter-departmental coordination is primarily done in special committees and by officials (Nannestad 2009: 79). At partisan level, the Social Democrats have been the largest party between 1924 and

2001; however, even together with the parties of the divided left, it did not obtain a majority. In this constellation, the smaller centre parties, especially the Radical Party, gained a pivotal role in coalition building.

Given the high degree of fragmentation in the party system, the necessity for cross-cleavage consensus politics becomes clearer. In order to obtain majorities, centre-left and centre-right parties have to find compromises. Thus, it becomes clearer why in Danish politics a relatively large welfare state has been combined with 'a relatively capitalist system, both in the sense of relatively strict private property rights and (for a long time) unusually free trade' (Christoffersen/Paldam 2006: 120). However, privatization policies took off relatively slowly in the 1990s and remained modest in international terms; public companies mostly remained in public hands (Petersen 2013: 182).

Being dependent on each other not only in the case of structural reforms, cross-cleavage compromises are much more likely. In terms of political compromises, 'the left obtained the welfare state and the right obtained rather strict capitalism' (Christoffersen/Paldam 2006: 121). This consensus politics of cross-party agreements for crucial arrangements has been stable and accepted for a long time, with major shifts only since the erosion of support for the Social Democrats in the early 2000s. Furthermore, as with Sweden, Denmark has not joined the Eurozone, following a negative referendum in the year 2000. Table 4.1 depicts the Danish coalition cabinets from the early 1990s to 2009 and their respective PPP activity (see also Petersen 2011). Despite the need for coalition partners, the Social Democrat Poul Nyrup Rasmussen managed to stay prime minister from 1993 to 2001, forming four cabinets in total. A rhetorical turn towards PPP occurred first in 1999, and an 'Action Plan' was published in 2004. However, from the seven possible pilot projects mentioned in the plan, only one was realized. Despite a rhetorical turn in favour of PPP, the government was in reality ambivalent or even sceptical towards PPP (Petersen 2011: 10). Regarding the two fiscal indicators government debt and deficit, Denmark was far from being under pressure in terms of need for private financing.[1]

According to the quantitative data in Chapter 3, Denmark is on average the least active PPP country in the sample examined in this book. This finding is consistent with the qualitative results of Greve/Mörth (2012), who observed only a limited number of PPP projects in Denmark (as well as in the other Scandinavian countries). Two of these projects were the National Archives at central level and at local level a new elementary school in Trehøje, Jutland (ibid.: 443). Overall, the Danish PPP policy is characterized by Greve/Mörth as lacking profile. 'The government [...] has been passive on or absent from the international scene, has had only

Table 4.1 Danish governments and their PPP politics

Years	Government	Parties	Action
01/1993–09/1994	Poul Nyrup Rasmussen I	Social Democrats (S), Centrum Democrats (CD), Radical Vernstre (RV) and Christian Peoples Party (KrF)	–
09/1994–12/1996	Poul Nyrup Rasmussen II	Social Democrats, Centrum Democrats and Social Liberals.	–
12/1996–03/1998	Poul Nyrup Rasmussen III	Social Democrats and Social Liberals	–
03/1998–11/2001	Poul Nyrup Rasmussen IV	Social Democrats, Radical Venstre	1999: PPP first mentioned by the government
11/2001–02/2005	Anders Fogh Rasmussen I	Venstre and Conservatives, tolerated by Dansk Folkeparti	2004: PPP action plan Seven pilot projects proposed, but only one (National Museum) realized
02/2005–11/2007	Anders Fogh Rasmussen II	Venstre and Conservatives, tolerated by Dansk Folkeparti	2006: PPP competence unit in the Danish Enterprise and Construction Authority established (dissolved in 2009) www.deaca.dk/publicprivatepartnership
11/2007–04/2009	Anders Fogh Rasmussen III	Venstre and Conservatives, tolerated by Dansk Folkeparti	

Note: Only Rasmussen I had initially been a majority cabinet.

Source: Own compilation.

a few showcase projects, and has not created a viable market for PPPs' (ibid.: 445). In general, the Treasury was not convinced of the financial advantages of PPP.

As in the other Scandinavian countries, an essential part of the PPP activity in Denmark is at the local level. In areas such as schools and hospitals, whose operation is primarily the responsibility of the regional level, PPPs in Scandinavia did not keep up (Greve 2003: 61). In contrast, the municipalities are responsible for providing the majority of direct services.

> Local governments provide primary and secondary school education, welfare for the elderly, childcare, and local doctors' help. Furthermore, local governments are responsible for cleaning of public buildings, waste disposal, and social and human services. To pay for this, local governments have independent taxation powers of the central governments, and are collecting 20% of citizens' income in tax. (ibid.)

Especially at local level, a certain number of ex ante evaluations have been carried out to assess whether a proposed project can be implemented as a PPP. These preliminary studies were often co-funded by the central government, which by 2010 had provided about DKK 12 million. In 2007 a structural reform came into force that has bound the activities of regional and local authorities for a long time. Under the reform, the number of regions was reduced to five and the number of municipalities to 98.

The regions became mainly responsible for such things as health and environmental issues, which could increase opportunities for PPP in the view of the EPEC. However, some projects, especially in the road sector, that were originally initiated by the regional authorities, had been transferred to the central level as part of the reform. 'Generally, this means that progress in these projects has been stalled until the projects are handed over', the European PPP Report (EPPPR 2007: 93) said optimistically. However, the mid-2000s saw some progress in Denmark in terms of PPP, first with the setting up of an inter-ministerial working group (Ejersbo/Greve 2005: 259) and then in 2006 a central PPP unit in the National Agency of Enterprise and Construction. Again, these attempts have been characterized as half-hearted (Petersen 2011). The Danish PPP unit was placed in the Danish Enterprise and Construction Authority (now the Danish Business Authority) within the Ministry of Economy. The department is responsible for developing competitive and market-based policies and, in cooperation with other corporate actors, preparing them for implementation.

> The Unit produces guidelines and acts as a key counterpart in valuable knowledge sharing in this field. The Unit can co-finance parts of the cost government organisations have in the initial research and tendering processes. It has a staff of five. The Unit has supported three PPP projects in different municipalities and regions since the beginning of the Task Force Unit. (OECD 2010: 98)

After the implementation of the policies, the government recommended 'competitive dialogue' as the most suitable procurement procedure for PPP. 'This procedure has been used for all current tenders (the Trehøje School and the National Archives)' (ibid.). In addition, after discussions about a school project (Vildbjerg), the Danish Central Tax Administration issued guidelines that must be met by the private contractors 'in order to gain VAT rebate on investments made in PPP projects equal to municipalities' access to VAT rebate on certain investments' (EPPPR 2007: 93). With the Finance Act 2010, PPP should be further promoted. The law offered the municipalities and regions DKK 10 million annually for such projects. In addition, a fund for the strengthening of PPP in the field of welfare state policies has been inserted.

At the end of 2009, however, the PPP Task Force and the co-financing pool, managed by the Ministry of Enterprise and Construction, were dissolved. Since 2010, PPP funding has been carried out jointly by the Danish Enterprise and Construction Authority, the Danish Competition Authority and Udbudsportalen and Udbudsrådet. Udbudsportalen (www.udbudsportalen.dk) is a platform that matches public authorities, especially municipalities, to private providers, and provides advice on all aspects of contracting and procurement, including the EU procurement directives and related matters. It helps to exchange experiences and also holds information about ongoing PPP projects.

The task of Udbudsrådet ('procurement council') is to promote competition in the public sector. For this purpose it talks to the public authorities, municipalities, regions and companies to evaluate past experiences and develop new proposals for tendering regimes and public–private cooperation. The Minister of the Economy appoints the chairman and one of the other 13 members. One member is appointed by the Minister of Finance, the Minister of Social Affairs, the Minister of Health and, inter alia, by the industry, the regions, the unions and the agricultural lobby (www.udbudsraadet.dk).

The general picture of a restrictive Danish privatization policy is supported by the major project of a 19 km fixed link (bridge or tunnel) between the German island of Fehmarn and the Danish island of Lolland, agreed with Germany in 2008 and realized by a project company under private law, but completely owned by the Danish state. Even though this company may charge a toll for the use of the planned tunnel, the project is neither a PPP nor full privatization, such as the Franco-British Eurotunnel, but only a formal privatization. However, according to the Danish–German agreement of 2008, subsequent substantive partial privatization of the project company is not excluded (Allen & Overy 2010: 82).

4.2 FINLAND

In the 'Scandinavian model' of welfare capitalism, Finland was the first country to start an encompassing liberalization and privatization policy, which it commenced in the early 1990s, partly as a reaction to a massive economic crisis following the boom of the 1980s, partly in preparation of the EU accession in 1995. After a period of expansion in the 1980s, public shares in companies had been reduced, as well as the state influence on the economy in general. Among the three Scandinavian cases in our sample, Finland pursued the most active PPP politics at central level. The emergence of PPP followed the liberalization of the telecommunications sector in the 1980s and the subsequent privatization and decentralization policies of the 1990s. In the area of e-government, partnerships helped in the acquisition of necessary know-how and spread risks more widely. Smaller authorities especially were challenged, with high demands on their employees to negotiate, monitor, manage and evaluate such projects (OECD 2003: 20). Depending on the level of governance, different models were applied. At national level, classic contract-based models were preferred; at local and regional levels more broadly defined models were discussed.

However, while the language of PPP prevailed, the term is also used in a broad, rhetorical sense. For example, some (rural) development programmes use the PPP semantics, while they are often just simple cooperations or 'joint ventures of either a contractual or corporate nature' (EPPPR 2009: 41). This creative use of the PPP term has also been euphemistically described as 'a great deal of innovative thinking about procurement and the ways in which PPP models can be adapted to provision of public services' (ibid.: 42). Among the promoting agencies there is the Association of Finnish Local and Regional Authorities, promoting and advising PPPs specifically in rural areas (ibid.: 41). A dedicated PPP unit does not exist; however, a joint unit of the Ministry of Trade and Industry (www.tem.fi) and the Association of Finnish Local and Regional Authorities (www.localfinland.net) offers general advice for public procurement (Leviäkangas 2013: 227). According to the Public Procurement Act 2007 (the main legal framework of PPP in Finland), procurement must be advertised publicly, if the contract value exceeds €15 000, in the social and health care sector €50 000 and in the construction sector more than €100 000. Furthermore, service providers need to be treated equally and the principles of sound economics must be considered (Huomo 2008: 442).

Although the first project using the PPP approach was realized in 1997, Finland is one of the low-activity countries among the sample in this book. The first project, the 68 km Järvenpää–Lahti motorway, was opened in 1999 for traffic. Its total investment amounted to €252.3 million. With a contract period of 15 years from opening, it was transferred to the Finnish Transport Administration in 2014. A second large-scale project at national level was signed in 2005 – the 51 km E18 Muurla–Lohja motorway – with a contract period of 21 years from opening to traffic (2009). The budget authority for the entire period of the contract is €700 million. 'Following criticism of the perceived generosity of the payment mechanism on the first PPP road scheme it can only be assumed that the terms on this one are tighter. The process too has been refined and shortened, cutting out the BAFO [Best and Final Offer] stage' (EPPPR 2007: 97). Overall, Finland is a small PPP market, which might limit the prospects for the PPP approach. Also, subsequent governments have focused on objectives such as efficiency and developed a range of mechanisms labelled partnerships (ibid.).

In fact, up to 2010, only two further projects have been signed, which were initiated by a Ministerial Working Group in 2009. In the first project a second railway track between Kokkola and Ylivieska (77 km) (2011–2014) was built and maintained; in the second project the highway section Koskenkylä–Kotka is going to be expanded into a motorway (17 km) and 36 km of new motorway is planned. For the first project costs of €660 million are projected, with pure construction costs at €263 million; for the second project costs of €650 million are projected, of which €285 million are construction costs. Together, both projects sum up to €1310 million of project volume (Letter of the Finnish Ministry of Finance upon request of the author, 9 February 2011). In autumn 2011, Finland's Transport Agency announced the successful bidder for the E18 Koskenkylä–Kotka motorway. This project is part of a highway development plan aimed at upgrading E18 to a motorway by 2015. 'The work from Koskenkylä to Kotka is one of four upgrades designed to improve the road transport infrastructure between Helsinki and Hamina in Finland, and Russia to the east' (www.pppbulletin.com/news/view/17602). Lenders include the EIB and the Nordic Investment Bank.

Politically, the first project in 1997 was started in the era of the social democratic prime minister Paavo Lipponen (1995–2003) and the following projects (2005 and 2010) in the era of Matti Vanhanen of the Centre Party (2003–2010). Vanhanen's first term was based on a coalition with the Social Democrats and the Swedish People's Party, the second term since 2007 on a coalition with the National Coalition Party, Green League and the Swedish People's Party (Table 4.2).

Table 4.2 Finnish governments and their PPP politics

Years	Cabinet	PPP action
04/1991–04/1995	Esko Aho (Centrum) (KOK, RPK, KESK)	–
04/1995–04/1999	Paavo Lipponen I (SDP) (KOK, RPK, SDP, VAS, VIHR)	1997: Järvenpää–Lahti motorway contract signed
04/1999–04/2003	Paavo Lipponen II (SDP) (KOK, RPK, SDP, VAS, VIHR)	–
04/2003–06/2003	Anneli Jäätteenmäki (Centrum) (RPK, KESK, SDP)	–
06/2003–04/2007	Matti Vanhanen I (Centrum) (RPK, KESK, SDP)	2005: Muurla–Lohja E18 motorway contract signed 2007: Public Procurement Act 2007 sets the legal framework for PPP
04/2007–04/2011	Matti Vanhanen II (Centrum) (KOK, RPK, KESK, VIHR)	2009: Ministerial Working Group established 2010: Contract signed for a) second railway track between Kokkola and Ylivieska (77 km) to be built and maintained; b) the highway section Koskenkylä–Kotka to be expanded into a motorway

Note: KOK: Conservatives, RPK: Swedish People's Party, KESK: Centrum, SDP: Social Democrats, VAS: Left, VIHR: Greens.

Source: Own compilation.

Overall, the Finnish PPP activities are characterized by a pragmatic approach. Public–private cooperation is utilized for political purposes such as the development of rural areas, the promotion of information and communication technologies (ICT) and environmental protection and the promotion of innovation and competition. These projects are rather small in volume and initiated from the local level. They are not considered in the survey of Kappeler/Nemoz (2010) due to the threshold value. A PPP task force does not exist in Finland.

The NPM reforms along with the extensive privatization of public functions and the opening of other public sectors for private competition brought changes not only for the functioning of the public sector, but also for its interaction with the private economy. These reforms have had a significant impact on the use of PPPs in the introduction of e-government. 'The need to find alternative ways to finance e-government projects and to share risk is probably two of the most important factors driving the development of e-government partnerships with the private sector' (OECD 2003: 153). However, PPPs in Finland are not exclusively commercial in nature: 'They also tie into the shared vision of developing an information society and commonly shared values of openness and stakeholder consultation' (ibid.). The Information Society Advisory Board (ISAB), with high-level public and private representatives, played an important role in this process (ibid.).

In recent years, new models of cooperation between public and private actors in the development of rural areas by private construction and development companies are increasingly used. According to Leväinen/Altes (2005), at local and regional level there are primarily four different forms of public–private cooperation used: the 'exchange' of land for building rights, the 'integral development' and the 'joint development' models, and the 'licensing model'. In the exchange model (land for building rights), development companies or construction firms buy land with potential for further development and sell it on demand for relatively low prices to the local community, which in exchange takes care of the building rights and land development and then returns or resells the lots/building sites. In the integral development model, the community takes care of the basic infastructure of the area, such as main roads, parks and water, while the details of the land development are transferred to the private partner. In the joint development model, duties are performed by a joint venture company of community and private shareholders. In the concession model, development is primarily done privately. Costs and risks of utilization are transferred to the private partner (ibid.). Furthermore, the Association of Finnish Local and Regional Authorities (Suomen Kuntaliitto), an association of the 18 regions and 336 municipalities, aims to promote business opportunities in rural areas through PPP models. Through special programmes, the role of small rural enterprises ought to be strengthened as a provider of public services. The project will also look for ways to increase the chances of small businesses in competitive tenders by state agencies.[2]

4.3 SWEDEN

Looking back at Table 3.2, Sweden has been the second least active user of PPP in our sample, surpassing only Denmark. Besides sharing features with Denmark such as minority governments, Sweden is characterized by some institutional features such as a strong corporatist tradition and social democratic influence. Despite its unitary state structure, the directly elected local governments in Sweden are comparatively strong. Additionally, 20 regional governments (Landstingen) exercise power especially in the health sector. Both levels levy their own taxes and are relatively independent from the central level, which holds its own administrative structures at regional and local level (Jahn 2009: 139). In general, administration in Sweden is relatively independent from (party) politics. However, in the course of the welfare state expansion that has occurred since the 1970s, the size of public administration as well as the share of government tasks and expenditures has been massively extended (Hancock 2007: 411).

In the socioeconomic dimension, a very high organizational density of interest groups and associations has led to a strong 'civil society'. The preference for organizing interests also led to a long and outstanding corporatist tradition of economic planning and policy making. In contrast to, for example, Irish corporatism, in the Swedish variant civil society actors such as unions are much more powerful. Furthermore, until 1990 members of the main association, the Swedish Trade Union Confederation (LO), automatically became members of the Social Democratic Workers' Party (Jahn 2009: 128). Given these peculiarities of the 'Swedish model' of welfare capitalism, the prospects for a transfer of the PPP approach to Sweden appear limited.

However, with the decline of corporatism also in Sweden, advocates of PPP have sensed their chance. According to Greve/Mörth (2012), PPP in the Scandinavian countries in general and especially in Sweden can also be seen as a new form of corporatism. It can be seen as a more pluralist form to serve the demands of northern welfare capitalism under changing international conditions of competition and cooperation. In contrast to the southern European countries, this northern PPP pluralism appears to be more oriented towards the involvement of 'society' and decision-making needs (ibid.: 447). A change in the pattern of corporatist policy has been observed since Sweden joined the EU in 1995 and had to open its markets. However, the intensified competition in formerly protected sectors and industries did lead to a change of rhetoric, including the PPP terms, but did not help to overcome a deeply rooted sceptical view of PPPs within politics and bureaucracy. Greve/Mörth (2012: 448) have observed in that context an emphasis on deregulation and the opening up for more competition in previously monopolistic sectors (e.g. electricity and telecommunications, postal services, domestic air traffic, and rail and taxi services). However, they find it difficult to assess the impact of these policies on PPP in Sweden, as the number of at least medium- and large-scale projects remains very moderate. Similar to Denmark, the Swedish population refused to introduce the Euro in a referendum in 2003 (56.2 per cent voted 'no').

At national level, the only PPP in a strict sense has been the 19 km high-speed railway from Arlanda airport to Stockholm, agreed in the early 1990s by the conservative Bildt cabinet and becoming operational in November 1999. The private partner was selected in 1994 to build the track and after completion exclusively operate the route. In return it had to finance half of the costs of SEK 6 billion. The route was opened for trains in 1999 and the network infrastructure remained in the hands of a public corporation. While the project shows most of the features of a PPP, it also has been questioned whether it is a 'real' PPP. 'It certainly looked like a PPP in the sense that it was a formal contract between the actors and there was a shared risk-taking between the actors'; however, towards the public sphere it was presented as a joint project between public and private actors, aiming to avoid the notion of a PPP (ibid.: 449). This was partly due to a change in government in 1994, leading to a 12-year period of social democratic government (until 2006). However, the incoming Carlsson III cabinet as well as the following Persson cabinets were bound to the contract, even if they did not like it. Thus, avoiding the notion of PPP is rather understandable.

The change in government in 1994 led to a standstill in further projects. The incoming social democratic minority cabinet, supported by the greens and the left, was not in favour of PPP. Only in 2006 did an incoming centre-right government lead to new preferences in the field of PPP, with all four coalition parties favouring the PPP approach. The EPPPR (2007: 98) mentioned optimistically the discussion of a ring-road PPP project around Stockholm and hoped for further applications of PPP in the field of transport infrastructure. The new government appointed a working group of representatives of the Swedish Road Administration (SRA), the Railway Administration (Banverket) and Nordic Road and Transport Research (VTI) in order to explore opportunities for PPP in Sweden (Reuterskiöld/Cope 2008: 463). The slow progress of the new PPP policy preference since 2006 is according to Reuterskiöld/Cope (ibid.) explained by the influence of SRA and Banverket as the main authorities in the field of road and railway development, and in the long-term infrastructure planning horizon, based in Sweden on a ten-year plan. While this plan 'can be revised as a result of government changes, boom or recession' (ibid.), it takes some effort to initiate such changes. A specific PPP legislation or task force does not exist (ibid.: 464).

Table 4.3 Swedish governments and PPP actions

Years	Cabinet	Type	PPP action
1990–1991	Carlsson II (SAP, Left)	minority government	No PPP activity
1991–1994	Bildt (Moderates, Centrum, Liberals, Christian Democrats)	minority government	1993: High-speed railway from Arlanda airport to Stockholm signed (operational since 1999)
1994–1996	Carlsson III (SAP, Left)	minority government	No PPP activity
1996–2006	Persson I & II (SAP, Left)	minority government	No PPP activity
2006–2010	Reinfeldt I (Moderates, Liberals, Christian Democrats, Centrum)	majority government	2006: A working group of the Road Administration (SRA), the Railway Administration and Nordic Road and Transport Research (VTI) established to explore opportunities for PPP

Note: SAP = Swedish Social Democratic Party.

Source: Own compilation.

At municipal level Collin (1998) has observed more activity than at central level. In a quantitative study on factors that make up the tendency of local governments to use (or not use) PPPs, he selected 64 of the 280 Swedish municipalities by size and geographic location, and conducted telephone interviews of current PPP projects. A total of 117 ongoing projects were determined. With the number of identified projects per municipality, the dependent variable 'intensity of PPP usage' was then created. In addition, a dummy variable was created to denote the inclination of the municipality to use or not use PPP (ibid.: 278). Of the explanatory variables analysed with multiple regressions, four proved to be relevant: population, fiscal capacity, and the relative size of the public sector and the service sector. 'Intensity in the use of PPPs is significantly influenced by the size of the population and taxability within the municipality. Transforming intensity to propensity removes the population effect and reveals an influence both of taxability and of the relative size of the public and the service sectors' (ibid.: 279f.). With an increase in the number of public sector employees, the tendency for the community to use PPP decreases, while it rises with the number employed in the service sector of a municipality.

4.4 CASE COMPARISON

In all three Nordic countries PPP activity at central level remained low, with Finland being the most active case and Denmark the least active. All three countries are unitary states and thereby 'neutralize' this trait in comparison to highly active countries such as the UK, Portugal and Greece. However, it could be argued that while the Nordic countries may formally be unitary states, in detail they have a much stronger local or regional level of self-government than the UK, Portugal or Greece. On the other hand, even the higher degree of local autonomy in the Nordic unitary state appears to be not sufficient to accumulate a significant number of projects if not supported by the central government. As the Nordic cases clearly illustrate, without a policy preference for PPP at the central level, it is hard for local governments to join the PPP bandwagon.

Less surprisingly, policy coordination within this group is, however, regarded as important, making the transfer of PPP more unlikely. The close policy coordination in a variety of forums makes it more difficult for an individual government to 'break out' of the regional policy consent. A large but efficient public sector, both in terms of staff and expenditure, and the corporatist tradition have also contributed to the rather sceptical stance with regard to the PPP approach. Each country has developed and signed a few pilot projects, in the case of Sweden as early as the 1990s; however, so far this has been the only large-scale PPP activity. In Denmark the National Museum remains the only project realized out of a PPP action plan with up to five pilot projects. Only Finland broke out of the Nordic consensus and pursued a more active PPP policy after 2005 under Matti Vanhanen from the Centrum Party. Whereas in Sweden the first PPP was initiated under a conservative cabinet (Carl Bildt) in 1993, the first Finnish PPP was initiated under a social democratic cabinet (Lipponen). Further Finnish PPP activities were initiated under the two Vanhanen cabinets. Thus, while in Sweden PPP was placed on the agenda under conservative prime ministers (Bildt and Reinfeldt), in Finland it was used under centrist or moderate left prime ministers (Lipponen, Vanhanen).

In terms of interest group structure, the Nordic countries, especially Sweden, are characterized by a strong corporatism. According to our empirical results from Chapter 3, this variable proved very influential in terms of supporting or hampering PPP activity. Also, fiscal policy in the Nordic countries is not a factor that could drive policy makers further along the PPP approach. These countries are regarded as European 'model pupils', with very low budget deficits or even budget surpluses. Thus, fiscal stress can in these cases be neglected as a driver for higher PPP activity. Also, the legal tradition of Roman-Scandinavian civil law produced a significant result in Chapter 3, suggesting that the Nordic variant of Roman civil law is least supportive of PPP. Finally, corruption (not tested in Chapter 3) is very low in the Nordic countries and the somewhat statist tradition is unlikely to be supportive towards the adoption of a PPP approach.

NOTES

1. 'In the period from 1999 to 2010, Denmark's government sector produced an average annual surplus of 1.7 percent measured against GDP, compared to an EU average of –2.9 percent in the same period [...]. Also, Denmark's general government debt was brought down from 58.1 percent in 1999 to 27.5 percent in 2007 (it thereafter rose to 43.8 percent in 2010 as a result of the global economic crisis, which compares to an EU average of 80.0 percent in the same year)' (Petersen 2011: 12).
2. www.localfinland.fi/en/authorities/regional-economic-development/Pages/default.aspx [4 July 2012].

5. United Kingdom and Ireland

In this chapter, the focus will be on UK and Irish PPP/PFI policies, including some differentiations in the British regions. The HM Treasury's 'PFI signed projects list' and the Irish Taoiseach's 'PPP project tracker list' provide useful cumulative information about the respective activities. The development of PPP/PFI in the UK since its introduction in 1992 is already well covered by the research literature. For Ireland, factors such as the politics of corporatism, sound public finances until the outbreak of the global financial crisis and the longstanding role of a predominant party (Fianna Fáil) in Irish politics can help to explain the lower PPP commitment compared to the UK.

5.1 UNITED KINGDOM

5.1.1 Institutional Context

The UK is a unitary state under 'asymmetric' devolution, with the Scottish Parliament claiming most powers, followed by the Welsh Assembly with only secondary legislation and the Northern Ireland government with long periods of suspended self-rule within the investigation period. As we will see later, among the devolved regions Scotland most intensely relied on PPP/PFI. Despite devolution, administrative as well as financial centralization is high, but not as high as, for instance, in Portugal and Greece.

Local governments were strengthened under the Blair cabinets commencing in 1997. However, there are still tight ties between central and local government, enabling 'Whitehall' to set incentives or to coerce local governments to act in certain directions which are particularly welcome to central government. Such a mixture of coercion and incentives has been created by the Treasury with PFI credits, a subsidy for local governments that was only available for projects carried out in the PFI mode. The strong influence of the central government on procurement and public management decisions at local or regional level can be illustrated by the London Underground PPPs. Clearly expressing his scepticism on the feasibility of the modernization of the Tube via the PPP mode, the then London mayor Ken Livingston was bypassed by central government in 2002/03. About five years later, in 2008, the first underground PPP Metronet was renationalized under the Conservative mayor of London Boris Johnson because of huge delays in the modernization programme and cost overruns; the second PPP operator, Tube Lines, followed in May 2010 (House of Commons 2012). This renationalization has been interpreted as a final 'settlement' in the quarrel between Johnson and the Brown government about the future of the London underground PPPs.

In contrast to most continental European cases, judicial review of political decisions is very weak in the UK. There is no powerful constitutional court as, for instance, in Germany or France; thus, executive and legislative decisions can hardly be controlled by the judicative. A Supreme Court distilled out of the judicial function of the House of Lords still has to find its place in the adversarial political culture of the UK (Gee et al. 2015). Besides the absence of a judicial veto player, other institutional or partisan veto players are rare. Only in 2010 did a 'hung parliament' force two parties which initially were not close friends into a coalition. Usually, the plurality vote enables a sufficient majority for one of the two 'big' parties and thus a smooth change of government and policies.

The near absence of veto players is accompanied by the common law tradition, which makes policy changes easier than in the continental European law traditions. In a nutshell, the common law tradition is more flexible and more 'malleable' to the will of a governing majority. This was also the experience under the Thatcher cabinets in the 1980s, with a massive cutback of union rights and the privatization of public utilities. When New Labour took over,

> there was little left in the industrial sector in the United Kingdom to privatize, although the welfare state still remains largely untouched by privatization. Apart from some competitive tendering for contracts, such as for the cleaning of hospitals and schools, and isolated examples of private companies being brought in to sort out underperforming educational and health services, the welfare state remains solidly state provided. (Parker 2006: 388)

Eventually, these sectors came under pressure from the coalition government commencing 2010. In 2012/13, for instance, the Conservatives addressed privatizing the Post Office, whereas they backed away 'in 1994 because of the potential adverse impact on rural post offices and because of the possible loss of uniform postal charges across the country' (ibid.).

Overall, the institutional context of the 'Westminster system' with its focus on parliamentary sovereignty and governability accompanied by weak institutional constraints for policy changes provide a supportive environment for the adoption of the PFI/PPP approach in the UK. However, this malleable institutional context might only be one side of the PFI coin. The other side is a political will for policy change and the ability to overcome scepticism and resistance. Thus, the next section goes deeper into the partisanship dimension of PFI/PPP in the UK.

5.1.2 Partisanship and Institutionalization

Over the whole investigation period, the UK has been Europe's most active country in the use of PPP/PFI. Introduced in 1992 by Chancellor of the Exchequer Norman Lamont under the Conservative prime minister John Major, PFI represented a policy change regarding the inclusion of private money in public procurement. After a period of extensive privatization in the mid-1980s, the concept of private financing of infrastructure was developed in the British Treasury, named after Sir William Ryrie ('Ryrie Rules'). These rules, which were imposed under Thatcher but abolished under Major, stipulated a strict separation of publicly and privately funded projects. Private investment could then only be executed instead of public investment, not in addition to it (Yescombe 2007: 33). Also, the efficiency of private funding and risk transfer by the private partner had to speak clearly for this option to be taken.

In the politics of the Thatcher government the Ryrie Rules were initially intended to discourage the private financing of public tasks, 'on the grounds that this would relax the constraint the government wanted to exercise over the public sector budget as a whole' (ibid.). Thus, the Ryrie Rules were meant as a self-disciplinary instrument to resist the temptation of bypassing budget limitations with the help of the private sector. The Ryrie Rules therefore prevented rather than facilitated private financing, but it soon became obvious that this policy had to be attenuated, since infrastructure investments were not being carried out by the public sector to a sufficient extent. Consequently, the 'substitution' part of the Ryrie Rules was abolished as early as 1989, three years before PFI was launched, with the intention of providing a framework for private financing of public infrastructure, which had already begun in 1987 with the Channel Tunnel linking England and France as well as the Dartford Bridge east of London 'and the second Severn Bridge between England and Wales (signed in 1990), all of which were Concessions' (ibid.).

However, these cases were not 'mixed' public–private projects like, for instance, the Channel Tunnel Rail Link. According to the Universal Testing Rule, introduced in 1994, the possibility of private funding for all public projects had to be checked, signalling a complete change of the policy to the Ryrie Rules. In 1997 the New Labour government finally dropped the Universal Testing Rule and introduced the concept of PPP, which incorporated PFI as well as expanded opportunities for joint ventures and contracting out. The idea of PFI itself had been transferred from Australia and New Zealand. However, as local governments initially were not allowed to act as contracting authorities, the use of PFI was still limited.

Seldon (1997: 336) reports that the Conservative government's economic policy was further elaborated by Lamont in a speech in which economic growth 'was to be supplied by protection for capital projects in what would be a tough autumn spending round, and by a new partnership between private finance and public sector projects called the Private Finance Initiative (PFI). […] The second prong bore Lamont's imprimatur, although Major was an enthusiast for it'. Keeping in mind that Major had been Chancellor of the Exchequer before becoming prime minister, as was Gordon Brown, three British chancellors, Major, Lamont and Brown have been among the most front running and fervent public–private enthusiasts. After the change in government in 1997, New Labour agreed to stick to the Tories' plan of tight spending ceilings. Thus, the first two years of government left little space for expansive policy changes. Whereas Blair's priority was to devote resources to health and education, Gordon Brown 'wanted to devote it to tax credits, an idea imported by Ed Balls from his professor at Harvard, Larry Summers, later US Treasury Secretary' (Powell 2010: 112).

Given the high degree of infrastructure privatization under Thatcher, options for further full privatization in the 1990s were limited. Also, further privatization was not popular among New Labour supporters. Consequently, most privatizations took the form of PPP or PFI. The intention was to combine the reputedly superior project management skills of the private sector with public service reforms in the transport, defence, health (NHS), education and other public sectors (Parker 2006: 389). Thus, the PFI model was rebranded and expanded as a core element of the 'third way' by then Labour chancellor Gordon Brown after the change of government in 1997 (NZZ 2011: 9). To enable PPP/PFI not only at national level, but also at the local level, the Local Government (Contracts) Act 1997 entrusted municipalities with using their own competences to conclude contracts. The responsibility for the PFI policy became part of the newly created Office for Government Commerce (OGC) (Yescombe 2007: 35).

Under the Blair/Brown governments, the aim concerning PPP/PFI was to be a European or even world 'leader' in the development of such hybrid policy forms. According to the former Chancellor of the Exchequer Gordon Brown, the UK's PFI model has been used as a reference model for policy transfers around the world. '[T]he UK has led the world in the development of PFI contracts. The UK model and guidance is widely drawn on around the world; and throughout the EU governments are setting up private finance units, based on the UK model, to take forward PPP projects' (HM Treasury 2008: 8). Led by the Treasury, the UK under New Labour developed the largest PPP programme in Europe, which included all sectors of civil and also military procurement. In 2003, according to Conor (2005: 44), about 10 per cent of all public investment was made as PPP/PFI, and in 2005/06 it was about 12 per cent (National Audit Office 2008: 2).[1]

In 2000, the operational tasks of the Treasury Task Force (founded in 1997) were transferred to 'Partnerships UK' (PUK), an information and promotion company (see www.partnershipsuk.org.uk). PUK itself was a PPP with a public share of 44 per cent held by HM Treasury and 5 per cent by the Scottish Executive. Among the private shareholders (51 per cent) were The Bank of Scotland, The Prudential Assurance Company, Santander, Sun Life Assurance Company, Barclays, The Royal Bank of Scotland, Serco and Global Solutions Limited (Hellowell 2012: 311). The operation of PUK, however, was at 'arm's length from HM Treasury' (OECD 2010: 78). Its responsibilities comprised advising public authorities and the development of a standard contract. However, there was also a division of labour within the PPP Policy Team which was responsible for the development of the PPP policy.

The PPP Policy Team was responsible for policy-related activities such as the approval of deals and the issuing of key texts, guidelines and statistics, but only in England – the devolved regions got their own policy units. The Policy Team was in charge of developing the PPP/PFI market through appropriate policies and ensuring 'value for money' for the deals initiated by central government departments or by local authorities. 'It also scrutinises PPP/PFI business cases and provides input to the Major Projects Review Group (MPRG) and the Project Review Group (PRG)' (ibid.: 77).[2] Complementing these responsibilites, the role of PUK was focused on technical support, capacity building and the promotion of PPP. Thus, British governmental activities were concentrated in two units: the PPP Policy Team and PUK (ibid.: 78), which later were integrated into Infrastructure UK (IUK), set up by the Chancellor of the Exchequer under the Labour government in 2010.

The Operational Task Force (OTF) was set up by the Treasury in 2006, with the mission to support public employees in regional or sectorial PFI teams in the management of ongoing projects. The objective of the OTF was to discuss issues of contract adjustment, benchmarking or refinancing with ongoing projects (ibid.: 78). The OTF has also become a part of IUK, which in turn is located within the Treasury. 'IUK has been set up as a separate unit within HM Treasury, providing advice to the Commercial Secretary to the Treasury who leads on infrastructure issues and who reports to the Chancellor of the Exchequer' (www.hm-treasury.gov.uk/ppp_infrastructureuk.htm). As there are no specific laws for decisions on PPP/PFI projects, the PPP Policy Unit has more discretion than policy makers in more legalistic polities. The result is a greater openness to political steering, especially by the Treasury through policy documents such as 'PFI: Meeting the Investment Challenge' (HM Treasury 2003), 'PFI: Strengthening Long-Term Partnerships' (HM Treasury 2006b) or 'Infrastructure Procurement: Delivering Long-Term Value' (HM Treasury 2008, see also OECD 2010: 77).

Characteristic of the British PPP policy under New Labour was strong public control and evaluation activity. In contrast to continental European governments, the audit authorities were more intensely involved to ensure value for money (Ball et al. 2000). In particular, the National Audit Office (www.nao.org.uk) has repeatedly evaluated British PPPs and reported to parliament (e.g. National Audit Office 2003). Issues under scrutiny are mostly the criteria of comparison with conventional public procurement, the construction of the public sector comparator (PSC) and the contractual design.

The distribution of the projects among the various commissioning authorities was rather uneven. As of September 2006, PFI projects with a volume of over £55 billion 'included 185 new or refurbished health facilities, 230 new or refurbished schools and 43 transport projects' (Dyton/Bavishi 2008: 529). For 2006, the percentage share of total capital value splits among the different government departments as follows: Department of Health 21 per cent, Department for Transport 18 per cent, Ministry of Defence 15 per cent, Department for Education and Skills 13 per cent, Devolved Administrations 13 per cent, and Department for Communities and Local Government, the Home Office and Department for Work and Pensions each 4 per cent (ibid.: 529).

The two sectors with the highest funding programmes are schools and hospitals. In school building, the programme 'Building Schools for the Future' (BSF) contributed to lots of new school buildings and renovations by means of PFI. Shortly thereafter, in health care, especially in hospital construction, a similar programme was developed to modernize the outdated British health system using PPP after the takeover by New Labour. At that time, the physical infrastructure of British hospitals no longer met modern requirements. The facilities often dated from the

Victorian era or from the 1960s. While the old buildings sometimes were in a better condition than those from the 1960s, they did not meet modern standards due to their spatial layout. Thus, a new hospital programme needed to be put in place (Jacob 2009: 17). In addition to the physical infrastructure, the NHS also needed other organizational reforms, as the British health system ranked far below the European average, for instance in terms of patient–doctor ratio. The then decided NHS Plan was the largest hospital building programme in the history of the NHS (ibid.).

5.1.3 PPP/PFI Under the Coalition

The coalition of Conservatives and Liberal Democrats which came to power in May 2010 did not initially prioritize PPP/PFI. The coalition agreement of 11 May 2010 did not mention PFI or PPP (HM Government 2010). However, the election manifestos and party convention statements of both coalition partners did mention PPP/PFI. In October 2008, David Cameron announced five points in a 'Plan for Change' that a Conservative government would like to change in relation to the existing PPP/PFI policy. Among others, it stressed including the liabilities from PPP projects in the regular budget of the government, according to the recommendation from the Financial Reporting Council's Accounting Standards Board (Conservative Party 2008: 36f., Helm/Inman 2009).[3] Furthermore, the liability of private companies as well as the proportion of the risk transferred to them should be increased. If the private partners are too risk averse, the projects are to be carried out exclusively by the public sector. Finally, the state should have an exit route in case of non-compliance with the agreed services and quality standards. However, none of these points were included in the election manifesto of the Conservatives; only general demands for increases in the private share of economic activities and the encouraging of private initiatives, as well as increased efficiency in the public sector found its way into it.[4] The Liberal Democrats argued in their election programme for a 'United Kingdom Infrastructure Bank' (UKIB), to attract private investors and in the long run promote the transition to a 'green economy'.[5]

At their party conference in September 2008, the Liberal Democrats called for the inclusion of liabilities under PFI contracts in the public budget to improve the independent verification and PFI competence of each authority. PFI projects should be undertaken only if the benefits of private financing can be clearly identified.[6] These pre-election statements, together with the lack of mention of PFI in the coalition agreement, point at the initial downgrading of PPP/PFI on the coalition agenda. Following the emergency budget of June 2010, IUK has been dedicated to long-term infrastructure goals. With participation of the private sector, for the next five years investment in infrastructure of about £200 billion in energy, transport, waste, science, water and telecommunications was planned. However, while the government soon began to rely on PFI again, the parliamentary parties remained sceptical. In mid-2011, the Conservative chairman of the Finance Committee called PFI a drug the country should come off. The Committee therefore called on the government to restrict the use of PFI to an absolute minimum (NZZ 2011: 9). Despite these critics, the Conservative Chancellor of the Exchequer, George Osborne, agreed in the first fiscal year of the change of government to a total of 61 new projects with an investment volume of £7 billion. According to the NZZ (*Neue Zürcher Zeitung*), the reason for this is simple: governments love PFI because the costs barely appear in the current budget (ibid.).

In the second half of 2010, the coalition started to put pressure on the PPP/PFI contractors in order to find ways of cutting costs. For this reason, in July the Cabinet Office minister arranged meetings with executives of the 19 biggest government suppliers in order to find ways of cutting costs for the services they provided for the government (www.pppbulletin.com/news/view/15977). For instance, there has been discussion as to whether to sell spare capacities of the £13 billion Future Strategic Tanker Aircraft (FSTA) project (heavily criticized before by the Commons Public Accounts Committee) to the French air force, giving it access to the new British fleet of refuelling aircrafts. Seeking ways to further squeeze operational PFI signed under New Labour was one of the priorities of the coalition government.

Another change in the coalition's PPP/PFI policy was the untying of PFI credits for local governments in autumn 2010, enabling the sponsoring departments to choose the best form of funding. Thus, according to the Comprehensive Spending Review of Chancellor Osborne, the responsibility for the revenue costs of local government PFIs had been transferred from local government to the sponsoring department. Local governments did not receive PFI credits for new building projects any longer, but were directly supported by the respective department. 'This means all projects will see the unitary charge paid for by the relevant department instead of by the local authority, which currently obtains the credits from the Treasury via the relevant department' (www.pppbulletin.com/news/view/16173). This also meant the end of social housing programmes of up to £1.9 billion based on PFI credits in 13 projects under preparation. Another move that squeezed the PFI programme in autumn 2010 was the scrapping of a planned £12 billion PFI in the defence sector, the new training facility in St Athan, South Wales (www.pppbulletin.com/news/view/16120). With regard to tendering regimes, at the end of 2010 the coalition downgraded the role of competitive dialogue as the prevalent procedure, simultaneously upgrading open, restricted and negotiated procedures by announcing detailed guidelines for their use.

The coalition government not only redeveloped and rebranded the Private Finance Initiative as ‘PF2’, it also used large subsidiary programmes to stimulate construction in the housing sector. In 2012, Chancellor Osborne introduced a four-year programme to subsidize mortgages by giving purchasers of new residential buildings an interest-free loan of 20 per cent of the house’s price. The programme aimed to push the construction and acquisition of new properties with purchasers only requiring a deposit amounting to 5 per cent of equity, while state loans covered a further 20 per cent and private banks the rest. In 2013, about 30 per cent of all new homes sold used the scheme, contributing to the surprisingly vigorous economic recovery. The beneficiaries of the programme, which was extended until 2020 after the Conservative re-election in 2015, have not only been homeowners. The property market, including real estate companies, as well as the construction sector started thriving again after a long period of stagnation (Rásonyi 2014: 10).

Despite some unrest from members of parliament and especially the Public Accounts Committee in relation to PFI, the commitment of the coalition to PPP/PFI is clearly expressed in one of the biggest rail contracts in the UK, the Intercity Express Programme (IEP). With the first plans for the modernisation project of the East Coast Main Line and the Great Western Main Line already launched in 2005, the contract for the two lines were finally closed in mid-2012. ‘Worth £4.5bn over 27.5 years, the contract will see Hitachi Rail Europe engaged as a subcontractor to supply a fleet of 92 trains, incorporating a total of 596 carriages, and maintain them for the duration of the deal. New depots will be built in Swansea, Bristol, west London and Doncaster to service the new trains. (www.pppbulletin.com/news/view/24039).

The PFI signed projects list offers an accurate documentation and database on British PPP/PFI activities. Table 5.1 shows, based on these data and differentiated by territorial and functional portions, the level of British PPP/PFI activity. Table 5.2 summarizes the main PPP/PFI activities of British cabinets between 1992 and 2012.

Table 5.1 Number and volume (£ million) of signed British PPP/PFI projects, 2000–2009

	England and Northern Ireland						Wales		Scotland		Total	
Year	Central		Local		NHS							
	No.	Vol.	No.	Vol.	No.	Vol.	No.	Vol.	No.	Vol.	No.	Vol.
2000	17	1 343	30	1 089	8	603	6	101	7	429	68	3 565
2001	12	937	27	749	4	281	1	25	7	257	51	2 249
2002	13	842	30	6 492	5	506	3	84	3	81	54	8 005
2003	9	1 882	30	1 484	6	671	1	41	5	209	51	4 287
2004	6	884	32	1 239	14	1 523	4	67	5	183	61	3 896
2005	6	474	34	1 641	5	1 016	0	0	5	367	50	3 498
2006	9	1 774	32	1 999	5	2 068	1	20	10	1 174	57	7 035
2007	3	475	30	1 878	13	2 027	1	28	10	1 113	57	5 521
2008	7	3 013	19	740	1	304	1	18	3	285	31	4 360
2009	3	1 395	29	2 809	0	0	0	0	3	508	35	4 712
Total	85	13 019	293	20 120	61	8 999	18	384	58	4 606	515	47 128

Sources: HM Treasury, PFI signed projects list (02/2010); own calculation.

Table 5.2 Main PPP/PFI activities of British cabinets

Years	Government	Action
1992	Major I (Con)	PFI enabling jurisdiction
1997–2001	Blair I (Lab)	1997: PPP Task Force 2000: PUK
2001–2005	Blair II (Lab)	2002: London Underground enforced as PPP (renationalized until 2008 by the Mayor of London, Boris Johnson (Con)
2005–2007	Blair III (Lab)	2006: OTF 2006: PRG
05/2007–04/2010	Brown (Lab)	2010: IUK
05/2010–05/2015	Cameron/Clegg (Con/Lib Dem)	2011: Policy and contracts review process initiated 12/2012: PF2 policy guideline published

Source: Own compilation.

5.1.4 The Regions

In terms of devolution, Scottish political institutions have gained the most powers among the three regions. Theoretically, this could be a source of resistance against PPP/PFI or it could be used to actively support or develop the PPP approach. In practice, at the beginning, Labour governments in Edinburgh actively supported the PPP policy. The Scottish National Party (SNP), while in opposition, strongly rejected this policy; however, once in government (first as a minority cabinet) learned to value its advantages. Already by the end of the 1990s under Labour, the Scottish Executive had participated with a 5 per cent share in PUK. Several Scottish governments have not only been favourably disposed to PPP/PFI, they later also developed variants such as Non-Profit Distributing (NPD) or implemented Tax Incremental Financing (TIF), and established the Scottish Futures Trust (SFT) in 2008 as well as the hub programme to accelerate public investment, including the use of PPP and PFI.[7] This indicates that Scottish governments have been very active in creating policies relating the PPP/PFI approach.

The Labour–Liberal Democrat coalition in the period 2003–2007 introduced, for instance, the hub programme and the NPD model. In the hub initiative, DBFM contracts are used for community facilities such as health centres, schools, and police and fire stations. As Unison Scotland (2011: 1) has observed, several projects that were originally set to use conventional public funding have been switched to NPD, such as the Edinburgh Sick Children's Hospital, the Dumfries & Galloway Royal Infirmary, the Scottish Blood Transfusion Centre and Inverness College. Furthermore, many school NPD projects have been switched to the hub programme (ibid.).

As an opposition party, the SNP was critical towards PPP/PFI and developed the idea of a SFT 'to "crowd it out" by providing Scottish Government bonds for cheaper conventional public financing of public infrastructure. […] The SFT is also advising councils on funding for a range of waste treatment infrastructure projects, which includes PPP contracts (e.g. in Glasgow and Edinburgh/Midlothian)' (ibid.: 2). Organizationally, the SFT is a quasi-autonomous government body which initially was meant to replace the role of PFI as proposed by the SNP. It was in charge of a £2.5 billion Scottish government PPP pipeline of NPD and hub DBFM projects in 2011, 'one of the biggest of its type in Europe' (ibid.: 1). With taking over government responsibility, the SNP started outsourcing operational responsibility to the SFT and developing derivatives such as the NPD.

As reported by the Scottish government in 2012, the SFT is 'delivering a £2.5 billion NPD pipeline of revenue financed infrastructure projects as announced by the Scottish Government in November 2010. This is being delivered in partnership with the Scottish Government, local government, NHS Boards and other public bodies'.[8] According to the Scottish government's Infrastructure Investment Plan 2011, it prioritized the following as means of maximizing available funds for investment:

- Using the SFT 'to get more infrastructure for the money that we are spending, to support the development of innovative financing methods and to facilitate collaborative procurement and asset management across the public sector;
- Taking forward a new pipeline of revenue funded investment worth £2.5 billion, to be delivered through the NPD model, including major projects such as completing the M8, Aberdeen Western Peripheral Route including the Balmedie to Tipperty Project, and the Royal Hospital for Sick Children in Edinburgh;
- Making full and appropriate use of the Regulatory Asset Base (RAB) to fund new rail projects (including Edinburgh– Glasgow Improvements Programme, Aberdeen–Inverness and Highland Mainline), to improve digital infrastructure and to upgrade the electricity transmission grid;
- Bringing forward regulations made under the Local Government Finance Act 1992 to pilot up to six TIF schemes to test their applicability under Scottish circumstances.

- Taking forward a second wave of the National Housing Trust (NHT) initiative, which leverages private sector funding and Council borrowing to support affordable housing' (Scottish Government 2011: 11).

By the end of 2012, three out of a total of 93 NPD and PPP/PFI projects had already expired, the others still being operational. The bulk of the 93 Scottish projects were PPP/PFI (88); only five were NPD, covering 7.5 per cent of the total capital value of these kinds of projects. All five NPD projects were operational in 2012. All contract periods are 30 years, except the Tayside project with 32 years, which is the only health sector NPD, while the remainder are in the schools sector.

Table 5.3 *NPD projects in Scotland*

Project name	Commissioning body	Financial close	On/Off balance sheet			Est. Total capital value (£ m)
			IFRS	UK GAAP	ESA 95	
Aberdeen City Schools NPD	Aberdeen City Council	24.12.2007	On	Off	Off	120.5
Argyll and Bute Schools NPD	Argyll & Bute Council	09.09.2005	On	Off		90.0
Falkirk Schools NPD	Falkirk Council	18.05.2007	On	Off		115.5
Mental Health Development NPD	NHS Tayside	18.06.2010	On		Off	95.0
Moray Schools NPD	Moray Council	22.06.2010	On		Off	43.9

Note: IFRS = International Financial Reporting Standards, GAAP = Generally Accepted Accounting Principles, ESA = European System of Accounts.

Source: www.scotland.gov.uk/Topics/Government/Finance/18232/12308/NPDpayment figures [27 February 2013].

Differentiated by sector, most PPPs/PFIs and NPDs are done by local government, followed by the health sector, Scottish enterprises and agencies, and water and sewerage (see Table 5.4).

Table 5.4 Scottish deals by sector

	No. of projects	Capital value £m	% of total value
Further Education	1	8.6	0.14
Health	31	1 332.0	21.55
Local Authority	45	3 594.2	58.15
Other Public Sector	1	3.0	0.04
State Enterprises & Agencies	5	663.0	10.72
Police	1	17.0	0.27
Water & Sewerage	9	562.3	9.09
Total	93	6 180.1	

Note: By type of deals, schools cover the largest share, with over 55 per cent of capital value, followed by hospitals and transport (see Table 5.5).

Sources: www.scotland.gov.uk/Topics/Government/Finance/18232/13368; own calculation [27 February 2013].

Table 5.5 Scottish deals by type

	No. of projects	Capital value £m	% of total value
Colleges	1	8.6	0.14
Hospitals	29	1 329.2	21.50
Health (Other)	2	2.8	0.04
Schools	38	3 409.4	55.16
Prison	2	112.0	1.81
Transport	4	612.5	9.91
Waste Water	9	562.3	9.09
Waste Management	2	46.7	0.75
Waste to Energy	1	43.0	0.69
ICT	3	21.6	0.35
Other	2	32.0	0.51

Sources: www.scotland.gov.uk/Topics/Government/Finance/18232/13368; own calculation [27 February 2013].

5.2 IRELAND

5.2.1 Institutional Context

Ireland's political system has a two-tier unitary structure with strong central–local relations. For a long period its party system was dominated by the national-liberal Fianna Fáil, with sometimes small coalitions or minority governments. The country has a strong tradition of social partnerships. After achieving independence from the UK in December 1921, the newly established governmental system resembled that of Westminster in many respects. Among others, a common law system and a highly centralized administrative system have been adapted from the UK. After independence from the UK, the focus was on central control by political and administrative means, leaving nearly no autonomy for local government and the regional dimension (Quinn 2010: 239). Currently, at regional level there are 34 county and city councils, five borough councils and 75 town councils all with relatively limited functions and finances. Put in a nutshell, local government is widely regarded as an executive function of central government. Lacking financial and political autonomy, its main task is administering central policies (ibid.: 240). A push towards regionalization has been set by the EU, leading to the setting up of indirectly elected regional authorities and assemblies (ibid.: 241). At central level, the electoral system of the Single Transferable Vote is a variant of a proportional representation (PR) system; after the erosion of Fianna Fáil dominance it often did not produce clear one-party majorities. Thus, coalition governments, or even minority governments, have become a common phenomenon. The collegial cabinet is headed by the Taoiseach (prime minister). The bicameral parliament has asymmetrical competences, with the Senate also having powers to initiate bills; however, the Dáil Éireann is considered the more influential chamber (ibid.: 244).

At local level, the elected councils are the primary policy-making bodies, exercising 'reserved functions' such as the passing of the annual budget or of local development plans. Other functions are exercised by the county or city manager, who performs the executive functions of the day-to-day tasks. Policy areas of local government encompass many fields: a) housing and building, b) road transport and safety, c) water supply and sewerage, d) development incentives and controls, e) environmental protection, f) recreation and amenity, g) aspects of agriculture, education and welfare, and h) miscellaneous services (ibid.: 245). Contrary to many other EU states, local authorities in Ireland have no responsibilities in the health and education sectors or in policing and social welfare. Thus, central government departments and executive agencies carry out these tasks (ibid.: 246). This means that central government can more easily apply pressure for the use of PPP as compared to the UK, where first the local communities had to be given the legal right to enter PFI contracts. Also, the instrument of PFI credits for local governments was not needed in Ireland. Once the central level was convinced of the advantages of the PPP approach, the Irish central government had much better chances of imposing the use of PPP on local authorities.

Party politics in Ireland was dominated by Fianna Fáil until a landslide election in 2011 (Krumm 2011). The structural transformation of the Irish party system was paved by the real estate and banking crisis commencing in 2008. Fianna Fáil, which had continuously governed for 13 years and 8 months, was hit so hard by the general election that a quick recovery seemed unlikely. Never before had the share of votes of Fianna Fáil fallen under 39 per cent. In the election to the Dáil Éireann, which was held early, on 25 February 2011, only 17.36 per cent of first preference votes had been given to Fianna Fáil. Due to the disproportionality effect in the PR Single Transferable Vote this led to them gaining only 12 per cent of seats. Between 1931 and the election in 2011, Fianna Fáil had been in government and provided the Taoiseach (or its institutional predecessor) for 61 years, whereas the second strongest party (Fine Gael) had been in government for nearly 17 years (see Adshead/Tonge 2009: 88 for explanations of Fianna Fáil's dominance). With Fianna Fáil being the predominant party, it was mainly this party that was in charge of deciding whether to adopt the PPP policy approach or not.

5.2.2 Socioeconomic Dimension

In the socioeconomic dimension, the long-term experience of the politics of social partnerships was one of the foundations for adopting the PPP approach. The politics of social partnerships emerged in the second half of the 1980s as a response to economic and social problems and has been described as a 'particularly Irish version of neo-corporatism'. Each of the several programmes covers a period of about five years according to the specific challenges involved. The programmes covered a broad variety of social and economic policy issues, such as wage agreements, in order to stimulate demand on the one hand but prevent inflation on the other. The programmes covered a range of public policies and also their mechanisms for implementation. Besides the traditional actors from the government, employers and the unions, the talks leading to agreements

Table 5.6 Results of the Irish election to the Dáil Éireann, 1989 to 2011

Year	Turn-out (%)	Fianna Fáil		Fine Gael		Labour		Sinn Féin	
		Seats (total/%)	Votes (%)	Seats (total/%)	Votes (%)	Seats (total/%)	Votes (%)	Seats (total/%)	Votes (%)
1989	67.66	77/46.39	44.15	55/33.13	29.29	15/9.03	9.48	0	1.21
1992	67.46	68/40.96	39.11	45/27.11	24.47	33/19.88	19.31	0	1.61
1997	65.26	77/46.39	39.33	54/32.53	27.95	17/10.24	10.40	0	2.55
2002	61.89	81/48.80	41.48	31/18.67	22.48	21/12.65	10.77	5/3.01	6.51
2007	66.41	78/46.99	41.56	51/30.72	27.32	20/12.05	10.13	4/2.41	6.94
2011	70.10	20/12.04	17.36	76/45.78	36.23	37/22.29	19.35	14/8.43	9.89

Source: Krumm 2011: 609.

increasingly comprised actors from the community and voluntary sector as well as the farming sector (Quinn 2010: 248).

Whereas local and regional government institutions have been characterized as rather weak, social partnership programmes did have a severe impact on these levels of government, as most of the partnership policies are implemented at subnational level, having territorial rather than sectoral relevance. For instance, various local development units have been established, among others, to implement projects using EU structural funds. Such policies have strengthened local partnerships and helped them to emerge in a 'bottom-up' process. 'National government has also progressively incorporated a partnership approach into subnational governance. Consequently, there are now 38 area-based partnerships, 33 community partnerships and 35 LEADER companies working to counter disadvantage in their areas and assist in the implementation of public services' (ibid.). In general, regional authorities were encouraged if not forced to adopt a working mode of partnership across sectoral boundaries such as public–public, public–private and public–voluntary. 'The Southern and Eastern Regional Assembly, for example, involves representatives from twenty nine state agencies on its operational committees. The activities of the regional bodies accord with the aims of the current partnership agreement Towards 2016 and the National Development Plan 2007–2013' (ibid.: 249).

Besides the politics of social partnership, a large financial sector has contributed to the adoption of the PPP approach in Irish politics. Among our sample of 14 states, Ireland showed the largest financial sector in terms of GVA. Between 1995 and 2009, 8.8 per cent of its GVA was produced by the financial sector. The size of the financial sector in this period was mainly due to the International Financial Services Centre (IFSC), a special tax area based in Dublin. This special tax area was installed in the late 1980s by the Haughey government under Fianna Fáil and attracted the headquarters of many international financial organizations (Palan et al. 2010: 144). Despite being criticized as a tax haven, this financial strategy also contributed to the rapid economic development of the country. From the late 1980s to the global financial crisis, Ireland performed very well and the high unemployment level as well as the high share of taxes to GDP went down, 'simultaneously moving from GDP per capita at perhaps 60 to 70 percent of the EU average to around 110 percent of the EU average' (Köthenbürger 2006: xv). These developments led to Ireland being branded the 'Celtic Tiger', often overseeing that the success was based on specific tax and regulatory policies as a main factor in attracting foreign investment and strategies to maximize the transfers from EU structural funds for domestic investment.

However, the large Irish financial sector was severely hit by the 2008 real estate bubble and the subsequent global financial crisis, forcing huge financial interventions by the Irish government. In autumn 2008, the government decided to guarantee the liabilities of six Irish banks. Up to the end of 2012, domestic banks were supported with €63 billion from the so-called 'troika' of the ECB, EU and IMF. Consequently, the Irish government held nearly all the shares of the Allied Irish Bank and still, at that time, some parts of the Bank of Ireland. Meanwhile, better capitalized banks and building societies still have to deal with defaults of residential mortgages.

In the course of the crisis the so-long moderate debt quota rose from 25 per cent of GDP in 2007 to 65.5 per cent in 2009 (EU 27: 74 per cent), the economy shrunk by about 7.6 per cent (EU 27: –4.2 per cent) and the deficit reached –14.4 per cent (EU 27: –6.8 per cent), while unemployment rose to 14 per cent in 2010 (Krumm 2011). In the second half of 2010, the problems of Irish banks became more and more obvious and the EU and IMF officials urged the government to join the 'rescue package' to stabilize the banks and prevent further spread of the crisis to other European countries. This move was very unpopular in domestic politics because of its austerity conditions and led opposition parties as well as the junior partner of Fianna Fáil, the Greens, to call for snap elections.

5.2.3 PPP Politics

As shown in Chapter 3, Ireland has reached an upper intermediate rank in the investigated sample of countries, although it is still considerably behind the UK. Indeed, the first privatization and PPP policies had already been introduced at the end of the 1990s under Taoiseach Bertie Ahern (Fianna Fáil, 1997–2008), especially since 1999 under a Fianna Fáil minority government. Given the formation of the Irish party system out of the nationalist cleavage in the 1920s, Fianna Fáil has been characterized as a nationalist and republican party with a considerable amount of populism. As the left–right cleavage is hardly appropriate, both major parties, Fianna Fáil and Fine Gael have pursued a liberal economic policy, with Fianna Fáil putting slightly more emphasis on actively stimulating (foreign) investments and getting the economic benchmark figures right, whereas Fine Gael's approach is more in line with continental Christian democratic (and conservative) parties.

In terms of party politics, the mid-1990s are characterized by changing coalition governments. After the split of a Fianna Fáil–Labour coalition in 1994, Fine Gael, Labour and Progressive Democrats formed a new coalition government (1994–1997). Less surprisingly, there was little consensus in favour of the PPP policy approach. However, the situation changed in 1997 with the incoming new Fianna Fáil cabinet under Bertie Ahern. Similar to the UK, the Finance Ministry took a leading role in the implementation of PPP. In June 1999 it announced eight PPP pilot projects, which started albeit slowly. However, by June 2001, there were already 134 projects at various (early) stages of development (Reeves 2003: 163). While pursuing its PPP policy, the government tried to ensure that the public investment in PPPs did not influence the calculation of the sizes of key fiscal aggregates (ibid.).[9]

Furthermore, the National Development Plan I (2000–2006) emphasized the role of PPP in national development. The Programme for Prosperity and Fairness (agreed in 2000) further established and anchored PPP on the government agenda. These programmes were meant to improve public services, the management of resources and the organizational processes, and customer and employee satisfaction, as well as strengthen transparency. They were also used to implement PPPs at municipal level. However, in these programmes PPP was only one issue among others. The support for PPP was further intensified with the State Authorities (PPP Arrangements) Act 2002, in which the legal institutionalization of PPP took shape.[10] This Act was initiated by the Finance Ministry to give the authorities and communities greater legal security in the use of PPPs. The law allows state agencies and local governments to draw up PPP contracts and to participate in institutional PPPs in the form of a company. It enables the transfer of public tasks to the private partner, but reserves jurisdiction for the state. 'Local authorities should note that the approval of the Minister for the Environment and Local Government is required before forming companies or entering into joint venture arrangements for the purposes of PPP arrangements' (Circular IPPP 01/02 2002).

Another step to further institutionalize the PPP approach has been the creation of the National Development Finance Agency (NDFA) in November 2002, shortly after the last general election of June 2002, with the aim to 'raise finance for infrastructure investment. It was envisaged that the NDFA would raise 2 billion Euro per annum, and that this would not count against the general government balance which the EU uses as a key fiscal aggregate' (Reeves 2003: 164).

However, with the setting up of the NDFA it was already clear that the EU would assess such projects on a case-by-case basis and that they are not off balance sheet per se – only as a function of the transferred risks. The role of the new agency was then changed, becoming a national supervisory authority and providing advice to government agencies involved in procurement and infrastructure (ibid.). In 2003 it also was decided that PPPs primarily are to be aligned to projects in 'urgent' sectors such as urban development.

Besides the implementation of PPP, a privatization programme has been pursued. By 2003 nine public enterprises were privatized, with sales revenue of €8.2 billion. The privatization and PPP policy since 1999 can be seen in particular in the context of Ireland's huge infrastructure deficit. In addition, investments strongly depended on EU transfers. From the late 1990s the next round of EU enlargement was foreseeable, and this raised fears of a break in the transfers from the EU to Ireland:

> Despite these vital injections of investment, rapid economic expansion meant that Ireland's physical infrastructure had reached a stage of acute crisis by the mid 1990s. [...] The increase in Irish living standards, and the forthcoming enlargement of the EU, paved the way for vested interests to urge Ireland's Government to consider largescale adoption of the PPP model. (ibid.: 163)

Following the logic of corporatist policy making, interest groups got involved in the implementation of PPPs in Ireland, too. Already in January 1998, the Irish Business and Employers' Confederation (IBEC) and the Construction Industry Federation (DIF) presented a detailed plan for the use of PPPs, including the argument that they can be used to reduce the Irish infrastructure deficits. An IBEC report identified a need for infrastructure investment 'of almost 18 billion Euro over the period 2000–2006. The new centre-right government, elected in 1997, was receptive to the overtures from the private sector' (ibid.). The foreseeable significant cuts in EU Structural and Cohesion Funds for Ireland, as well as the financial effort to achieve membership of the single European currency have helped Irish finance ministers looking for ways to relieve the Treasury. Thus, for the Irish government the popularity of the PPP model was due to the fact that these investments could be held off the balance sheet (ibid.: 164).

In Circular 04/04 of the Infrastructure Public Private Partnership Unit (Circular IPPP 04/04 2004), local politicians were alerted to the expiry of a fund to support local PPP projects at the end of 2004. The fund, with assets of more than €5 million, was established in late 1999 to support local governments in the development of PPP projects that were not eligible for 'mainstream investment programs': 'To date a total of 49 projects and € 3.88 m in funding has been approved. Therefore, € 1.19 m remains to be committed before the end of this year' (Circular IPPP 04/04 2004).

The EIB (2004: 6) spoke of an ambitious Irish PPP programme for roads and schools and the EPPPR (2007: 144) refers to the PPP market in Ireland as buoyant and 'expanding from the high-profile toll road programs into social infrastructure such as accommodation, schools and healthcare'. The main agencies involved in PPP projects are the National Roads Authority, the Railway Procurement Agency, the National Development Finance Agency and local authorities. 'A suite of Guidance has been issued by the Department of Finance on PPPs. In addition the NDFA is the statutory financial adviser on all PPPs regardless of who is the procuring authority' (EPPPR 2009: 86). Table 5.7 summarizes main activities of Irish governments between 1992 and 2011 in the field of PPP.

Table 5.7 Irish governments and their PPP action

Years	Cabinet	PPP action
1992–1994	Albert Reynolds (FF/Labour)	–
1994–1997	John Bruton (FG/Labour/PD)	–
1997–06/2002	Bertie Ahern (FF/PD) minority government since 1999	06/1999: PPP pilots announced 1999: National Development Plan I (2000–2006) emphasized the role of PPP 2001: The Transport (Railway Infrastructure) Act
2002–2007	Bertie Ahern (FF) minority government	03/2002: State Authorities (PPP Arrangements) Act 2002 11/2002: Formation of the National Development Finance Agency (NDFA) 01/2003: National Development Finance Agency Act 2006: Formation of the Inter-Ministerial Committee for PPP
2007–2008	Bertie Ahern (FF/Greens/PD)	National Development Finance Agency (Amendment) Act Central PPP Policy Unit: www.ppp.gov.ie/
2008–2011	Brian Cowen (FF/Greens/PD)	–

Note: FF = Fianna Fáil, FG = Fine Gael, PD = Progressive Democrats.

Source: Own compilation.

According to the Irish constitution, not all policies are eligible for PPP; a number of duties shall exclusively remain within public competences. In this way, the Irish constitution is more similar to continental European ones like in France and Germany. In particular, activities in the sectors of defence, policing and justice, as well as the execution of sanctions imposed by the courts, are restricted to the public administration. In the remaining fields, OECD (2010: 103) counted 34 PPP projects worth €4 billion which had been approved since March 2006.

The institutional development of the policy framework was continued in 2006 with the creation of the Inter-Ministerial Committee for Public and Private Partnerships, whose task was the formulation of policy objectives for the wider use of PPPs, including an approval process, a governmental role in the financing process and payment mechanisms for the private partner (ibid.). The Committee encompassed the Economy and Finance Minister, the Minister of Development, the Minister for the Environment and the Minister of Public Works as well as other ministers interested in PPP. As in the UK, the projects must be approved centrally. In contrast to the UK, the Inter-Ministerial Committee, rather than the Treasury, is responsible for approving projects, making its decisions based on the recommendations of the Special PPP Secretariat (ibid.). The Special Secretariat is assigned to the Ministry for Finance and Economic Affairs and has general advisory functions, such as identifying projects eligible for PPP, promoting PPP across levels and sectors of government, evaluating projects and monitoring the implementation of PPP contracts. The Special Secretariat encompasses legal, technical and financial advisers and is chaired by a Special Secretary who is in charge of reporting to the Minister of Economy and Finance. 'Afterwards, the Special Secretariat notifies the interested public entities and invites them to submit an application before the Inter-Ministerial Committee that expresses their consent to implementing the project under the PPP structure' (ibid.). This structure of new PPP institutions, with a Special Secretariat responsible for operational and promotional issues and an inter-ministerial PPP committee at cabinet level, resembles the structure that had been set up in Greece one year before, in 2005. Thus, it can be inferred that Irish politicians closely monitored what other PPP active countries were doing.

Additional to these central PPP units, a number of ministries, such as the Ministry of Transport and the Ministry of Education and Health, have their own special PPP units or agencies. For instance, in the Transport (Railway Infrastructure) Act 2001, the Railway Procurement Agency was established 'as an independent statutory public body to procure new metro and light rail infrastructure and services through public–private partnerships, joint ventures or other means, as determined by the Minister for Transport' (ibid.: 104). Table 5.8 presents a brief quantitative overview of Irish PPP projects from 2003 to 2011, based on the 'project tracker list' as of mid-2011. As the list reports only project volume bands, we have calculated our estimation of project volume using the band mean of each project. Given these limitations, the figures have to be interpreted very carefully. Starting with the number of signed projects in a given year, 2005 shows the lowest and 2009 the highest figures. The same is true for the estimated project volume. With the peak occurring in 2009, these figures suggest that the global financial crisis commencing in 2008 has had a long-term rather than short-term impact on the PPP level in Ireland. This is somehow understandable considering the long-term planning horizon of PPP projects; the projects signed in 2009 can be expected to have a lead time of several years. Thus, the impact of the crisis commencing 2008 is reflected in the estimated average project volume only in 2011, three years after the crisis outbreak.

Table 5.8 'Tracked' number and estimated volume of PPP projects in Ireland, 2003–2011

Year	No. of projects	Estimated project volume (€ m)
2003	1	375
2004	5	635
2005	0	0
2006	3	785
2007	7	1 970
2008	8	740
2009	18	3 770
2010	8	1 930
2011	7	175
Under preparation	1	1 000
Not allocatable	4	450
Total	62	11 831

Note: The source list indicates only investment bands for each project. This table was calculated using average values. Thus, it offers only a general estimation.

Source: Project tracker list 2010 (06/2011), www.ppp.gov.ie/ppp-projects/ppp-projects.

However, the high activity in 2009 can also be seen as an effect of the austerity restructuring measures following the financial crisis, partly enforced by the EU/ECB/IMF troika. In this view, it is an attempt to switch public procurement to the PPP route as a way of keeping the deficit and debt figures of the public budget under control. However, because of internal economic developments (capital availability, e.g. willingness of banks to fund projects) and externally enforced requirements (especially austerity measures), the PPP policy lacked a clear direction. Several major projects had been cancelled or delayed in the mid-term aftermath of the crisis. For example, in 2010 the toll road operators felt the squeeze due to there being fewer toll road users than initially projected. The problem of drivers avoiding toll roads, especially in times of economic crisis, is also known in countries such as Spain and France, which largely have relied on similar models.

In Ireland, for example, the M3 (Dublin–Cavan) and the Limerick tunnel were hit by traffic rates falling by over 20 per cent below the expected levels, thus raising demands for compensation ('bailout') to be paid out by the government's National Roads Authority (NRA), the leading Irish procurement agency (www.pppbulletin.com/news/view/16053). Among the delays is the tendering of the Gort to Tuam highway (€500 million), which stalled in early 2011, 'due to concerns over Ireland's sovereign debt situation. Procurement agency the National Road Authority (NRA) said it is committed to the 57km scheme but the timing of financial close will now be delayed' (www.pppbulletin.com/news/view/17286). Traffic risks as well as the countries sovereign debt crisis, for example, made it harder to acquire the necessary private funding for PPPs.

In early 2012, after the landslide election of February 2011, the new Fine Gael/Labour coalition announced that they would invest solely in road maintenance projects in the next four or five years, as new roads were not affordable at that moment (www.pppbulletin.com/news/view/21945). However, only a year later, a major PPP road scheme (N17/N18) was set into motion. In other sectors, the effects of the crisis on PPP began to come clear, too. In mid-2010, a planned PPP prison in North Dublin (Thornton Hall) was switched to conventional procurement. 'Minister for Justice Dermot Ahern said the phased approach made sense in an industry where construction costs had fallen and would mean Thornton Hall could open earlier than expected' (www.pppbulletin.com/news/view/15563).

Social housing has been hit less hard, because different levels of government are involved, such as, for example, Dublin City Council, which launched in October 2010 a new housing project, 'becoming the first housing PPP project since the collapse of the council's €900m regeneration programme in 2008' (www.pppbulletin.com/news/view/16099). In 2008, three large social housing redevelopment PPPs collapsed in the aftermath of the property downturn and 'are now all to be rebuilt using only public money' (www.pppbulletin.com/news/view/18160). Two large projects cancelled after the credit crunch in autumn 2011 were the Metro North (€3 billion) and the Dart Underground project (€2 billion). A third project, however, but only worth €170 million, was continued. 'The Luas scheme will connect two existing lines running south and north in the centre of Dublin, and form part of a new line connecting Luas services with a suburban rail station to the west of the city centre' (www.pppbulletin.com/news/view/20825). However, the starting date was pushed back towards 2014, indicating a low priority.

Despite this caution with PPP up until autumn 2011, the government launched a stimulus investment package worth €2.25 billion in mid-2012, using also PPP to target roads and schools. In a first phase the investment volume of €1.4 billion was expected to come from private investors as well as the EIB, the National Pension Reserve Fund and domestic banks in Ireland, and the remaining €850 million from privatization proceeds and the national lottery.[11]

5.3 CASE COMPARISON

The UK and Ireland both show relatively centralized state structures not only in the administrative dimension, but also in terms of fiscal relations between the different levels of government, making the implementation of a policy change easier than in more decentralized or federal systems. Overall, Ireland was even more centralized than the UK in the period under investigation. In the UK the institutional setting up of a PPP enabling framework started earlier and reached a more sophisticated level, including, for instance, the PFI credits to 'convince' local governments to participate in the PPP approach. In contrast, Ireland set up important units later than the UK and did not reach the former's level of sophistication. However, given the smaller size of the Irish state and the more centralized executive and administrative structures, such detailed steering institutions were not necessary in the Irish case. PPP steering was more easily done by direct central government directives than in the UK with its more complex institutional environment (such as the devolved regions).

Both countries participate in the more flexible common law tradition, making a policy change and implementation easier than in the continental law tradition with codified administrative rules and strong constitutional courts. However, in contrast to the UK, Irish law is more strongly 'codified' and in this sense more similar to the continental European law tradition. While the Irish polity originates out of the so-called 'Westminster model' of government, it misses a core element of it: the plurality vote. Applying the Single Transferable Vote, a variant of the PR system, does not often lead to single party governments as in the UK prior to 2010. As we have seen in Chapter 3, a low number of governing parties is one of the best predictors for a policy change in favour of PPP. Despite cases of 'hung parliaments', plurality voting has proved to be an effective way of producing single party governments and thus enabling smart policy changes. This condition of a single party majority cabinet was present in the UK during the whole of our investigation period, but not in Ireland.

In the socioeconomic dimension, the Irish system of interest groups is more corporatist than the British one. Additionally, British unions were suppressed in the 1980s under Thatcher and lost influence on the Labour party in the 1990s. Given the pluralist structure of interest groups as well as limited political influence, British unions were hardly able to slow down the policy change towards PPP/PFI. In particular, Unison, the largest public sector union in the UK, issued policy papers on PPP/PFI, but was hardly able to achieve policy changes from the Labour government. This pluralist institutional background of interest groups plus the weakened unions provided favourable conditions in the UK for PPP which were lacking in Ireland. There, the corporatist structures of policy making by 'social partnerships' potentially provided better conditions for PPP sceptics to exercise influence. However, as the high level of PPP commitment expressed by the policy programmes of 'social partnershipping' as well as by successive Fianna Fáil governments shows, these conditions were not realized in practice.

As shown in Chapter 3, the size of the financial sector also plays an important role in the adoption of a PPP policy. In Ireland we have on average one of the largest financial sectors in our sample of 14. This is due to the industrial and economic policy of Irish governments since the late 1980s, trying to attract the headquarters of large international companies to Ireland, especially to a special tax zone in Dublin. In relative figures as a share of GDP, the Irish financial sector even trumped the British one with its core at the City of London. Besides this sector, a low corporation tax rate contributed to the overall economic growth in that period. While financial sector GVA in absolute terms is bigger in the UK, as an average share of total GDP it is bigger in Ireland, as shown in Chapter 3. Thus, we can assume that in both cases the PPP policy also was seen as an instrument to support domestic financial markets, which in the UK primarily is located in the City of London.

In the partisan dimension, in both cases a massive 'onset' of PPP policies took place after a change in government in 1997. Both incoming new governments faced financial restrictions. Whereas in the UK the incoming New Labour government stuck to a self-imposed debt ceiling in order to avoid the 'tax and spend' image of old Labour, in Ireland the financial restraints were primarily imposed by European developments. For the UK, Eurozone membership was not a desirable option. For Ireland, with a very low public debt quota, Eurozone membership was less of a problem. Rather the EU Eastern enlargement in 2004 made it foreseeable that in the medium term large amounts of EU subsidies would be redirected towards the new member states. Thus, Irish politics had to consider alternatives to allow for the breakaway of EU funds.

In both cases the finance ministry has had a crucial role in adopting PPP policy. However, Ireland never reached the level of PPP/PFI activity and support attained in the UK. Institutional adjustments were more extensive and innovative in the UK than in Ireland. The formation of the Special Secretariat and the Inter-Ministerial PPP Committee in Ireland in 2006 illustrates a belated high level of support, but also a similar pattern of top PPP institutions as in Greece (chapter 9.3). Whether Irish policy makers copied Greek institutions or both were inspired by another source remains open to further research.

NOTES

1. Despite its pioneering role in the development and use of PPP models, theoretical and qualitative political science studies on the development of relevant policies in the UK dominate the research (Clark/Root 1999, Edwards et al. 2004, Flinders 2005, Greenaway et al. 2004, Hellowell 2012, Maass 2002, Shaw 2003), in contrast to those with economic or administrative focus, or accountability and advisory focus (Barlow/Köberle-Gaiser 2008, Broadbent/Laughlin 2003, Broadbent/Laughlin 2004, Dyton/Bavishi 2008, Froud 2003, Grout 1997, Sadka 2007, Sawyer 2005, Shaoul 2005 and 2012, Spackman 2002).
2. The Policy Team is also responsible for the guidance of the Operational Task Force (OTF) and the Treasury Infrastructure Finance Unit (TIFU), and the evolution of the standard contract model SoPC4. The director of the Policy Team also heads the Project Review Group (PRG). 'The Project Review Group oversees the approval process for local authority PFI projects that receive Government support. It is the gatekeeper for the delivery of PFI credit funding to the local authority PFI programme' (ibid.). The private PPP Forum, founded in 2001, is there to supplement the support and advisory bodies from the private sector. The Forum is supported by six employees of private companies of the UK-based PFI industry and has, inter alia, lobbying duties (www.pppforum.com).
3. See also www.pppforum.com/government/ [Government & Politics: Conservative Party on PFI] [30 November 2010].
4. The Conservative Manifesto 2010. *An Invitation to Join the Government of Britain*. London, http://www.conservatives.com/Policy/Manifesto.aspx [30 November 2010].

5. Liberal Democrats: Liberal Democrat Manifesto 2010. *Building a Fairer Britain*. London, p. 24, http://network.libdems.org.uk/manifesto2010/libdem_manifesto_2010.pdf [30 November 2010].
6. www.pppforum.com/government/ [30 November 2010].
7. www.scotland.gov.uk/Topics/Government/Finance/18232/IIP [27 February 2013].
8. www.scotland.gov.uk/Topics/Government/Finance/18232/12308 [27 February 2013].
9. See also the Irish government's PPP website at: http://www.ppp.gov.ie/ [16 June 2010].
10. See *The Cross Departmental Team on Infrastructure and PPPs: Fourth Progress Report, 2002*, accessed at http://www.taoiseach.gov.ie/eng/Publications/Publications_Archive/Publications_2006/Publications_for_2002/4thProgReportOnInfrastructureAndPPPs.pdf [19 October 2011]
11. 'The funding follows the €17bn Infrastructure and Capital Investment Framework announced last November, which stemmed from exchequer funding. However, critics of the announcement have said it will do little to offset government spending cuts of the past few years' (www.pppbulletin.com/news/view/23939).

6. Belgium and the Netherlands

This group consists of two very different countries, e.g. in terms of both federal–unitary structures and also PPP activities. In Belgium, the regions play an important role in policy making, whereas the Netherlands has unitary structures. There, the push for public sector modernization has had a huge impact on the adoption of the PPP approach. Furthermore, public tendering in the 'Benelux' countries is also known for its transparency and standardized procedures, which might reduce the chances of alternative methods such as PPPs. At central level, the Belgian federal government was very reluctant towards adopting PPP; at regional level, Flanders was the most active jurisdiction.

6.1 BELGIUM

6.1.1 Institutional Context

Among the 14 states in our sample, the Belgian polity is the most volatile. The federalization of Belgium began in the 1970s and has not yet come to a standstill. After almost every federal election, the coalition negotiations led to a further step of institutional reform, with an overall tendency to transfer powers to the regional level. At regional level there is a unique feature: there are two state entities for each of the two main language groups, one in charge of cultural and social matters (the communities) and one in charge of territorial matters (the regions). This functional split results from the incongruence of territorial and cultural lines of separation (Krumm 2015). The 'cleavage' of Flemish and francophone identities shapes most areas of Belgian politics. Forming a new coalition after an election at national level has increasingly become a highly challenging task, as the party system has split along the borders of the language communities. This means, each political group usually contributes two parties to a coalition, one from the French-speaking and one from the Flemish side. This leads to huge delays in government formation and raises the number of partisan veto players up to the level of the second Italian republic.

While the capital, Brussels, is only a region (not a community), the German speaking population in the east of Belgium forms only a community; its territorial interests are represented in the Walloon region. Among the three federal systems in our sample, Belgium has the most 'devolved' system with an increasing number of powers transferred to the three communities or regions. Whereas the communities are the French, the Flemish and the Germans, the regions are Wallonia, Flanders and Brussels-Capital. In order to increase synergies, the parliament and government (council) of the Flemish community and the Flemish region have merged.

As is typical for federal systems, the central level is in charge of policies such as foreign affairs, defence, justice, the finances, the social security system, public health and internal affairs. It is also in charge of tax legislation and civil and commercial law as well as public procurement regulations. In contrast, the communities are responsible for policies in the fields of 'education, culture, audio-visual media, youth, health, sports and use of languages. Of significance to PPPs, the Communities are largely responsible for school infrastructure' (EPEC 2012a: 4). Finally, the regions exercise legislation over topics related to the economy, employment, housing, public works, energy, transport, the environment and spatial planning.

The Walloon and Flemish regions are also subdivided into five provinces. However, these provinces do not have significant decision-making powers. Roads or highway projects, waste management, public transport and light rail, as potential candidates for PPP, are implemented at regional level (ibid.). In contrast, matters concerning railways and national airports are decided at central level. The regions also decide on regional airports, inland shipping and, together with the local authorities, bus services. Issues relating to sea ports (e.g. Antwerp) are mostly decided at local level (van den Hurk/Verhoest 2013: 21).

6.1.2 The Central (Federal) Level

The central level is also called the federal level, with Brussels as its capital. Given the heterogeneous institutional setting as sketched above, the central level does not have the most promising prerequisites for adopting intense PPP policies. However, despite these institutional and linguistic (cultural) limitations, EPPPR (2007: 64) noted that Belgium 'punches well above its weight', but this is particularly due to the Flanders region. At the central level and in the Brussels region, there is no PPP legislation. In Wallonia an Infrastructure Agency (SOFICO) has been established, which can engage in long-term contracts such as those in PPP. In November 2008, a decree of extraordinary funding of programmes for the renovation and expansion of schools through PPP was adopted (Allen & Overy 2010: 41). The Walloon and the Brussels-Capital regions will be covered in section 6.1.4 in more detail.

At central level, as well as in the regions, the DBFO (Design, Build, Finance, Operate) model is prevalent. However, policy making at central level is difficult and requires a good deal of consensus and bargaining. Coalitions usually encompass more than two parties and have to be balanced in terms of linguistic and partisan diversity. For example, Liberals and Socialists are often bound together in one cabinet, with the Socialists from the francophone Walloon region and the Liberals from the Flemish region. Up to 2007, federal governments had a smaller format and were more stable. They usually survived the maximum period of four years. However, towards the end of our investigation period, cabinets became more heterogeneous and short-lived. For instance, the Verhofstadt III cabinet survived only for four months, the following Leterme I cabinet nine months. Details are provided in Table 6.1.

Table 6.1 Belgium federal governments, 1995–2009

Years	Government	Parties
06/1995–06/1999	Dehaene II	CVP, SP
07/1999–07/2003	Verhofstadt I	Liberals, Socialists, Greens (rainbow coalition)
07/2003–12/2007	Verhofstadt II	Liberals, Socialists
12/2007–03/2008	Verhofstadt III	Liberals (Open VLD + MR), Flemish Christian Democrats (CD&V), francophon Humanists (cdH) and francophon Socialists (PS, without Flemish Socialists SP.a)
03/2008–12/2008	Leterme I	Liberals (Open VLD + MR), Flemish Christian Democrats (CD&V) and francophon Zentrumshumanisten (cdH) and Socialists (PS)

Note: CVP = Christelijke Volkspartij, SP = Sozialistische Partei, VLD = Vlaamse Liberalen en Democraten, MR = Mouvement Réformateur, CD&V = Christen-Democratisch en Vlaams, cdH = Centre Démocrate Humaniste, PS = Parti Socialiste, SP.a = Socialistische Partij Anders.

Source: Own compilation.

As can be expected from the results of Chapter 3, coalition governments and especially socially heterogeneous cabinets provide among the most 'unfriendly' conditions for high PPP use. Consequently, we do not find much PPP activity at central level. In the area of e-government (ICT), the OECD found, in a study of Belgian activities, that the private sector is mainly used on an ad hoc basis for the outsourcing of services. More encompassing public–private cooperation appeared unsystematic and limited, as each government kept its power of procurement and its capabilities in-house. Scale effects or synergies thus have not been realized to the optimal degree. 'Public–private partnerships are limited among the governments, and no commonly agreed policies exist' (OECD 2008b: 27). According to the OECD, through a more coherent framework for partnerships with the private and voluntary sectors, as well as through outsourcing, the Belgian authorities, especially at regional level, could improve the efficiency and bargaining power of the public sector as a whole (ibid.: 28).

> There is no framework in place governing public–private partnerships to enable better public sector service delivery; additionally, the governance structure is perceived as being too complex to identify opportunities for such cooperation. Clearer insight into ongoing and planned projects in the public sector and the creation of single points of contact for private sector partners would be helpful. (ibid.: 115)

Allen & Overy (2010: 39) identified as further obstacles to a more intensive use of PPP the strict rules for the use of languages and 'regulatory barriers' which lead to higher initial costs for the private investors. 'Procurement procedures also tend to be long and complex with a high risk of litigation.' As in most other countries, PPP activity in Belgium is critically monitored by the Court of Auditors (Rekenhof 2009; see also Deloitte 2009 and van Montfort 2008). For instance, the Belgian Court of Auditor monitored PPPs in the Flanders region in 2008. Examining the early stages of 11 projects, they observed that initially a high emphasis was placed on budget neutrality. They also criticized the Flemish government's risk and cost assessment of the projects. 'The general lack of far-reaching standardization has led to high transaction costs, increased complexity and limited transparency. Despite frequent reporting in Flemish Parliament the information supply remains incomplete, above all as far as PPP budgetary impact is concerned' (Willems/van Dooren 2011: 522).

From the perspective of the private sector, according to OECD interviews, the federal government structures are too complex and confusing to identify realistic opportunities. They recommended more transparency in ongoing and planned public sector projects 'and to create single points of contact for private sector partners. The private sector is not necessarily perceived as a potential partner by the public sector, but rather as a potential competitor' (OECD 2008b: 131). Overall, the OECD observed a relatively low use of PPPs in the development and implementation of e-government in Belgium. Some larger projects were initiated after the global financial crisis in the prison sector at central level. In 2011, four prisons were tendered by the Buildings Agency, and a fifth followed in 2012. In February 2012, a tender for a €300 million prison PPP in a suburb of Brussels was launched by the Belgian Ministry of Justice. For the four prisons PPP, a Beheersmaatschappij Antwerp Mobiel (BAM)-led consortium was named the preferred bidder in the tendering 'on the Dendermonde and Beveren schemes and Eiffage on the 312-capacity prison in Marche-en-Famenne and SNC-Lavalin on the fourth in Leuze-en-Hainaut' (www.pppbulletin.com/news/view/21819). A €70 million police headquarter in Charleroi contracted in 2011 was another project at central level. However, all these projects were launched after the end of our investigation period in 2009 and thus did not contribute to the quantitative exploration in chapter 3.

6.1.3 The Flanders Region

In the Belgium system of 'checks and balances' between the different communities and regions as well as between the regional and the federal level, the Dutch language group is probably the one pushing strongest for more self-rule. In terms of PPP, Flanders is by far the most active and set up in mid-2003 in the Flemish Government Policy Service its own competence centre (OECD 2010: 98, see www2.vlaanderen.be/pps) as well as developed its own standardized DBFM contract form (EPPPR 2007: 64).

Unlike countries where compliance with the Maastricht convergence criteria could have played a role for the early onset of PPP schemes, the Flemish PPP programme began relatively late, in 2003. Especially during the 2004–2009 legislature, they started with broad PPP investments (around €6 billion) in such diverse fields as roads, housing, education, health care, sports and tourism, using the DBFM contract model. The governments preferred to participate in PPPs via a public holding company. 'The financial participation of the government is supposed to lower the barriers for the private partners. It is also supposed to deliver an extra financial return. Contract or concession PPPs are used less frequently by the Flemish authorities' (Willems/van Dooren 2011: 520). Furthermore, Flemish governments highly prioritized off balance sheet financing with regard to the ESA 95 standard for their PPPs. With only a few exceptions, 'ESA neutrality was perceived as the sine qua non' (van den Hurk/Verhoest 2013: 23).

The higher use of PPPs by the Flemish government is also explained by the historically active use of outsourcing as a procurement instrument in this region (OECD 2008a: 127). The Flemish PPP Expertise Centre (or Knowledge Centre) was established by a Flemish PPP decree from 18 July 2003 and is responsible for the preparation, monitoring and evaluation of such projects. Other sector-specific funding agencies were established or realigned according to needs. The setting up of the PPP unit was part of the PPP law adopted by the Flemish government on 18 July 2003. Its aim was to encourage and facilitate PPP initiatives in Flanders. The law defines, inter alia, various types of PPP and the role of the competence centre, and outlines a number of changes to existing laws (Vlaamse Regering 2003).

Within the Anglo-Saxon model variants, the DBFM model is particularly encouraged, for instance by providing a standard contract. Regional development is on the agenda of the PPP unit, too. The unit also maintains a project database. Whereas the Flemish PPP Knowledge Centre is purely focused on 'publiek–private samenwerking' (PPS), the role of the special investment company Participatiemaatschappij Vlaanderen (PMV) is much broader. As an independent investment company (founded in 1995 as a division of GIMV (Gewestelijke Investeringsmaatschappij voor Vlaanderen) and made an independent organization in 1997) with a portfolio of €900 million, its investment focus is on renewable energy, biotechnology, cleantech, life sciences and the modernization of public infrastructure. It invests in particular in companies and projects, from which an economic or technological 'leverage' is expected (www.pmv.eu).

Another corporation acting in this field is the BAM, set up in September 2003, which provides integrated traffic management for the Antwerp region. 'The Flemish Government aims to sort out the Antwerp traffic problem. Flanders cannot afford any further debt. That is why it created BAM, a company under public law, to implement the Antwerp Mobility Masterplan' (www.bamnv.be). BAM was built with the support of all parties by decree. Its task is to improve the notoriously bad traffic situation in the region through financing, management and operation from a single source. For this, the company has been assigned a number of statutory powers, including the possibility of expropriation for the use of infrastructure development. The majority of BAM is in the hands of the Flemish government, which grants annual operating grants. Administrative control remains with the government and parliament (www.bamnv.be).

PPP has been used most intensely in two policy fields: sports facilities and school infrastructure (education, see van den Hurk/Verhoest 2013: 23). In the area of school infrastructure, the 'Agentschap voor Infrastructuur in het Onderwijs' (AGIOn) was established on 7 May 2004 by decree as an agency under the supervision of the Flemish education minister. Its task is to subsidize the purchase, construction and renovation of schools. The ceilings of subsidy by AGIOn are: in primary education, 70 per cent; and in secondary education, 60 per cent. In 2007 AGIOn was assigned €124 million from the government (http://www.agion.be). The largest Belgian project is the company 'DBFM Schools of Tomorrow', founded in 2009. Private partners contribute 75 per cent, the public sector 25 per cent (of which half was held by the Flemish SA School Invest and AGIOn). Its task is to modernize 200 schools in Flanders with the DBFM model between 2010 and 2016 (by 2014 plans for all schools should have been completed). After completion, the project company will be responsible for building maintenance for 30 years. The total cost amounts to €1.5 billion. The PPP project is a collaboration between AGIOn and the Flemish Investment Company (together Invest SA School) on the one hand and Fortis Real Estate (Ageas) and Fortis Bank (together FS Scholen) on the other. The project is similar to the British BSF programme (Building Schools for the Future) and thus can be further analysed in terms of PPP 'policy transfer' from the UK (Sack 2009: 63).

In November 2007, the Flemish prime minister Peeters introduced the policy paper 'Public Private Partnerships 2008' to parliament. It included, inter alia, a list of major projects and the relevant sectors to be addressed in future by the government. It also included a commitment to the expansion of the PPP policy, for instance by establishing a network of experts within the Flemish government and the elimination of cumbersome regulations (www2.vlaanderen.be/pps/English). Again, the focus was on the use of DBFM contract models, especially in roads infrastructure. This huge emphasis of the Flemish government on PPP has probably contributed to the rising commitment of the Belgian federal government to PPP. In 2009/10, the federal government made several procurements for prison buildings using the DBFM model (Allen & Overy 2010: 39), suggesting a 'bottom up' policy stream from the Flemish region to the central government. Furthermore, in the Flemish region a number of ad hoc laws for specific projects were approved. This was meant to clarify in particular financial and property issues on specified projects. 'More recently and in response to the liquidity crisis, such ad hoc legislation has also introduced additional guarantees from the Flemish Region in order to make certain projects more attractive to financiers' (ibid.: 41). Differentiating the number and volume of the

Table 6.2 Flemish governments and their PPP politics

Years	Government	Party	Action
02/1992–1999	Luc Van den Brande	CVP, SP	
07/1999–06/2003	Dewael	VLD, SP, Agalev and VU	PPP first mentioned 2002: PPP Knowledge Centre established
06/2003–07/2004	Somers	VLD, Spirit (VU), SP.a, and Groen	07/2003: PPP law passed 09/2003: Beheersmaatschappij Antwerp Mobiel (BAM) founded 05/2004: Agentschap voor Infrastructuur in het Onderwijs (AGIOn) founded
07/2004–06/2007	Leterme	CD&V, N-VA, SP.a & Sociaal-Liberale Partij, Open VLD	
06/2007–06/2009	Peeters I	CD&V, N-VA, SP.a & Sociaal-Liberale Partij, Open VLD	11/2007: Policy paper on PPP 2009: DBFM School of Tomorrow founded

Note: VU = Volksunie, N-VA = Nieuw-Vlaamse Alliantie.

Source: Own compilation.

Flemish projects, 2005 saw the highest number of projects, the total for that year being nine, while 2009 saw the highest investment volume, even though it only involved two, albeit large-scale, projects.

The active PPP policy during the global financial crisis in 2008/09 clearly illustrated the priorities of the Flemish government. It did not scale back like many other countries. In the following years, more PPPs were signed by Flemish authorities. In 2012 for instance, the construction of nine sports halls or complexes in Flanders via PPP had been signed with a contract time of 30 years. Also, the Ghent South highway PPP (R4) was signed by Flemish authorities, with a contract time of 30 years.

6.1.4 Wallonia and Brussels

Wallonia and the capital Brussels have had hardly any experience with PPP in the investigated period (EPPPR 2007: 64). The Walloon government primarily relied on public companies for providing services and PPPs were little known and without significant political support. Consequently, there no PPP programme was set up and no PPP project has been implemented at the regional or community level in Wallonia. 'The preferred solution for delivering public services is often a type of "public–public" partnership between the Region and one of its public companies (e.g. water, environment and road sectors)' (EPEC 2012a: 6). The PPPs located in the Walloon region are commissioned by the federal government in Brussels. However, there have been plans to utilize PPP as a means of business promotion and in the area of social policy and social housing (EPPPR 2007: 64), which have not (yet) been realized. However, in the last few years, PPP has gained more attention in Wallonia, too.

As reported by the EPEC (2012a: 6), the regional political programme for 2009–2014 referred repeatedly to PPP, especially for refurbishment investments, but also for housing, energy efficiency, tourism, river transport, sport facilities and schools. However, the government programme also remained vague when it came to the details and what PPP exactly means. While at regional level PPP was so far absent, the local level appeared different (ibid.). The EPEC report lists a total of 18 municipal projects for Wallonia, 13 of which were in the field of housing and accommodation, two were police stations, one a fire station, one a city hall and one a waste management system (ibid.). Thus, at the local level in Wallonia there is some PPP activity, in contrast to the levels of the region and the community (ibid.: 5).

Ironically, despite the absence of PPP activity at regional and community level, Wallonia set up an advisory unit (Cellule d'Informations Financières, CIF) in 2005 as a special purpose body, with responsibility also for PPP since 2009. Politically, the CIF[1] is responsible to the Regional Minister of Budget and Finance. Its mission is to monitor and advise public companies in Wallonia and scrutinizing 'draft budgets and accounts of public companies and issuing opinions to government regarding the financial state of these organisations. Since 2009, its competencies have been extended to issuing opinions on PPP projects within the Walloon Region and the FSC' [Francophone Speaking Community] (ibid.: 7). It is completely financed by public funds, without contributions from users, industry or the EU (ibid.). Other activities such as attempts to adopt a legal or policy framework for PPPs have not been observed for Wallonia. However, in 2008 a decree was adopted outlining a PPP school building programme,

> which has not and, according to CIF, will not be carried out. Political scepticism and the lack of public support towards PPPs make it unlikely that a PPP policy framework and a PPP programme will emerge in the near future. There is, however, a willingness to develop a strategy for the next multiannual financing framework to blend EU grants with PPPs. (ibid.: 9)

At least one regional project in Wallonia was signed in 2012. The Liege tram PPP with a length of 17km (€320m) was approved by the Walloon government in March 2012, following months of political debates. The project will run until 2043 (27 years, see www.pppbulletin.com/news/view/22415).

The capital region of Brussels is slightly more active than Wallonia. It first initiated a PPP project in 2006, the Aquiris waste water treatment plant (www.aquiris.be). One of the few e-government projects in the capital Brussels conducted with the PPP approach is the high-speed telecommunications network IRISNet (www.bruxelles.Irisnet.be), providing an intranet and a public internet platform for schools, administrations, hospitals and other institutions in the region (OECD 2008b: 131). In June 2011, the Brussels authority for transportation infrastructure announced the appointed of an advisory board for the modernisation of the Leopold II Tunnel; three companies have been contracted as legal, financial and technical advisers to support the authorities. 'The 100m tunnel is located in the centre of the Brussels capital, running over the Belgium canal, and requires major restructuring' (www.pppbulletin.com/news/view/18530).

6.2 THE NETHERLANDS

6.2.1 Institutional Context

The political system of the Netherlands has long been regarded as a prototype for consociational democracy (together with Switzerland, see Lijphart 1989). In contrast to Switzerland, it is a unitary system with 12 provinces and more than 400 local governments. Whereas the unitary structure could provide a context for fostering PPP, the consociationalism can be expected to have a negative impact on it. Consensus in the Netherlands works on the basis of voluntarily cooperation of the political elites despite 'overlapping cleavages', with increasing polarization, and increasingly weaker 'pillarization' (Oosterwaal/Torenvlied 2010). Even if pillarization has become more loosely tied compared with the 1970s, the consensus culture is still dominant at the level of policy making. The party system is structured with a social democratic and green pole, a Christian centre and a strong liberal pole. Right-wing populist parties (Pim Fortuyn, Wilders) have challenged the culture of consensus and further contributed to polarization at the political level. Thus, coalition formation can take a relatively long time, but less so than in the fragmented Belgian system.

The consensus culture might not provide the best social environment for introducing a contested concept such as PPP. Consensus enables political groups to exercise some kind of informal veto in the case of policy change. Also, unlike the cases of the UK, Portugal, Spain and Greece, which all favour one party governments, coalition governments might not contribute to a fast and easy adoption of the PPP approach.

The consensus culture is also mirrored in the structure of the government, with the constitution giving the prime minister only very limited additional powers compared to the other ministers of the cabinet. One of these additional powers is to suggest the members of his cabinet, before they are appointed by the monarch. Thus, the hierarchical structure of the cabinet is very different to that of the UK and resembles the non-hierarchical cabinet system of the Swiss federal council (Bundesrat). Historically, the modest powers of the Dutch prime minister evolved from a strongly inclusive, non-hierarchial system created to accommodate certain representational requirements. Compared with the UK, this system does not provide good conditions for fast and easy policy transfer.

Privatization policies have played a certain role in the Netherlands, albeit limited due to a traditionally smaller-sized and more efficient public sector. Historically, state involvement in the economy was comparatively low (e.g. in contrast to France), limiting also the scope for privatization policies, which were more focused on sectors similar to natural monopolies. 'The Netherlands is one of the few EU countries that implemented the EU directives targeted at these sectors in a timely way' (Köthenbürger 2006: xvii).

At regional level there are 12 provinces, which make up the second tier of government, each having a directly elected council, chaired by a governor who is formally appointed for six years by the Crown on recommendation of the provincial council. 'The council also appoints the executive board (between three and nine people), which is chaired by the governor' (Keman/Waldendorp 2010: 270). A certain degree of decentralization may de jure exist, but in practice the system is strongly centralized and governed 'top-down' by The Hague. In the early 1990s, 'grants and subsidies to the lower tiers were redistributed according to 'objective' criteria and by means of revenue sharing across the polity. All in all the legal framework of the Dutch state concerning intergovernmental relations between the different layers is basically top-down organised and controlled through the power-of-the-purse by central government' (ibid.).

At local level there are 443 'well-equipped' municipalities with

> a considerable bureaucracy, many responsibilities and a substantial budget. On the other hand, central government sets local agendas and restricts decisions which might lead to differences in local service provision. Municipalities have limited fiscal autonomy and many of their responsibilities are defined by the central government. (ibid.: 272)

Despite some attempts of decentralization in recent time, the powers of central government still prevail. For example, functional agencies have been set up in many areas, such as in water management, the police and health care. Whereas the water boards are directly elected by the respective population, in the other areas agencies are directed 'top-down'. In these cases, the management of government functions is geographically 'devolved' to areas 'that coincide with neither municipal nor provincial boundaries. These include, for example, the 25 police areas, the 35 transport and traffic areas, the 40 regional health authorities and the 150 regional labour market offices', for which central government still sets the standards and controls its performance; these administrative structures can therefore also be described as deconcentrated tasks (ibid.: 271).

In the field of socioeconomic interest group relations, the corporatist system in the Netherlands is also to a certain degree hierarchically structured, with central government as the leading actor in this process. Together with associations of trade unions and employers' organizations, the government tries to exert influence on issues of income policy and social and economic policies. Despite its overall characterization as being in decline, corporatism is still considered as an important consensus and cooperation mechanism and has, at least regarding policy implementation, 'the same centralist flavour as other features of the Dutch political system' (ibid.: 278).

6.2.2 PPP Politics

PPP activity in the Netherlands is not as high as could be expected due to factors such as the centralized state structure or the overall dynamics in public sector reform. For example, elements of the NPM approach have been warmly adopted since the 1990s and more recently e-government tools were broadly taken up. In 2012, the UN Public Administration Network e-government index (UNPAN 2012) ranked the Netherlands second in its worldwide comparison of the introduction and use of forms of e-government.[2] Thus, Dutch politics on the one hand has high aspirations for public sector reform and modernization, but remains on the other hand sceptical towards PPP. Koppenjan (2005: 135) has observed that, despite high expectations, especially in the area of transport infrastructure, the development of PPP projects has stalled. The modest role of PPP in the Netherlands can be linked with the consociational style of policy making (Lijphart) with a relative high number of veto players. In contrast to Belgium at national level, the conflict lines in the Netherlands are not linguistically but confessionally based.

Originally, in the Netherlands PPP was used for transportation projects such as high-speed rail lines, roads and bridges on estuaries; later, the programme was extended to the fields of education and justice (prison). One of the flagships in PPP was the high-speed railway line from Amsterdam, via Schiphol and Rotterdam, to the Belgian border, connecting the Netherlands with the PBKAL (Paris, Brussels, Cologne, Amsterdam and London) high-speed rail network (EIB 2004: 6).

Conducive to PPPs has been that organizations with mixed public–private structures in the areas of health, housing and education were (are) quite common. Nevertheless, Koppenjan (2005) and EPPPR (2007: 58) estimated a medium level of activity, with a slight increase in 2006, prior to the general election in November.

> The current transport policy document 2010 to 2020 contemplates a total investment in transport infrastructure of € 80.5 bn of which € 30.5 bn is to come from private sources. The main unknown is the impact of the regional and local governments on the decision-making process (typically adverse and driven by environmental concerns). (ibid.)

Similar to the UK (and Ireland), in the Netherlands, in 1998, a social–liberal coalition under Prime Minister Wim Kok faced their second spell in government with major challenges in the field of public transport infrastructure. Given the necessary austerity measures at the eve of the introduction of the Euro in 1999, they searched for alternative financing options. In this context, the PPP approach was put on the political agenda. For this purpose a variety of suitable projects in which private partners could be involved had been identified by central government, encompassing several motorways, 'the expansion of the Rotterdam dockland area, a new railway between the Rotterdam Port and Germany for the transportation of goods, 'and high-speed railways between Amsterdam and the Belgian and German borders' (Koppenjan 2005: 136f.).

As early as 1999, a PPP Expertise Centre was established in the Ministry of Finance. Its tasks were to develop a public sector comparator, checklists for various contract types and standard tender documents as well as guidelines for contract management and project procurement. 'The Knowledge Centre consists of industry experts and policy makers appointed by the government' (OECD 2010: 105). It has the task of promoting public–private cooperation in capital-intensive projects, and is controlled by an advisory council[3] and a steering committee. PPP legislation does not exist. The results of the first plans of the Kok II cabinet commencing in 1998 are expected to be sobering (Koppenjan 2005). By 2005, only a few projects had been brought to contract maturity, such as a high-speed rail route, the A59 Geffen–Oss road project and a land development project in the municipality of Voorburg (Sijtwende project) (ibid.). 'While expectations of PPP are high, there is little understanding of either the problems that attempts to create these partnerships encounter or the manner they should be dealt with' (ibid.).

In response to the slow start of the PPP programme at central level, in mid-2006 the competence centre was integrated into the Ministry of Finance as a new, separate department (PPP Asset Management). This department also provides an overview of the PPP actors and activities in the Netherlands (www.ppsbijhetrijk.nl/english). The website maintained by the Ministry of Finance provides both an overview of ongoing national projects as well as planned procurement; it is supplied with relevant PPP information by all relevant ministries. These include the Department of Defence, the Government Buildings Agency (Rijksgebouwendienst), which carries out the tendering of construction projects, and the Directorate-General for Public Works and Water Management (Rijkswaterstaat), which advertises and supervises the infrastructure projects. Furthermore, the Ministry of Health, Welfare and Sport is involved in the tendering of PPP in the health-care sector. Similar to the NHS Trusts in the UK, the Dutch health-care facilities can invest in property and building at their own discretion.

> This causes the ministries of Health, Welfare and Sport and of Finance to play their role from a distance: obstacles for PPP application in the healthcare sector are cleared by adjusting rules and regulations, and the ministries can assist interested healthcare institutions in their thinking about developing the application of PPP to required property development.[4]

In the area of schools, the School Construction Service Centre (Servicecentrum Scholenbouw) is responsible for PPP (ibid.). The PPS Network Nederland is an information and advocacy platform, which was founded in 2007 by actors in the Dutch PPP market to convince national, regional and local decision makers of the benefits of the model and to stimulate the flow of projects (EPPPR 2007: 58).

Among the more recent funding activities of the government was the lowering in October 2008 of the threshold of investment volumes that is necessary for a project to be implemented as a PPP, the threshold being decreased from €112.5 million to €60 million. Also, the government has developed a standard contract for construction, defence and transport (EPPPR 2009: 75). Major projects in the rail sector included the high-speed link between Amsterdam and Paris, which was the first Dutch PPP and closed in October 2001. In the road sector, 2009 saw some major projects come to a close, for example the A15 project connecting Rotterdam harbour with the 'hinterland' and the A12 project as well as the second Coentunnel project, west of Amsterdam. Also, the sector of facility and accommodation saw some major projects close in 2008 and 2009, such as detention centres in Zaanstad and Rotterdam, the justice complex in Schiphol, the Defence Ministries' headquarters project in Utrecht and tax office projects in Groningen and Doetinchem (Allen & Overy 2010: 51).

As already mentioned, public sector reform and e-government were placed high on the Dutch reform agenda. In the field of e-government, the private sector is involved on the basis of individual decisions. The project management is carried out by public and private corporate bodies such as ICTU (ICT Uitvoeringorganisatie) on public order (OECD 2007: 126). ICTU was founded in 2001 by the Home Office and the Association of Dutch Municipalities (VGN) and operates specifically for government procurement and implementation of ICT. 'In doing so, ICTU aims to achieve coherence in all facilities and programmes, as well as collaboration between policy and implementation on all layers of government' (www.ictu.nl/english). In this field, guidelines for the use of contracting out, PPPs or similar instruments do not exist; however, the government is trying to strengthen their control of respective institutions, which are also described as 'arms-length organizations' (ibid.: 106).

Focusing on the post-investigation period, in 2010 an international consortium was awarded a €1 billion DBFM contract to upgrade and maintain parts of the A15 motorway, running for 30 years. Later in the same year, two more road PPPs were signed, one worth €260 million (A12), the other €1.5 billion (A15), again applying the DBFM model (www.pppbulletin.com/news/view/16002). In May 2011, BAM PPP set up a joint venture (€390 million) with a pension fund to invest in PPP projects in the social and transport sectors of the Netherlands, Belgium, the UK, Ireland, Germany and Switzerland (www.pppbulletin.com/news/view/18203). In March 2012 the Dutch Minister for Infrastructure and the Flemish Minister for Public Works signed an agreement on a Belgian–Dutch PPP, in which a private partner will be contracted (DBFO) for a €1 billion sea-lock PPP at the port of Ghent, which was lacking capacity due to a fast growing cargo sector and also an increase in the size of ships. 'The new lock should improve access to the port of Ghent and ensure a smooth passage of vessels between the Netherlands, Belgium and France' (www.pppbulletin.com/news/view/22343). Also in 2012, the PPP for the new Museum of Defence in Soesterberg took shape, as a 25-year DBFM contract worth €100 million. Further projects in this period after the global financial crisis included the N33 road PPP (€150 million), the Groningen Tram PPP (€310 million) and 'the A1/A6 and the first section of the huge €4bn Schiphol–Amsterdam–Almere road. Outside transport, a new government policy HQ and a National Institute for Health and Environment came to market in 2012' (Partnerships Bulletin/Deloitte 2012: 6).

6.3 CASE COMPARISON

Geographically close neighbours, the Belgian and Dutch polities differ in several aspects. Most obviously, the linguistic differences in Belgium have since the 1970s led to a federalization of the political system and a decentralization of administration. On the other hand, the Kingdom of the Netherlands still has a unitary polity with 13 provinces at arms lengths from central government. Both polities apply an electoral system of PR, leading to relatively fragmented parliaments and multi-party cabinets. However, due to the linguistic differences, policy making in Belgium has become much more complex than in the Netherlands. Given the thus high number of partisan veto players at governmental level in Belgium, it is less surprising that PPP support at central level has remained rather moderate. The case of the Netherlands also corroborates that a unitary state structure (such as in the UK, Portugal and Greece) does not necessarily foster higher PPP activity (see also the Nordic countries). Comparing the Netherlands with the UK in this regard, the cabinet format with respect to veto players is the more crucial factor.

Despite an early setting up of an administrative unit in charge of PPP in the Netherlands, both countries are latecomers in terms of PPP activity. In the case of Belgium, only the Flemish region developed a significant

PPP programme after 2003, whereas at national level as well as in the Walloon region nearly no PPPs could be identified for the investigation period. For the Flemish region, the criteria of budget neutrality (i.e. off balance sheet according to the ESA 95 standard) took a high priority. In contrast to the federal level, different Flemish cabinets comprised members from the same parties over a longer period of time, thus giving more continuity to policy making.

The Netherlands contrast strongly with this pattern. Firstly, at national level a policy commitment to support PPP had already been introduced in the late 1990s, and a PPP unit was set up short thereafter. The policy support of the Kok government can be seen in the context of neighbouring modernizing centre-left governments (New Labour in the UK and the red–green coalition in Germany). However, in contrast to these larger neighbouring countries, in the Netherlands the early PPP plans did not take off at a pace. This situation changed in 2005/06, and even after the global financial crisis there was a constant flow of projects, some even large scale as the A15 motorway with €1.5 billion of volume.

Regarding the federal/unitary state structure, unitary states do not necessarily provide a better context for more PPP activity. As the Flemish case within the federal Belgium illustrates, a federal system can provide a space for single jurisdictions within a federal system to move ahead (similar to e.g. North Rhine-Westphalia in Germany). While in some other federal systems, such as Germany and Spain, there were asymmetries at subnational level too, the Flemish case in Belgium is probably the most obvious. For Belgium, a relatively high level of budget deficit (and sovereign debt) could also be a potential 'driver' for PPP. However, in this case the fragmented partisan landscape seems not only to prevent the deficit from being reduced, but also to affect the amount of PPP activity at the national level.

A factor that has to be considered for the Netherlands is its strong corporatism. As we have seen in Chapter 3, the structure of interest groups has a strong influence on a country's willingness or ability to adapt to higher levels of PPP activity. In this aspect, the Netherlands can also be compared with the Nordic countries or Austria.

NOTES

1. 'The Walloon Region has established a small dedicated unit within a government agency – Cellule d'Informations Financières (CIF) – that offers legal and financial advice to the regional government and the FSC on projects before they are put to tender. At the request of a procuring authority (regional, Community or municipal), the unit may assist in the

preparation, procurement and implementation of PPPs, although in practice this has not been the case so far' (EPEC 2012a: 5).

2. The index is composed of the 'weighted average of three normalized scores on the most important dimensions of e-government, namely: scope and quality of online services, development status of telecommunication infrastructure, and inherent human capital' (UNPAN 2012: 120).
3. The advisory council encompasses 'private sector experts that meet informally two or three times a year in a personal capacity to discuss the working of the Knowledge Centre and formulate recommendations about the work of the Centre to the Steering Group. The Steering Group consists of representatives from government departments and is responsible for determining the work programme of the Centre. All policy documents and progress reports prepared by the Centre for the Council of Ministers must be first approved by the Steering Group. It does not closely monitor the progress of individual projects' (OECD 2010: 105).
4. www.ppsbijhetrijk.nl/english/Projects/ [10 January 2011].

7. Germany and Austria

Whereas Germany started its PPP policy after the takeover of the red–green coalition government in 1998, in Austria it began with the incoming centre-right government in early 2000. At federal level in Germany, large projects such as 'Toll Collect', the satellite-based calculation of truck tolls, the modernization of the computer and telecom infrastructure at the armed forces and the armed forces carpool contributed to a considerable amount of investment. At the level of states (i.e. state level), some governments were inclined towards PPP, too. In Austria, due to frequently practised 'grand coalitions' at the national level and oversized proportionality cabinets at the state level, PPP never did receive much political support – except from the ÖVP (Austrian People's Party) led Schüssel cabinets commencing in 2000.

7.1 GERMANY

7.1.1 Institutional Context

In contrast to the 'model pupils' such as the UK and Portugal, the political system of Germany includes some institutional features which do not favour a quick policy change towards a high level PPP involvement. Firstly, Germany is a federal state comprising 16 states of various population size and economic capacity. Each state has its own parliament and government, with the governments sending delegates to the second chamber, the Federal Council (Bundesrat). Via the Federal Council, states have relatively broad opportunities to suspend or even completely veto legislation which touches the interests of the states. Until the federal reform of 2006, up to 60 per cent of federal legislation needed the consent of the second chamber. After the reform this share was still up to 40 per cent (Krumm 2015).

While some of the vetoes of the Federal Council can be outvoted by the first chamber (Bundestag), others cannot (consent and objection bills). Compared to Austria and Belgium (the other federal systems in our sample), the German Federal Council has the strongest powers to block a policy change at federal level. However, these formal requirements are often not the crucial obstacle for a policy change as, for instance, financing and implementation of policies are shared between the federal and the state level, giving the states an opportunity to negotiate for a relatively high federal share of financing or yielding federal subsidies or other forms of compensation. Thus, while in theory the Federal Council is an important veto player, in practice state governments prefer to make deals and compromises with the federal government.

In contrast to the UK prior to 2010, Germany used to have coalition governments. Due to its electoral system of PR, a coalition partner is needed by the winning party. Mostly this is a small party, either the Liberals or the Greens. From 2005 to 2009, however, a 'grand coalition' consisting of Christian Democrats (CDU/CSU) and Social Democrats (SPD) was required to reach the necessary absolute majority of seats. This coalition still supported the PPP approach, but enthusiasm was reduced compared to its predecessors, the two 'red–green' coalitions between 1998 and 2005. In general, coalition governments raise the number of partisan veto players. These are parties whose consent is needed in order to execute a policy change (Tsebelis 2002). Thus, under conditions of coalition government, a change of policy (in favour of PPP) can more easily be blocked by another (governing) party. Although the number of coalition parties is relatively small in the German case, it is a feature that distinguishes it from the UK, Portugal and Spain as the leading PPP countries.

Another institutional factor has to be kept in mind: German corporatism. Although not being among those countries with the strongest corporatist ties (such as the Nordic countries or Austria), there was a revival of corporatist policy making under the two 'red–green' coalitions, labelled, for instance, as 'alliance for employment' (Bündnis für Arbeit). These negotiation forums provided room for talks, for example on the appropriate level of wages and other employment promoting measures. According to section 3.4.3 of this study, a corporatist structure of the interest group sector also has a negative impact on the level of PPP activity.

Furthermore, in contrast to the UK and Portugal, Germany was a latecomer in terms of privatization of public utilities. A first wave of privatization and liberalization policy did take place in the sectors of telecommunication and electricity in the 1990s. In a second wave, among others, Deutsche Telekom was privatized and placed on the stock exchange ('Volksaktie') in 1996 and 1999. Furthermore, the railway corporation Deutsche Bahn was transformed into an SOE (Köthenbürger 2006: xvii). Despite several attempts, a full (material) privatization of

Deutsche Bahn has not been successful so far. At federal level a first step towards the involvement of private capital in public procurement was made under the Christian–Liberal coalition (Kohl IV) in 1994 with a law on the private financing of federal highways (Fernstraßenbauprivatfinanzierungsgesetz, FStrPrivFinG). The law was drafted by the Federal Ministry of Transportation under the then minister Matthias Wissmann, who also pushed forward other privatization projects during his term in office.

However, the highway construction private financing act may claim to have laid the foundations for later PPP development in the infrastructure sector. It was meant to open up possibilities for private participation in the construction of tunnels, bridges and passes (so-called F-model). So far, however, with the 'Warnowquerung Rostock'and the 'Herrentunnel Lübeck', the model has only been used twice (Allen & Overy 2010: 79). In the last legislation period of the Christian–Liberal coalition (Kohl IV), from 1994 to 1998, a stronger focus had been set on privatization of public enterprises and liberalization of regulated sectors, such as the telecommunication market in 1998. In the telecommunication sector, for example, the impulse for liberalization came from the European Commission, which published its influential green paper on the development of a common market for telecommunications services and equipment in June 1987 (Commission of the European Communities 1987).

Subsequently, the market-based opening of previously nationalized sectors was often managed in three steps: liberalization, privatization and regulation. This sequence can, for example, be clearly observed in the opening of the telecommunication sector since 1998. The marketization of the sector was introduced by several reforms of postal services in the 1990s, which ended the de jure monopoly in this sector and led to a stiff decrease in prices and an introduction of new services such as the 'call by call' service. In 1989 the first reform act for postal services led to the split of the formerly unitary public postal corporation into three sector-specific public corporations: Deutsche Bundespost, Postbank and Telekom. It also led to a liberalization of the market for terminal equipment (e.g. telephones), initializing the separation of restricted sovereign and liberalized entrepreneurial tasks, which also enabled service users to act as 'customers'. However, despite the splitting up of 'Bundespost', public ownership was not questioned. In 1995 the second postal reform (Postneuordnungsgesetz) took place. The legal form of Deutsche Telekom was transformed into a public corporation (Aktiengesellschaft) and in 1996 and 1999 large shares of stocks were sold on the stock exchange.

In 1996, the third postal reform was passed by parliament (Telecommunication Act, TKG) and led to a scrapping of the network and voice service monopolies in 1998. Also, the regulatory agency for telecommunication and postal services (Reg TP, in 2005 merged into the Bundesnetzagentur) was set up in 1997/98 under the supervision of the then Minister of Economy, Günter Rexrodt. The agency was initially projected to run for only ten years, but it prevailed as a most important actor for the regulation of network services in the fields of energy, telecommunications, post and rail (www.bundesnetzagentur.de). Less surprisingly, the telecommunications sector faced similar problems to public transport infrastructure in terms of increasing traffic (bitstream volumes) and public underinvestment. However, only in the transport infrastructure sector has PPP been able to take root, whereas, for example, the costs of broadband expansion was expected to be shouldered by conventional public or private investments. In conclusion, the reform activities of the late Kohl government in the 1990s were focused on liberalization and accompanying regulatory frameworks. Only after the change in government in 1998 did PPP have a chance to spill over from the British New Labour government to the centre-left ('red–green') coalition in Germany.

7.1.2 Federal Level

The incoming red–green coalition soon took the PPP approach from the British New Labour government and began to develop PPP activities both in a programmatic and practical dimension. However, in the coalition agreement of 1998 the term PPP and its equivalents were not yet used. But soon thereafter the defence and transport sectors in particular became inclined to use PPP. In the transport sector, a large funding gap was recognized and acknowledged by the Pällmann Commission in the year 2000. To at least mitigate the gap, the commission recommended in its final report to consider the inclusion of private funding in public infrastructure projects.

As a consequence, a new financial model as well as a new technical system in truck tolling and road infrastructure financing was introduced in 2002. The new satellite-based truck toll calculation system was soon tendered (by competitive dialogue) and the contract with the preferred bidder was signed on the eve of the 2002 general election, the government utilizing the event for public relations purposes. However, due to the technical problems which soon appeared, the starting date of the new system had to be postponed several times, leading to revenue losses of several billion Euros. The new distance-based truck toll replaced the older time-based toll system and contributes to covering the substantial underfunding of highway construction.

The technical infrastructure has been developed, financed and is operated by private companies, which in turn are funded by a share of the toll revenue. The PPP procurement process began in early 2000, half a year before the commission for the reform of transport infrastructure funding (Pällmann Commission) published its findings. This Commission recommended an expansion of user financing, through a distance-based toll of 14 cents per kilometre, to bridge an overall financing gap of €3.8 billion per year (Pällmann-Kommission Verkehrsinfrastrukturfinanzierung 2000: 59). The Commission also contributed the idea of creating the transport infrastructure finance company (Verkehrsinfrastrukturfinanzierungsgesellschaft, VIFG), which was founded in 2003. VIFG reinvests the proceeds from the truck toll into transport infrastructure.

The concession agreement, publicly signed just before the general election, initially remained secret; however, parts of it were made available by a newspaper (FAZ 2004: 12). Only following considerable public pressure was the contract made available to members of the parliamentary transport committee. Presumably, the federal government did not scrutinize the contract in any great detail in order to be able sign it before the election (Sack 2009: 188). A range of policy objectives was linked with the tolling contract, which the British newspaper *The Economist* characterized as follows: '[a]s well as collecting tolls, it is supposed to gather traffic flow and vehicle-specific data, offering an opportunity to pioneer "smart vehicle" technology, and help national champions such as DaimlerChrysler and Deutsche Telekom to establish a leading position in it' (Economist 2004: 74). Instead of 2003, the system became partly operational only in 2005 due to technical difficulties and then fully functional in 2006.

According to Fleischer/Halbritter (2004: 365) the case of Toll Collect reveals remarkable professional administrative deficiencies regarding the promotion and implementation of technical innovations. Complex tasks were transferred 'en bloc' to the private industry hoping, or even naively trusting, that a solution would be easily found and implemented. The administrative implementation was largely immune to political monitoring and review and thus from the influence of the executive and legislature. Furthermore, the advisory bodies of the parliament for the introduction of new technologies were not used, since these bodies rather aim at estimating long-term trends (ibid.).

The distance-based toll for lorries over 12 tonnes in weight was initially on average 12.4 cents per kilometre and was increased in 2007 to 13.5 cents per kilometre. On 1 January 2009 a further increase to around 16 cents took place, achieving additional revenue of €800 million. As part of the 'climate package' of the federal government the pollutant-dependent increase intends to foster the conversion of the truck fleet to environmentally friendly vehicles. In return the road tax of domestic carriers was lowered. The toll thus plays an important part not only in public funding, but also in setting differentiated policy goals, not only towards environmental issues but also the cross-subsidization of other transport modes, such as railways and waterways. Toll revenue totalled €3.08 billion in 2006 and €3.4 billion in 2007. After deduction of the shares of the Toll Collect consortium and the Ministry of Transport, the net revenue of VIFG was €2.3 billion, of which €1.09 billion was invested in roads, €954 million in railways and €265 million in waterways (see www.vifg. de). As a result it should be noted that, besides the budgetary effects, extensive policy goals played a role, via the introduction of the electronic truck toll system, as a powerful instrument of governance. While innovation risks were transferred en bloc to the industry, without adequate control options regarding the fulfilment of the agreed goals, the financial risk of a delayed introduction remained largely with the state as the ultimate responsible actor.

The PPP support in the defence sector can partly be explained by a similar constellation. Huge costs for upcoming large procurement projects in combination with only moderate support for defence policy in the German public sphere convinced the then defence minister Rudolf Scharping (1998–2002) to intensify the use of PPP in his department. The armed forces carpool and the modernization of the telecom infrastructure of the armed forces (project Herkules) are examples of large-scale PPPs in the defence sector. In 2002 a limited company comprising the car fleet of the Army with 26 000 vehicles and 400 employees (as well as 1400 civilian-supplied drivers) was privatized in the form of a PPP (www.bwfuhrpark.de/profil_13.html). At the end of 2006 the other major project (project Herkules) was signed by the Ministry of Defence. Project Herkules aimed to modernize 140 000 computer workstations, including the telephone systems, with 300 000 new devices. The project is rather an outsourcing contract than a PPP, with a contract time of ten years and involving 2950 employees. The budget volume originally was €7.1 billion over the whole period. In contrast to the privatization of the fleet, the results of this project have been subject to severe criticism (Krampe 2010, Scheidges 2010).

At programme level, the second 'red–green' coalition (2002) included PPP in their coalition agreement. It was agreed that PPP should be promoted in the construction sector and a steering committee should prepare the ground for a competence centre, which should advise local governments and private firms on the planning and implementation of public–private collaboration (Coalition Agreement SPD–Bündnis90/Die Grünen 2002: 60). Moreover, the collaboration of government, business and civil society should be promoted as instruments of development policy to solve global problems of development and to make technology, knowledge and capital better available for developing and transition countries (Coalition Agreement 2002: 84). The steering committee was established in the same year at the highest administrative level in the Ministry of Transport, Building and Urban Affairs, with members from federal, states and local authorities as well as from the construction and banking sectors (Fischer et al. 2006: 544).

Its task was to improve the framework for PPPs and to establish expert networks. While the steering committee and the embedded inter-ministerial working group were located at a strategic level, the PPP Task Force established in 2004 in the Ministry of Transport, Building and Urban Development focused primarily on the project level, and is in particular responsible for the implementation of pilot projects and the standardization of processes (ibid.). At state level a number of task forces and centres of excellence have since been established, too.

During the second red–green coalition (2002–2005) the PPP policy gradually gained top priority and was also used for symbolic politics, such as Chancellor Schröder's announcement at the end of February 2004 of a new, revised tolling agreement, after the termination of the existing contract.[1] The second red–green coalition is also characterized by large policy transfers from the UK in relation to PPP and the development of central and federal PPP funding structures in Germany.

Commencing in October 2004 a project working group of the SPD parliamentary group drafted a 'PPP Acceleration Bill', which was finally passed by the Bundestag prior to its dissolution (and re-election) in 2005. The Law was adopted in the first chamber (through the votes of the SPD and Greens. The then opposition of Christian Democrats and Liberals had abstained in the Bundestag, however, backed it in the Federal Council, where the federal government lacked a majority. The PPP Acceleration Law introduced a number of adjustments to other existing laws (law article) 'including those for procurement, tax, public road fees, budget and investment – to eliminate impediments related to PPPs. Although public–private partnerships were legally possible prior to the Law, they were considered legally disadvantaged relative to traditional public procurement' (OECD 2010: 55). Furthermore, the Law formulated some policy goals such as the development of model contracts and the establishment of centres of excellence. Subsequently, policy guidelines have also been developed by several ministries and at state level since the 2005 Acceleration Law was passed. 'These cover the legal framework for public–private partnerships, project assessments and contract relationship management. Some also focus on particular sectors (e.g. education)' (OECD 2010: 55).

After snap elections in September 2005, the new grand coalition between Christian Democrats and Social Democrats still supported PPP, though less emphatically. Their coalition agreement in 2005 reflected a significant expansion of the theme in quantitative terms, as indicated by five mentions in the document.

Starting in the section 'revival of investment activity', with a kind of general legitimating, the coalition agreement (Coalition Agreement CDU/CSU–SPD 2005: 21) states: 'Public–Private Partnerships are a promising way to close gaps in the provision of public services' (own translation). The PPP Acceleration Law should be amended and 'discrimination' eliminated, for example in the Hospital Financing and Social Assistance Law, the Investment Law and in the Highway Construction Private Financing Law, as well as removing the barriers for the involvement of small and medium enterprises in PPPs (ibid.). Transport policy should be mobilized to attract more private capital for road construction (ibid.: 55). The construction sector should be helped to develop a positive context for PPPs in buildings and roads, for instance by raising the number of pilot projects, strengthening the Task Force, providing standardized contract structures and introducing generally accepted rules for the economic analysis in the tendering process (ibid.: 62). Finally, the financial market policy and the armed forces are mentioned as areas for development using PPPs (ibid.: 155). The PPP experience report of the federal government (BMVBS 2007: 4) draws an initial assessment of previous experiences with PPP and announces a PPP Simplification Act (not realized) at the federal level.

In the coalition agreement of the Christian Democrats and Liberals dated 26 October 2009 there are only three mentions of PPP. In the section on small and medium enterprises/companies (Mittelstand) it says that a High-Tech Start-up Fund is to be set up as a PPP and this will build on the experience of a previous fund. In addition, they wanted to mobilize private capital for a venture capital fund (ibid.: 25). In the section on 'high performing transport infrastructure' a more general policy goal is formulated: 'We will take forward the models for private participation in PPP projects' (ibid.: 35). The section 'development cooperation' stated that their focus will be on the key areas of good governance, education/training, health, rural development, climate, protection of environment and natural resources, and economic cooperation by means, for example, of PPP, microfinance systems and infrastructure support (ibid.: 128). Compared to the coalition agreement of 2005 the support for PPP is much more moderate, but still present.

During the late grand coalition, on 9 July 2008, the framework contract for the new ÖPP Deutschland AG (www.partnerschaften-deutschland.de) was signed, which became operational in early 2009. It is financed with 60 per cent coming from the public sector and 40 per cent from the private sector, and organized as a PPP (OECD 2010: 62). It is the successor to the Task Force, and was established with the involvement of the Treasury and the Federal Ministry of Transport, Building and Urban Development. It is supported by ten states, 82 municipalities, 33 other public corporations and more than 70 companies. Its tasks include advising potential public contractors, project monitoring and evaluation, as well as basic work such as the evolution of frameworks and standards, knowledge transfer and the development of new PPP application fields (see www.partnerschaften-deutschland.de). ÖPP Deutschland AG has a staff of 21 and two executive directors. It is funded by fees from consulting services provided to public institutions and has shareholders from the public and private sectors. 'At present, public shareholding within ÖPP Deutschland AG is by the federal government, by the federal states Schleswig-Holstein and North-Rhine Westphalia, and by the German Association of Towns and Municipalities (DStGB). The intention is that more federal states and municipal governments become shareholders in 2010' (OECD 2010: 61f.). At the federal level, the Federal Ministry of Finance and ÖPP Deutschland AG primarily share responsibility for PPPs.

A standardized model contract for PPP projects does not exist in Germany, in contrast to the UK, France and the Netherlands (Allen & Overy 2010: 52). Instead, individually created contracts are used, contributing to higher transaction costs in the contract awarding phase. On major projects competitive dialogue is used as the preferred method of tendering. In the planning and procurement process efficiency also must be calculated. This is provided by section 7 of the Federal Budget Code (BHO) and the relevant paragraphs of the state's budget regulations (LHO). After examining the measure's efficiency the cost of operation of the measure has to be reviewed. This is done by comparing the cost of a conventional procurement with that of an alternative, for example, PPP.

As Sack (2009) has shown, the promotion of PPP in Germany was largely through partisan consensus. Mause/Krumm (2011) showed by comparing the activities of the states that the participation of the Party of Democratic Socialism (PDS)/The Left Party has a significantly negative effect of the government's willingness to use PPPs as a procurement tool. A second significant effect is linked with the status of a state in the federal fiscal equalization scheme. Receiving states have a lower willingness to use PPP as a procurement option than giving states. Decidedly critical statements on the financial profitability of PPPs are given by the audit offices, mostly based on a case-by-case basis. For example, the Bavarian Supreme Auditing Court (ORH), in its annual report for 2006, reported the following in relation to two PPP road projects in Bavaria: 'The ORH has not identified any cost benefits in the investments that would not have been attainable with conventional implementation. In contrast, the private pre-financing makes the measure more expensive' (Bayrischer Oberster Rechnungshof 2006: 53, own translation). Table 7.1 summarizes the German cabinets between 1991 and 2009 and their main PPP policies.

Table 7.1 German federal governments and their PPP policies, 1991–2009

Years	Cabinet	Parties	Action
01/1991–10/1994	Kohl IV	CDU/CSU/FDP	09/1994: Highway Construction Private Financing Act laid the basics for infrastructure PPPs (operator model) under transport minister Matthias Wissmann
11/1994–10/1998	Kohl V	CDU/CSU/FDP	Several privatization projects pursued (e.g. telecommunications, Lufthansa)
10/1998–10/2002	Schröder I	SPD/B'90 and Greens	Policy transfer of PPP from the New Labour government started 2000: Final report of the commission on transport infrastructure funding 2002: PPP tender of a satellite-based Toll Collect system
10/2002–11/2005	Schröder II	SPD/B'90 and Greens	2002: Steering committee set up 2004: PPP Task Force set up 2005: PPP Acceleration Law passed
11/2005–10/2009	Merkel I	CDU/CSU/SPD	11/2008: ÖPP Deutschland AG (successor of Task Force) founded

Note: CSU = Christian Social Union in Bavaria, FDP = Free Democratic Party, B'90 = Bündnis90.

Source: Own compilation.

7.1.3 State Level

In many fields of public policy, the federal level needs the consent of the states for a policy change. This was strongly given by the government of the largest state, North Rhine-Westphalia, which took a leading role at state level. At this level, North Rhine-Westphalia was the forerunner in implementing the PPP approach, including under the red–green coalition governments (until 2005). In contrast, Baden-Württemberg was a latecomer in terms of PPP, but developed an intense political commitment and project flow later in the investigation period. Given that high PPP activity is found in states regularly governed both by Christian Democrats (Baden-Württemberg, Hessen, Saxony-Anhalt) and Social Democrats (North Rhine-Westphalia and Schleswig-Holstein until 2005), party politics does not seem to play an influential role when it comes to adopting the PPP approach at state level.

Mause/Krumm (2011) have developed a PPP activity index for the German states. The index ranges from 0 (no activity) to 5 (highest activity) with the rating being based on four factors: mention of PPP in a coalition agreement (or, if not available, an electoral programme), existence of PPP institutions (e.g. task force), number of projects at state level (double weighted) and number of local projects in a state (ibid.: 532). According to their findings, North Rhine-Westphalia reached the highest ranking in this period, followed by Baden-Württemberg and Hessen. At the bottom they ranked four states with the same overall score of 0.6: Mecklenburg-Vorpommern, Rhineland-Palatinate, Saarland and Saxony. Over the whole of their investigation period (2002 to 2009), Bavaria, Berlin and Saxony show no increase in PPP activity; for Hamburg the index value even shrank. On average the index value increased by 0.8 points during the period, with the largest increase for Baden-Württemberg and Schleswig-Holstein.

A good indicator for the institutionalization of PPP at state level is the establishment of PPP task forces. In some states such structures were first established in 2001, in others later, with peaks in the years 2004/05 and 2008 (see Table 7.3), suggesting three 'waves' of institutionalization at the state level.

In the rest of this section, we will take a more detailed look at the health and prison sectors at state level. Due to Germany's federal structure, state and local governments play important roles in setting regulatory frameworks and providing subsidies in the health sector. As a 'third type' of actor, health insurance funds, encouraged by politics, have changed from being just payers to also being players in the health care sector. They still face severe restrictions regarding their autonomy, for

Table 7.2 PPP activity level of the German states, 2002–2009

State	'02	'03	'04	'05	'06	'07	'08	'09	change 02–09	range 02–09	mean 02–09
North Rhine-Westphalia	2.0	2.5	3.0	2.5	3.0	2.5	2.5	2.5	+0.5	1.0	2.6
Baden-Württemberg	0.3	0.3	1.0	1.5	2.5	3.5	5.0	3.5	+3.2	4.7	2.2
Hessen	1.3	1.3	1.3	2.0	2.5	4.0	2.0	2.0	+0.7	2.7	2.1
Saxony-Anhalt	1.2	1.2	1.2	1.5	4.0	3.0	2.0	2.0	+0.8	2.8	2.0
Schleswig-Holstein	0.3	0.3	1.0	2.0	3.0	3.0	4.0	2.5	+2.2	3.7	2.0
Hamburg	1.3	1.3	1.3	1.3	1.3	2.8	0.8	0.8	–0.5	2.0	1.4
Bavaria	0.3	0.3	1.8	1.7	2.2	2.2	1.7	0.3	0.0	1.8	1.3
Brandenburg	0.3	0.3	0.3	1.3	1.3	2.0	2.5	1.5	+1.2	2.2	1.2
Lower Saxony	0.8	0.3	0.3	1.2	1.7	1.2	1.7	1.7	+0.8	1.3	1.1
Thuringia	0.3	0.3	1.0	1.0	1.0	2.0	1.0	2.0	+1.7	1.7	1.1
Bremen	0.3	0.3	1.3	1.3	1.3	0.8	0.8	0.8	+0.5	1.0	0.9
Berlin	0.8	0.8	0.8	0.8	0.8	0.8	0.8	0.8	0.0	0.0	0.8
Mecklenburg-Vorpommern	0.3	0.3	0.3	0.3	0.3	1.3	0.8	0.8	+0.5	1.0	0.6
Rhineland-Palatinate	0.3	0.3	0.3	0.3	0.3	1.0	1.5	1.0	+0.7	1.2	0.6
Saarland	0.3	0.3	0.3	0.8	0.8	0.8	0.8	0.8	+0.5	0.5	0.6
Saxony	0.3	0.3	0.8	0.3	1.3	0.8	0.3	0.3	0.0	1.0	0.6
mean (all states)	0.7	0.7	1.0	1.2	1.7	2.0	1.8	1.5	+0.8		
range (all states)	1.7	2.2	2.7	2.2	3.7	3.2	4.7	3.2	+1.5		

Source: Mause/Krumm 2011: 533.

example the fixing of contribution rates, and are not directly comparable with NHS funds in the UK; however, 'their ability to contract with selected providers and to build up preferred provider networks of some kind increased. The selective-contracting toolbox was filled with new and more effective instruments for implementing innovative health care concepts', according to Greiling/Häusler (2011: 174). As a health care system with a decentralized structure, public–private collaboration in respect to contracting for health care services has a long tradition in Germany.

Table 7.3 Institutional development of PPP at state level

	Year	Unit(s)	Ministerial oversight	Sector	Level	Steering committee
Bund	2008	ÖPP Deutschland AG	Federal Ministry of Finance	Construction	F, S, M	N
	2008	Transport Infrastructure Financing Corporation	Federal Ministry of Transport, Building and Urban Development	Transport	F	N
BW	2004	PPP Task Force	FS Ministry of Economy	Construction[1]	S[1]	J[1]
BY	2004	PPP Working Group	Supreme Building Authority FS Ministry of Home Affairs	Construction and transport	S, M	J[2]
BE			Finance Administration		S, M	N
BB	2004	Department	FS Ministry of Finance	Construction and transport	S	N
HB	2004	Department	Senator for Environment, Construction, Transport and Europe	Construction and transport	S, M	N
HH	2004	Department	Finance Authority	Construction and transport	S, M	N
HE	2005	PPP Centre of Excellence	FS Ministry of Finance	Construction and transport	S (building) M (consulting)	J[3]
MV	2008	Department	FS Ministry for Transport, Building and Regional Development	Construction and transport	S	N
		Department	FS Ministry of the Interior	Construction	M (financial supervision of the municipalities)	N
NS	2005	PPP Competence Network	FS Ministry of Economy, Employment and Transport	Construction	S, M	J
NRW	2001	PPP Task Force	FS Ministry of Finance	Construction and transport	S, M	N
RP	2001	PPP Competence Network	FS Ministry of Finance	Construction and transport	S, M	J[4]

SL	2001	Department	FS Ministry of Economy and Employment	Construction and transport	S, M	N
SN	2001	Department	Saxon State Ministry of Finance	Construction and transport	S, M	N
ST	2005	PPP Task Force	FS Ministry of Finance	Construction and transport	S, M	N
SH	2004	PPP Team	FS Ministry of Finance	Construction and transport	S, M	N
TH	2004	PPP Working Group	FS Ministry of Construction and Transport	Construction and transport	S, M	N

Notes:

BW = Baden-Württemberg, BY = Bavaria, BE = Berlin, BB = Brandenburg, HB = Bremen, HH = Hamburg, HE = Hessen, NS = Lower Saxony, MV = Mecklenburg-Vorp., NRW = North Rhine-Westphalia, RP = Rhineland-Palatinate, SL = Saarland, SN = Saxony, SA = Saxony-Anhalt, SH = Schleswig-Holstein, TH = Thuringia.

F = federal level; S = state level; M = municipal level; FS = federal state.

[1] Baden-Württemberg: Transport projects are the responsibility of the Ministry of Home Affairs; state projects are the responsibility of the Ministry of Finance; steering committee established in November 2004.

[2] Bavaria: Steering committee includes representation from Building Authority, Ministry of Finance, Ministry of Economy, Ministry of Home Affairs, municipal associations, association of building industry, audit institutions.

[3] Hessen: Advisory Board, Group 'PPP in Hessen'.

[4] Rhineland-Palatinate: Working group established in December 2005.

Source: OECD 2010: 59–60.

There are currently around 150 health insurance funds which act as purchasers (payers) of health services and primarily state and locally owned hospitals as well as private hospitals and those owned by non-profit organizations. Furthermore, investment in hospital facilities and infrastructure is often subsidized by state governments (ibid.: 168). Thus, the German health care (hospital) market for PPPs is much more diverse (and larger) than the Austrian market, leaving more opportunities for, for example, special forms of project management and ownership. However, the pressure for competition and cost efficiency in the privatized and partly privatized hospital sector is immense and private providers in some cases have tended to rigorously close down certain services or promise new treatments that are then not offered to patients to cut costs. This has most recently led to a more careful public consideration of large-scale PPPs in the hospital sector or even of a re-transfer to public ownership (for the case of the university hospital Giessen/Marburg, see e.g. Zimmer 2009).

Compared to the Anglo-Saxon countries, privatization of prisons or certain functions of imprisonment is far less common in Germany. However, towards the end of our investigation period, prison sector PPPs slowly gathered pace. For example, in September 2010 the €512 million Burg Prison PPP was signed with the Projektgesellschaft Justizvollzug Burg consortium. The consortium is led by Bilfinger Berger and for 25 years is in charge of planning, financing, constructing and operating the prison (case 2 in Table 7.4). The project is located in the state of Saxony-Anhalt, according to Table 7.2 the fourth most active PPP state. With the Hünfeld prison PPP closed in 2005, Hessen (third case in Table 7.4) was the first state to introduce PPP in the prison sector. In October 2010, the €50.5 million Bremervoerde project in the state of Lower Saxony reached financial close. For the state's first PPP a DBFM model was used with a contract period of 25 years. The project included 'the construction of a 300-inhabitant prison, the provision of catering, education, training and security services as well as the construction of work spaces for 135 prisoners' and went operational in 2013 (www.pppbulletin.com/news/view/16197).

The PPPs listed in Table 7.4 are mainly pilot projects, as the options to privatize prisons are limited by the basic law. Exercising sovereign tasks, as for instance the potential use of violence in encounters with imprisoned persons, is restricted to public employees and cannot be transferred or outsourced to private companies (Article 33, paragraph 4 of the basic law). Thus, while for planning and construction of prisons private sector collaboration is possible, for the day-to-day operation of a prison it has to be distinguished which tasks should be performed by a private company

Table 7.4 PPP in the prison sector at state level in Germany

	Offenburg	Burg	Hünfeld	Munich
Opening	2009	2009/10	2005	2009
State	Baden-Württemberg	Saxony-Anhalt	Hessen	Bavaria
Government	CDU/FDP	CDU	CDU/FDP	CSU
Private Partner, Building / Construction and Finance	Züblin	Syndicate of Bilfinger Berger Project Investments and Kötter Justizdienst-leistungen GmbH	State Hesse (Finance), Züblin (Planning and Construction)	BAM Deutschland GmbH and LHI Leasing GmbH
Private Partner Operating Services	Kötter Justizdienst-leistungen GmbH	Syndicate of Bilfinger Berger Project Investments and Kötter Justizdienst-leistungen GmbH	Serco Group	Müller-Altvatter-Gebäude-management GmbH
Operating Services that are assumed by the private partner	Auxiliary tasks e.g. at the outer gate, care of the inmates (kitchen, purchasing, etc.) facility management with cleaning service, medical, psychological and social assistance, also academic and job-related education, prisoner employment	All non-sovereign auxiliary, care and supervision tasks concerning the inmates, e.g. emergency service at the outer gate, services in the library, medical services by own physicians and nurses	Facility Management (maintenance, cleaning), supply management (kitchen, linen, health care, purchasing), supervision management (employment, recreational activities, social assistance), party of custody (control of technical equipment, service at the observation monitor)	Technical services, energy and media supply

Sources: Edel/Grüb 2011: 37, own addition.

and to what degree privatization is meant to take place. Only partial privatization is possible, namely of such services where the actions of the private partner do not assume a sovereign character and power of intervention is not needed. Complete privatization, including the transfer of sovereign tasks, is prohibited by the basic law (Edel/Grüb 2011: 38).

As in other sectors, for example the health care sector, the use of PPP and privatization is contested and opposed by public sector unions. Similar to the prison sector, there are also limits for the health care sector. In contrast, in the Anglo-Saxon countries privatization of such services usually has fewer legal limitations than in Germany. Thus, coordination of public and private activities within a PPP in Germany is more complex and challenging. Due to the prohibition of privatization of sovereign tasks and the resulting need of a precise sharing of tasks between the private and the public employees (i.e. partners), transaction costs can be higher than in pure public or private fulfilment. 'In the completely privatized prison the partners only cooperate via contract and not within the organization as all employees in the prison are affiliated to the private company' (ibid.: 42).

7.1.4 Accumulated Figures

Having analysed sector- and level-specific activity, the question arises as to how the overall accumulated activity in Germany can be assessed. ÖPP Deutschland AG (www.ppp-projektdatenbank.de), which was founded in 2009, provides a database that can be used for this purpose as it provides information regarding the extent and distribution of PPP activities in Germany. The projects registered since 2002 are based on voluntary project information from sponsors and contractors. While it does not cover the 'real' level of activity in the sectors, it is one of the best currently available sources of information. With appropriate caution some developments can be interpreted from the available data.

Firstly, it is striking that in the areas covered by the ÖPP Deutschland AG projects a peak was reached in investment volume in 2007 and the sums invested via PPP continuously dropped, dramatically in 2010. The number of projects in 2010 dropped by 38 per cent and the investment volume by around 70 per cent compared to the previous year 2009. The moderate decline in 2008 and 2009 can be explained largely by the global financial crisis. Given the long preparation time for a PPP, the 2010 decline can also be seen as a delayed impact of the crisis. Additionally, a political explanation could be the change of government in October 2009. With the Social Democrats losing power, the strongest proponent of PPP was no longer represented in federal government.

Table 7.5 Numbers and volume of projects in the building and construction sector, 2002–2010

	Number of projects	Volume (€ m)
2010	16	366
2009	26	1 187
2008	27	1 414
2007	38	1 506
2006	22	592 + 7 100[1]
2005	16	508
2004	12	350
2002/2003	2	7 400[2]

Notes:
Not included in the database, but included in the table, is the contract for the modernization of the communication technology of the armed forces since late 2006 with an initial planned volume of €7.1 billion (later corrected to €7.8 billion) and a contract period of ten years (project Herkules). Not included also is the contract for the electronic collection of truck tolls with a volume of €7.4 billion, a term of 13 years (September 2002–August 2015) and an extension option on behalf of the government of up to three years.

[1] Project Herkules (own addition).
[2] Project Toll Collect (own addition).

Source: ÖPP Deutschland AG (2011) PPP project databank as of 31 December 2010.

Within the incoming Christian–Liberal coalition, inclinations towards PPP came more from the Liberals than from the Christian Democrats. In general, the political support for PPP at central level can be seen as decreasing with the change of government in late 2009. Finally, an economic reason could be the introduction of economic stimulus package II. According to ÖPP Deutschland AG, the funds provided by the federal government as part of the economic stimulus package were mainly used for short-term conventional projects and thus were in competition with the PPP option. 'Already planned PPP projects were partly structured differently or completely cancelled, because the planning capacity of the administration was bound otherwise' (ÖPP Deutschland AG 2011: 3, own translation). This effect of the economic stimulus package II on the PPP activity can be interpreted as a kind of competition between classical Keynesian demand stimulation under corporatist conditions and more pluralistic policy tools such as PPP applied under the influence of 'privatized Keynesianism' (see chapter 10.4).

Table 7.6 PPP investment volumes (building and construction, in €million) at different political levels

Year	Federal	States	Local
2010	0	148	218
2009	500	147	533
2008	710	360	344
2007	580	438	488
2006	7 100[1]	405	175
2005	245	51	212
2004	0	0	350
2002/2003	7 400[2]	0	64
Total	16 535	1 549	2 384

Notes:
[1] Project Herkules (own addition).
[2] Project Toll Collect (own addition).

Source: ÖPP Deutschland AG (2011) PPP project databank as of 31 December 2010.

Table 7.6 shows the volumes of the construction and civil engineering sector. Comparing the different political levels, a consistent participation of local authorities but, conversely, a significant variation in the participation of the federal government stands out. At state level, the highest investment volume was achieved in 2007; at a local level in 2009. The states' share in recent years was at 30 per cent of the investment (ÖPP Deutschland AG 2011). Comparing the activities of the states, Baden-Württemberg, Bavaria, Hessen and North Rhine-Westphalia have accumulated most projects. At municipal level, North Rhine-Westphalia, Lower Saxony, Hessen, Baden-Württemberg, Bavaria and Saxony-Anhalt have been running the most projects since 2002 (ibid.).

The German Institute of Urbanism (DIFU 2009: 47) estimated on the basis of its own survey a 2014 nationwide average PPP rate of 4.8 per cent of total capital expenditure for the cities and municipalities. They also estimated a rate of 3.5 per cent for the counties and 4 per cent for federal and state governments. These quotas are considerably higher than those of the PPP project database in 2010; the information is drawn from (self-)assessments of the decision makers and experts at the various political levels. The study also shows a significant levelling-off of the estimated future importance of PPP. Across all areas of infrastructure less than 5 per cent estimated an important future role for PPP, in contrast to 9.9 per cent in 2005. Education and schools still represent the fields with the highest expectations, followed by the IT sector and energy supply (ibid.: 6).

7.2 AUSTRIA

7.2.1 Institutional Context

Similar to Germany, the Austrian political system is federally organized, but comprises only nine states. Compared to Germany and also to Belgium, it is much more centralized. This has also led to its description as a 'Unitarian' federal system. The nine states have their own parliaments and governments and are represented in the second chamber at federal level, the Federal Council (Bundesrat). The number of representatives of the states in the second chamber varies between 3 and 12, depending on each state's population. They are elected by the states' parliaments by proportional representation after each election of a new state legislature. Thus, there is a permanent or 'rolling' renewal of the Federal Council with each state parliament election. In terms of fiscal centralization, the federal level and the social insurance funds collect approximately 80 per cent of public revenues, the states up to 8 per cent and the local level about 11 per cent (Scherrer 2013: 3).

Compared to its equivalents in Germany or even Switzerland, the second chamber is not very strong. It primarily has powers to suspend legislation in certain fields of polity where the interests of the states are touched directly. Its main instrument is to veto bills passed by the first chamber, the National Council (Nationalrat), which, however, in most cases can easily be overruled by the National Council. Thus, the Federal Council in most cases can only delay federal legislation. The latter has the power to overrule this veto by simple majority. Only in a very limited field of constitutional matters do the states and the Federal Council respectively need to be in agreement before the constitutional amendment can come into force. Given this relatively weak federal institutional setting, it can be expected that individual state legislatures or governments do not have sufficient power to slow down a possible policy change at national level in favour of the PPP approach. It is also improbable that states will act as agenda-setters in terms of PPP, unlike, for example, North Rhine-Westphalia in Germany or the Flemish region in Belgium. Policy change in Austria is unlikely to happen bottom-up, driven by (some of) the states. Focusing only on subnational public spending in Austria, the share of about one third is relatively high compared to the c.27 per cent on average in the UK and the c.12 per cent in Portugal (Krumm 2013). Given this relatively large capacity for fiscal discretion, subnational jurisdictions seemed surprisingly unwilling to use it in favour of PPP.

This reluctance can be explained by the coalition format at states and at federal level. Whereas in Germany grand coalitions occur only occasionally, in Austria they are very common. Grand coalitions in Austria are either led by the Austrian People's Party (ÖVP) or (more often) by the Social Democrats. Grand coalitions are usually less open to a policy change in favour of new and still contested policies such as the PPP approach. Less surprisingly, PPP gained most support at federal level under small coalitions between 2000 and 2006. These coalitions were formed by ÖVP and the smaller FPÖ (Freiheitliche Partei Österreichs or Freedom Party of Austria) and their splinter group BZÖ (Bündnis Zukunft Österreich or Alliance Future Austria) later on. In contrast to the social democratic parties in Germany and the UK, the Social Democrats in Austria never took up the modernization and reform drive of New Labour under Blair or the Social Democrats under Schröder at the end of the 1990s. Instead, in Austria these impulses came from ÖVP under Chancellor Schüssel, after forming a small coalition cabinet with the (right-wing) Liberals in 2000.

Another factor is the strong corporatism that prevailed in Austria until the 1990s, when stronger emphasis was put on privatization and market-based allocation, replacing the remnants of 'Austro-corporatism'. Concerning social partnerships, research literature has periodically discussed the end of Austro-corporatism as well as consociationalism (e.g. Tálos 1997). After World War II, the proportion of public corporations soon grew to a relatively large size through nationalizations. Soon the phrase Austro-Keynesianism emerged. According to Pelinka/Rosenberger (2007: 50), Austro-Keynesianism ceased in the 1990s, especially with the EU accession in 1996. This may have laid the foundation for the policy changes of the small coalition of ÖVP and FPÖ/BZÖ commencing in 2000. Despite several failed attempts at reprivatizing the nationalized industries since the end of the 1950s, some further efforts were launched at the end of the 1980s which turned out to be successful. The real breakthrough, however, was managed after 2000 by ÖVP–FPÖ coalition with the privatization of most parts of the (still) nationalized industries (Weber 2011: 126). The Schüssel I and II cabinets deployed a strict austerity policy, including a zero deficit goal for federal government (Pelinka/Rosenberger 2007: 55). However, first, privatization programmes were initialized in 1987 and then in 1996 to shrink the size of public corporations. Public corporations were managed and operated by Austria's state holding company Österreichische Industrieholding AG

(ÖIAG). In 2000, an ÖIAG law was passed at federal level. 'In line with the Catholic ethic of market mistrust, state involvement in a variety of non-network industries was dominant in Austria' (Köthenbürger 2006: xvi). The changes of the 1990s led to an increase in privatization proceeds, leading to a 'strong correlation between the degree of privatization and the country's overall economic performance measured by GDP growth rates' (Köthenbürger 2006: xvi; for privatization politics between 2000 and 2006 see also Pichler 2009: 255). The politics of state intervention in the economy by Austrian governments since World War II can be split into five phases, as depicted in Table 7.7. With regard to these institutional and socioeconomic factors, the Austrian political system offers no clear support for a policy change in favour of PPP. Institutional factors such as frequent grand coalitions at federal and state level and (decreasing) corporatism do not institutionally support the implementation of the PPP approach.

Table 7.7 Phases of economic policy making in Austria

Phase	Period	Politics dominated by
1	1945–1960	Reconstruction
2	1960–1975	Structural crisis
3	1975–1985	Response to new national and international challenges
4	1985–2000	Crisis and pressure for privatization
5	2000–2010	End of nationalized industries

Source: Adapted from Weber 2011: 127; own translation.

7.2.2 Partisanship

In terms of partisanship, at federal level only the Schüssel governments between 2000 and 2006 showed a greater enthusiasm for PPP. Their support for PPP was embedded in a broader policy change ('Wende') including a commitment to a zero deficit policy and a broader policy transfer from the UK (Dirninger 2013: 219). Especially in early policy documents after the new coalition took over in 2000, the policy change that occurred in the UK under the Blair government is positively referred to (Dachs et al. 2006: 617; for delegation of public services to the private sector see Dachs et al. 2006: 206). This is somehow surprising in terms of partisanship, as the ÖVP–FPÖ coalition can be characterized as centre-right, whereas the New Labour government in the UK was located as centre-left on the traditional left–right political landscape. Thus, the

ÖVP–FPÖ coalition in Austria was in a similar position in relation to a policy transfer from the UK as its red–green counterpart under Chancellor Schröder (1998–2005) in Germany. In Austria, the new centre-right cabinet 'initiated a comprehensive reform process, including extensive privatization. It claims that Austria has successfully privatized the majority of its large manufacturing firms and will continue privatization in order to consolidate the budget' (Belke/Schneider 2006: 97).

At federal level, little more than a handful of pilot projects had been realized under the small coalition up to 2007. In 2007, majorities switched again in favour of a grand coalition. As a result, it should be noted that federal PPP projects in Austria have primarily resulted from the political momentum generated by the Schüssel I government (ÖVP–FPÖ coalition, 02/2000–11/2002), realized by the year 2002. The planned establishment of a PPP Expertise Centre falls within the period of the second Schüssel government (Schüssel II, ÖVP–FPÖ/BZÖ, 02/2003–09/2006). Although the idea of an expertise centre was still added to the government programme of the grand coalition of SPÖ (Social Democratic Party of Austria) and ÖVP (chancellor Gusenbauer, 01/2007–09/2008), it was not realized, and the plans were later terminated during the period of the coalition. Also, the grand coalition of December 2008 under the chancellorship of the Social Democrat Werner Faymann brought no new life to the federal PPP policy. Concerning the coalition format, it is obvious that the ÖVP-led small coalitions operated a much more PPP friendly policy than the previous and subsequent grand coalitions with social democratic chancellors.

Table 7.8 Austrian federal governments and their PPP policies

Years	Government	Parties	Policy
01/1997–01/1999	Klima	SPÖ–ÖVP (grand coalition)	No PPP action
02/2000–11/2002	Schüssel I	ÖVP–FPÖ	Support for PPP in the context of a 'zero deficit' financial policy
02/2003–10/2006	Schüssel II	ÖVP–FPÖ/BZÖ	Support for PPP continued; plans for a PPP competence centre
01/2007–09/2008	Gusenbauer	SPÖ–ÖVP (grand coalition)	Plans for a competence centre were cancelled
12/2008–	Faymann	SPÖ–ÖVP (grand coalition)	No PPP action

Source: Own compilation.

Angerer/Hammerschmid (2005: 152) come to the overall conclusion that PPP in Austrian politics was hardly understood as a new governance mechanism, but merely as a convenient way of infrastructure funding despite financial restrictions, especially those in the Maastricht criteria. 'In Austria, the current institutional rules, roles and habits, based on a traditional representative democracy and a fragmented policy system did often not fit with the cultural demands within a PPP' (ibid.). At state level, Austria's capital Vienna, one of the nine Austrian states, set out plans for a PPP law in early 2012. The Public–Private Education Facilities and Infrastructure Act was meant to facilitate PPPs 'and to allow the town to solicit private companies to carry-out building work independently from main government' (www.pppbulletin.com/news/view/21756).

7.2.3 PPP Politics

Due to the reasons mentioned above, Austria has not developed significant PPP activity. However, some projects were initiated. At the federal level there have been only a few large-scale projects, such as the A5 motorway with a length of 52 km. The planning for this highway expansion between the Beltway, Vienna, and the Czech Republic was begun in late 2003 by ASFINAG (Autobahnen- und Schnellstraßen-Finanzierungs-Aktiengesellschaft or the Autobahn and highway financing stock corporation); three years later the contract was signed. The concession period is 30 years, the investment volume amounts to approximately €800 million and the present value of compensation payments is €933 million. The fee is based on a combined remuneration model, consisting of 30 per cent of the traffic volume risk (a shadow toll per vehicle kilometre) and 70 per cent of availability payments. For the latter no traffic volume risk is transferred; the payment is based only on the actual availability of road sections (BMVIT/BMF 2008: 3).

The private refunding of the construction costs of about €800 million, financed externally (not by ASFINAG), and the operating costs are covered through the payment of an annual allowance of about €64 million, depending on the amount of shadow toll and availability payment (ibid.: 4). Originally, the project was planned only as a 'first package' of similar projects in the eastern region with a total investment volume of €3.1 billion (ibid.). These plans, however, were not continued, because of dwindling political support. Finally, ASFINAG announced that there would be no further road renewals using the PPP model. Furthermore, projects in the rail sector in medium term are unlikely according to EPPPR (2009: 25), similar to further projects in the roads sector. 'The waste and healthcare sectors seem to be the only ones where any significant activity can be expected. Overall, companies will continue to find the financing of projects difficult until the credit crisis diminishes' (ibid.).

The Austrian truck tolling system was also planned in 2002. The concession agreement had a term of ten years from the start of the operational phase in 2004 and provided for the design, construction, financing and operation of the distance-based tolling for vehicles with a gross vehicle weight of 3.5 tonnes on motorways and highways. Through the technology open tender (in contrast to Germany) the Austrian government tried to transfer as many technical decisions, and thus also risks, to the private sector. The setting up of the system started in July 2002. Construction costs were approximately €200 million, pre-financed by the EUROPPASS Truck Toll System GmbH, which annually receives about €100 million for construction and operation, including a performance-related variable share (BMVIT/BMF 2008: 2).

Another PPP that was discussed at this time was public safety radio (digital radio BOS Austria), planned by the Ministry of the Interior. In this project, also initiated in 2002, the planning, construction, financing and operation of a bug-proof radio system for all emergency organizations (police, fire, ambulance, army) with approximately 1600 locations was awarded for 25 years to a private consortium (ibid.: 6). The aim of this project was to guarantee quick and coordinated digital communication among public safety and security organizations in Austria. 'The project under responsibility of the federal government was coordinated by the Federal Ministry of the Interior (MoI) with strong involvement of the Ministry of Defence and conceptualized as an PPP with a total capital expenditure estimated to range between EUR 250 and 370 millions' (Angerer/Hammerschmid 2005: 140). The refinancing of the operators should be managed through the user fees of the participating authorities. The political drive for the project has to be seen against the background of the push for federal budget consolidation during the first Schüssel cabinet. 'The HERAKLES project attracted a high level of political and public attention as indicated by the strong presence in public media' (ibid.: 140f.). The fee for the operator, totalling about €35 million, may be reduced in the case of limited performance of the system. As it was initially open as to which parts of the authorities and which states would participate (or alternatively develop their own systems), the consortium had taken, besides the operating and maintenance risks, also a demand risk (BMVIT/BMF 2008: 7). Further projects listed in the Austrian PPP report (Table 7.9) are the IMC Fachhochschule Krems (IMC University of Applied Sciences Krems), established in 1994 as a limited company with public and private partners, the redevelopment of a swimming pool, and a project for improving energy efficiency in public buildings, which was announced in 2003 by the Federal Real Estate Company. The ten-year concession for renovating 500 federal buildings began on 1 January 2004.

Table 7.9 PPP projects in Austria

Contracting Authority	Project	Period (years)	Model	Date	Investment vol.
ASFINAG	truck toll	10	DBFO	2002	c. €200 million
ASFINAG	A5 north highway	30	DBFO	12/2006	c. €800 million
Schieneninfrastruktur-Dienstleistungs-gesellschaft (SCHIG)	Güterterminal Graz/ Werndorf	34	DBFO	09/2000	€65 million
Schieneninfrastruktur-Dienstleistungs-gesellschaft (SCHIG)	Klima Windkanal	37	DBFO	06/2000	€59 million
Schieneninfrastruktur-Dienstleistungs-gesellschaft (SCHIG)	Rollende Landstraße Regensburg	21	DBFO	06/2005	€2.4 million
Bundesministerium für Inneres	Digital radio BOS Austria	25	DBFO	06/2004	c. €130 million
Bundesimmobilien-gesellschaft (BIG)	Bundes-contracting 500	10		2003	c. €15.2 million
BM für Wissenschaft und Kultur	IMC Fachhochschule Krems		GmbH	1994	

Source: Adapted from BMVIT/BMF 2008.

Considering the regional level, hospital management associations have gained some influence on health care PPPs (Greiling/Häusler 2011). Such regional hospital management associations were built by the states starting from the 1980s to subsequently include the local hospital management. They act 'quite frequently as the public partner in health-care PPPs. Therefore local and state governments are not directly involved as public partners. With a few exceptions only a few PPPs exist on the local governments' level. This has to do with the general trend that local governments transfer their hospitals to the state hospital management associations' (ibid.: 167). This development confirms two trends in wider public sector reform: firstly, a transfer of traditionally public tasks to special purpose units or public enterprises (formal privatization), and secondly, a transfer of local tasks to the regional or state level in order to realize effects of scale. Thus, the most important drivers for PPPs in the Austrian health sector were located at state level, but functionally separated in special purpose vehicles (SPVs). 'The state wide hospital management associations are under pressure to operate efficiently as there is a budget ceiling for the hospital sector' (ibid.: 167f.). In contrast to Germany, health insurance funds commissioned only three PPPs in Austria (ibid.: 168).

The biggest health care PPP has a volume of up to €400 million. Greiling/Häusler (2011: 166) depict 16 examples of health care PPPs. Among the most active private partners is VAMED AG. It was founded as part of a former public utility, privatized in 1996 and now owned with a majority share held by the German Fresenius Group and with minor shares by the Austrian privatization agency Österreichische Industrieanlagen AG and the Bank Austria group (ibid.: 167). 'The first Austrian PPP was in the hospital sector. Since 1996 a PPP has existed between the AKH Vienna and the VAMED AG' (ibid.: 165). Already in 1996 the federal government and the city of Vienna agreed to complete the AKH Vienna (Vienna General Hospital) via PPP. Thus, this can be regarded as the first PPP in Austria. EPPPR (2009: 26) considers the health care sector along with the waste sector 'as the only ones where any significant activity can be expected in Austria'.

7.3 CASE COMPARISON

Although there are some general institutional similarities such as a federal state organization, the German and Austrian political systems differ in a number of ways. Such differences are obvious – for example regarding the institutionalization of federalism, the degree of corporatism and 'statism', the coalition format and the spillover of the Anglo-Saxon public sector reform agenda since the late 1990s. However, despite such differences, the Austrian and the German cases were ranked at neighbouring positions in Table 3.2 (per capita rank 10 and 11 respectively). Taking into account the much smaller total amount of public investment compared to Germany, Austria even ranked better than Germany in our quantitative approach in Table 3.2 (rank 7 and 9 respectively), despite Austrian cabinets' moderate support for PPP since 2007.

Germany, as the largest state in terms of population and total GDP in our sample, also provides a large market for PPP proactive firms and businesses. Given the size of the economy and public budget, Germany would need many more PPPs in total to reach a similar share of the GDP or public investment as Austria. In terms of inhabitants Austria would only need one tenth of the German PPP activity to reach a similar level. Given the larger size of the PPP market in Germany and the more intense political commitment over time, PPP in Germany provided more of a laboratory for various forms and fields of PPP application.

In contrast to this, in Austria political support at federal level was limited to the period of the small coalitions under Chancellor Schüssel between 2000 and 2006. However, this period seemed to be sufficient to stimulate a considerable amount of PPP activity at federal level. At state level governments were more reluctant to use PPP, mainly due to the requirements for party proportionality at cabinet level in most of the states. In Austria, apart from some exceptions in the city of Vienna, states widely abstained from PPP. The only actors at state level are semi-independent bodies such as the regional hospital management groups which have been under general pressure to improve cost efficiency in the health sector. At federal level in Austria, the public motorway corporation ASFINAG and the public railway corporation SCHIG (Schieneninfrastruktur-Dienstleistungsgesellschaft mbH) developed some PPP projects in the early 2000s. However, this has to be seen in the light of the then ÖVP–FPÖ coalition.

In terms of party politics, the situation was the inverse of that in Germany. Whereas in Germany the Social Democrats under Chancellor Schröder got 'infected' by the PPP idea from the UK, in Austria it was the (conservative) People's Party, while the Austrian Social Democrats remained immune. They even used their influence in the grand coalition commencing 2007 to block further PPP developments such as the setting up of a proposed competence centre.

At state level in Germany, the picture is very heterogeneous. While some states such as North Rhine-Westphalia were forerunners, others such as Saarland and Saxony remained sceptical. This variation in political support at state level is lacking at the level of Austrian states. One institutional feature that might have influenced the reluctance in parts of the political elite is the structure of interest groups. Typically for small states, Austria has a higher density of organized interests than Germany. According to Lijphart (1999), Austria is among the most consociational systems in Europe with a value of 0.62 (similar to the Nordic countries), whereas Germany is slightly less corporatist (1.38

from 1971 to 1996). Thus, it can be expected that unions have more veto power in Austria than in Germany to resist a policy change. It is also said that Austria has a more conservative and therefore traditional political culture, which can limit policy transfer.

In both countries the PPP approach was in competition with classic Keynesian demand stimulation and corporatist arrangements. Besides the Nordic countries, Austria and, to a lesser degree, Germany have a tradition of corporatist steering of the economy that limits space for policy tools such as PPP, which develop better in pluralistic interest group environments. Both countries showed a tendency towards grand coalitions during the investigation period, being more pronounced in Austria, which sometimes is also labelled the 'Grand Coalition state'. However, in this dimension it is significant that the only PPP incentives at federal level came from centre-right small coalitions between 2000 and 2006. Thus, in terms of partisanship, Austria comes closer to a southern European pattern, where PPP is preferentially adopted by conservative parties when in government. Such a southern style pattern of centre-right or conservative parties encompasses the ÖVP in Austria, the Forza Italia under Berlusconi in Italy and the People's Party in Spain under Aznar. The Nea Dimokratia in Greece up to the financial crisis has also to be mentioned.

These cases illustrate a policy diffusion of PPP from its European forerunner, the New Labour party in the UK, overcoming traditional party political borders of 'left' and 'right' (see also chapter 10.3). In contrast, in the UK and Germany it was modernizing left-wing parties that included PPP in their programme portfolio. This close relationship between New Labour and the Social Democrats in Germany led, for instance, to the so-called Schröder–Blair manifesto, in which the German Social Democrats tried to couple to the British way of state modernization, while the Austrian Social Democrats abstained. This can be seen also in the context of the interest group variable. Taking the corporatism/pluralism dimension into consideration, it might be easier for centre-left parties to 'emancipate' from structurally conservative interest groups such as the trade unions. This emancipation seems to be easier under pluralistic systems of interest group formation.

The different attitudes towards PPP become clearer if we directly compare the different truck tolling projects. While in Germany the project ('Toll Collect') was a prestigious one, involving multiple functions such as industrial policy and research and development policy, in Austria the transfer of decisions (and related risks) was a top priority. While in Germany the project was pushed by a centre-left government under Chancellor Schröder, in Austria it was pushed by an incoming centre-right coalition government (ÖVP–FPÖ, cabinet Schüssel I).

Neither Germany nor Austria were among the forerunners in introducing PPP. In Germany, there was more and longer political support at federal level, due to the government participation of the Social Democrats from 1998 to 2009. In Austria the support at the highest level was more limited. However, Austria could compensate for this to a certain degree not at state level but in the hospital sector. However, Greiling/Häusler (2011: 177) described the German health care PPP market as more advanced and having greater variety than the Austrian one.

> It is noticeable that, to a greater extent, one finds hospital management associations or subsidiary companies of the hospital associations as public partners in Austria. This has to do with the way public hospitals are organized at the level of the Austrian federal states. A very prominent difference between Austrian and German PPPs is that in Germany, at least some of the public partners are much more aware of the potential of PPPs for strategic positioning. (ibid.: 176 f.)

In contrast to Germany, the discussion about integrated care solutions, managed by health insurance funds, is still at an early stage in Austria. In general, for the adaption of PPP to the infrastructure sector in Austria, off-budget financing of modernization projects under the centre-right cabinets played an important role. Given the priority of austerity policy or 'zero deficit' by the early Schüssel cabinet, the motivation for PPP was similarly too many other European cases, primarily driven by budgetary concerns.

NOTE

1. See *The Spiegel*, 20 February 2004, 'Schröder verkündet Einigung mit Toll Collect', www.spiegel.de/wirtschaft/0,1518,288487,00.html [15 October 2015].

8. France and Italy

8.1 FRANCE

8.1.1 Institutional Context

With some institutional features similar to the UK and Portugal, France (at least theoretically) might be a promising PPP candidate. The semi-presidential system of France has – similarly to the system in the UK – been highly centralized for a long time. A first attempt at decentralization was introduced between 1982 and 1984 by the newly elected François Mitterrand, the first socialist president of the Fifth Republic. However, more influential has been the constitutional reform of 2002, in which the regions and their powers for the first time were mentioned in the constitution (Article 72). The municipalities, departments and regions have direct contacts to the central level and have no hierarchical powers among themselves. The regions, for instance, are in charge of policy coordination of the departments and the municipalities, of deliberating on regional development goals and programmes and coordinating inter-regional measures (Zimmermann-Steinhart/Kazmeier 2010: 178). Whereas the regional presidents are elected by the regional assemblies, the prefects of the regions and departments are appointed by central government. At department level the most powerful person is the elected president of the general council (conseil général).

At central level, the Senators of the second chamber are indirectly elected by the territorial collectivies; the Senate is less powerful than the National Assembly, which is elected with qualified majority in the first ballot, and simple majority in case of a second ballot. The directly elected, powerful president appoints the prime minister; however, he cannot dismiss him or her without the dissolution of parliament. Calling for referendums on contested topics or to legitimize presidential policies is one of the instruments in the hands of the president. However, contrarily to the US president, he has no veto powers against parliament. As the prime minister depends on a parliamentary majority, presidents might have to appoint a prime minister from other parties than his or her own, called 'cohabitation'. In 1986, President Mitterrand appointed the conservative Jacques Chirac as prime minister, and in 1997 President Chirac appointed socialist Lionel Jospin. Under cohabitation, presidents focus more on foreign policy and the prime minister on domestic issues such as the economy. Thus, under cohabitation the influence of the president on economic policies is reduced.

Focusing more on political culture, French governments have developed a strong statist tradition over time, revived after World War II. This was due to the financial problems of some private corporations or poor services offered, for instance, in the railway, telephone, steelmaker, and later the ICT sectors. Also, the statist tradition was legitimized by avoiding private firms in 'strategic' sectors becoming too influential and their decisions having a substantial impact on general economic policies, for instance in the banking, energy, transportation and defence sectors. In order to be able to better influence economic and social policy outcomes, 'the government concluded it had to own the largest companies in the country. This was especially crucial after World War II, when the infrastructure had to be built as fast as possible, but it also inspired the nationalization policy of 1982' (Berne/Pogorel 2006: 164). Historically, the pattern of an economy serving the state had already been developed under mercantilism and implemented by Jean-Baptiste Colbert, finance minister under Louis XIV. Patterns of government supervision of the economy are from time to time revived, as after World War II and in 1982 under the early Mitterrand presidency. The influence of the statist tradition on the PPP policy becomes clearer if we keep in mind that France, through the workings of its Conseil Constitutionnel (Constitutional Council), is the only country in our sample where rulings have delayed the PPP policies (in the mid-2000s) of a government (see below).

Mitterrand soon proceeded on a more pragmatic course, abandoning much of the socialist rhetoric that had helped him to grasp power in 1981 (ibid.: 164). Thus, the international trend of liberalization and privatization that started in the UK under Thatcher in the 1980s, reached France only belatedly and in several phases, depending on the electoral cycle, which was a crucial factor. In France, the centre-right parties headed by the Rassemblement pour la République (RPR, since 2002 Union pour un Movement Populaire, UMP) initiated the drive for privatization in 1986 after gaining a parliamentary majority (cohabitation), but were cautious regarding the unpopular privatization of public services. On the other hand, the Socialists struggled after their nationalization episode of 1982 to agree on the proper course of economic policy. Even much later they had (and still have) 'diverging opinions about the management of state firms' and the proper course of economic policy (ibid.: 167). Even after the global economic crisis commencing in 2008, ideas of state supervision of the economy became influential again and contributed to the election of the socialist president Hollande in 2012.

Both decentralization and privatization policies illustrate a common internal struggle of French policy makers between attempts to reform on the one hand and creating obstacles and blockades on the other. Reform attempts (not only) in these two fields face similar challenges in terms of intense ideological debates. In the field of privatization policies, the obstacles were strongly based ideological platforms such as a socialist belief that public ownership 'is in all cases superior to private ownership, the "Dirigiste" (Colbertiste, Bonapartist, and Gaullist) tradition, which highlights the superior knowledge and vision of the state, a Christian-inspired social doctrine that advocates public property in the name of the public good and social solidarity' (ibid.: 193).

Thus, whereas formally some similarities with the UK and Portugal are promising in regard to efficient policy changes, other, more informal aspects (political culture), as well as the option of a 'cohabitation' of a president and a prime minister from different parties (first realized in 1986), are hampering fast-track policy changes. Once convinced, the centralized institutional structure with the directly elected president at its centre offers a great potential for political steering from the centre. In practice, institutional factors such as 'cohabitation' or a politically influential Constitutional Council, as well as an often ideologically heated political culture, clinging to statist traditions, slow down these options.

Besides the statist tradition and cohabitation, the Constitutional Council had some influence in hampering the national government's PPP policy due to rulings made in 2003. Only in 2008, under the Sarkozy presidency, could a legal clarification of the details criticized by the Council be reached. Despite these facts, France has developed a comparatively high level of PPP activity, according to quantitative data available from MAPPP (see below), the central PPP unit. This can partly be explained by the centralized structure of government and partly by modernizing presidents. A more systematic PPP policy has developed since around 2002 and been centrally imposed to the functional and regional administrative bodies. However, despite having similar capacities of administrative steering from the centre as the UK, France has never developed a similar level of PPP commitment.

Historically, local authorities could often not afford the cost of construction or extension of services like gas, electricity and water supply. Thus, forms of public–private collaboration in France had already been used for public infrastructure, commencing in the seventeenth century, as types of concession models.[1] Similar to Spain and Portugal, many highways were planned and built under such models. 'In the 1980s, decentralisation made contracting-out easier, but it was the lack of public funds and the increasing need for investment in relation to EU environmental regulations that underpinned the last phase of PPP expansion' (Ribault 2005: 512).

Concession models are still today the most popular form for the provision of 'commercialized' public services and infrastructure and have led, for example, in the fields of water supply and treatment plants 'to the growth of the large, diversified French utility companies such as Vivendi and Lyonnaise des Eaux (Suez-Lyonnaise)' (Grimsey/Lewis 2005b: xiii). However, the number of PPP operators is limited. In the mid-1990s Lyonnaise des Eaux and Vivendi controlled about 60 per cent of the water supply market and 36 per cent of the sewage market. In the field of water disposal, PPP was still limited but also expected to grow. At the same time, both firms controlled '75% of the urban central heating market, 80% of refuse treatment, 55% of cable operation, and 36% of the refuse collection market. They are known as multi-utilities as they are horizontally diversified' (Ribault 2005: 512f.).

8.1.2 Partisanship and Institutionalization

Public policy changes are often less pragmatically and more ideologically debated than in neighbouring Germany. The overall approach in France can be characterized as torn between scepticism and a pragmatic utilization of PPP for political aims. Broader political support for PPP took off relatively late but became very obvious in the last years of the Sarkozy presidency. At first glance, statist and dirigiste traditions in relation to economic affairs may not provide an ideal framework to make France a pioneering country in terms of PPP. However, similar to the early experiences in Germany, large-scale PPPs could be utilized for industrial policy.

Since the opening up of the economy in the 1960s due to decolonization and the formation of the European Economic Community (EEC), de Gaulle and his successors have practised a rather interventionist industrial policy, including an accelerated growth policy and a merger and acquisition policy to grow 'national champions' – large public corporations more or less under the direct control of the government. Further elements of this policy were the redirecting of public funds to the private sector in order to accelerate private investment; the creating of industry development plans; the controlling of foreign direct investments in strategic sectors, such as military and nuclear technology; and the promoting of large-scale technological projects under government leadership (Schild/Uterwedde 2006: 162). The latter has also been characterized as 'high-tech-Colbertism', leading to a series of innovative major projects such the high-speed TGV, the nuclear energy systems, the Concorde aeroplane and the Ariane space missile, as well as the Airbus project, which due to high development costs could not have been conducted by a purely private initiative (ibid.: 163). However, interventionism and 'planification' were repeatedly questioned. The global oil crisis commencing with an economic crisis in the 1970s, the 'neoliberal' turn in the early 1980s, the new dynamics of European integration in the 1990s and the global credit crunch of the late 2000s have set incentives for reform (ibid.: 165). A first push for privatization and deregulation was made in 1986, but faced severe resistance and never reached levels such as in the Anglo-Saxon countries.

Sectoral industrial planning and policy are much more difficult now, not least due to the increasing influence of the Brussels competition authority and more recently the ECB in Frankfurt. Furthermore, international linkages ('globalization') and the European Stability and Growth Pact have contributed to the transfer of formerly national decision-making powers to supranational organizations as well as quasi autonomous international public bodies (such as the ECB). Thus, the predominant steering mode has changed from 'dirigisme' to (indirect) regulation. This includes an attitudinal change from an often prevalent policy against the market to a policy utilizing market tools for infrastructure or research and development objectives. However, the share of public involvement in the economy increased continuously, up to 54.3 per cent in 2003, catching up with Denmark and Sweden (ibid.: 167).

Furthermore, a relatively pluralistic organization of interest groups (Siaroff 1999), except in some sectors such as agriculture, where neo-corporatist patterns can emerge (Keeler 1987), provides conducive conditions for the implementation of the PPP approach. In contrast to Germany, self-government by associations and neo-corporatist forms of (economic and social) policy making have never become prevalent. Interest groups and trade associations are relatively fragmented and thus weak in pursuing and aggregating private and civil society interests. Membership numbers in the fragmented and competitive unions are among the lowest across Europe, and forms of partnership and cooperation between corporations (e.g. professional training) were only moderately institutionalized. For a long time individualism and paternalism have prevailed (Schild/Uterwedde 2006: 170, 253). Given the moderate institutionalization of interest groups on both sides of the labour relationship, the withdrawal of the state from (para)public tasks may open gaps to be filled by new arrangements between state, market and civil society (ibid.: 170).

Table 8.1 Economic policies of French governments, 1988–2008

President	Prime minister	Political direction	Main economic measures
Mitterrand 1988	Rocard 1988	Left	RMI; CSG: beginning of tax financing of social security systems
	Cresson 1991	Left	Maastricht Treaty: Euro
	Bérégovoy 1992	Left	Maastricht referendum: 51% yes votes Currency crisis; sticking to the policy of 'strong franc'
	Balladur 1993	Right (Cohab.)	Pension reform in the private sector
Chirac 1995	Juppé 1995	Right	Pension reform in the civil service failed
	Jospin 1997	Left (Cohab.)	35-hour week, job creation scheme for young people; cautious flexible working Denationalization Treaty of Amsterdam: Stability and Growth Pact; open coordination of employment policies (Luxembourg process)
Chirac 2002	Raffarin 2002	Right	Pension reform 2003: Second wave of decentralization New industrial policy: Innovation agency
	De Villepin 2005	Right	Innovation policy: National Research Agency, Cluster Policy (pôles de compétitivité) Failure to introduce flexible labour laws in first time employments (CPE) Interventionist industrial policy: merger GDF/ Suez; protection of domestic corporations European constitutional referendum: 53% no votes
Sarkozy 2007	Fillon 2007	Right	Tax package: tax cuts for high earners Reform programme: employment, labour administration, undermining of 35-hour week, reform of the special regime in the pension system, university reform, constitutional and administrative reform Interventionist industrial policy Protectionist demands in EU (préférence communautaire; agricultural policy)

Note: RMI = Revenu minimum d'insertion (a very basic form of social benefit for unemployed), CSG = Contribution sociale généralisée (general social contribution), CPE = Contrat Première Embauche (a law introduced in 2005 to relax regulation for dismissal of young employees, withdrawn by government after mass protests).

Source: Adapted from Uterwedde 2009: 92 (own translation).

The French toll motorways are an example of experiences with concession models. Also, there has been a stronger, high-level commitment to the PPP approach since the second Chirac presidency. EPPPR (2007: 70) confirms that France's PPP policy has developed a degree of central control and planning which is a good compromise between the extremes of Italian and Spanish market-led and the British government controlled implementation of PPPs. PPPs are applied under the Délégation de gestion regime, which allows public bodies to transfer tasks and duties to a private party under two different models: concession and affermage contracts. Whereas concessions resemble Build, Operate, Transfer (BOT) or Design, Build, Operate, Transfer (DBOT) models, affermage contracts are focused only on design and building, or only on operation. They do not include project financing, which is provided by the public sector, similar to maintenance services, which, however, are often contracted out. 'Such contracts are awarded through a public tendering process. For small projects, the bids are price-based; for larger projects, tendering is based on the project design and price' (Ribault 2005: 511).

The French PPP market has become more dynamic under the second Chirac and the Sarkozy presidency, not least due to the support of a task force. Recent developments in France are summarized by Lichère et al. (2009), Pignon-Xardel et al. (2009) and Bezançon et al. (2009). Among the PPP supporting institutions are the 'Mission d'appui à la réalisation des partenariats public-privé' (MAPPP), the 'Agence de maîtrise d'ouvrage des travaux du ministère de la Justice' in the Ministry of Justice, the 'Mission nationale d'appui à l'investissement hospitalier' in the Ministry of Health, the 'Institut de la gestion déléguée' (IGD) and the 'Centre d'expertise français pour l'observation des partenariats public-privé' (CEF-O-PPP, see OECD 2010: 99).

Founded in May 2005, the central task force MAPPP is assigned to the Ministry of Finance (www.ppp.bercy.gouv.fr). Their main function is to review planned projects at the national level in terms of legal, financial and qualitative aspects before they are approved by the Minister of Finance and the tendering procedure can be opened. MAPPP checks the feasibility studies of the responsible ministries. However, the final say is with the Ministry of the Economy, Industry and Employment. MAPPP provides its services for public sector entities for free and is advised by a committee of stakeholders from local and central government and from the private sector. 'It is not compulsory for public authorities to engage the services of the MAPPP for a PPP project. MAPPP is made up of ten people who are experts from the public and private sectors' (OECD 2010: 100). MAPPP does not have a right of review for regional and local projects; however, it offers its expertise. It also collects project data and issues guidelines to harmonize French PPP practice (EPPPR 2009: 43f.).

The IGD was founded in April 1996 as a private promotional organization for PPPs. Together with MAPPP they founded the CEF-O-PPP in June 2006 to further analyse PPP projects, 'exchange ideas and experience, and issue recommendations. The CEF-O-PPP is currently situated within the official premises of the IGD and is operationally managed by the IGD' (OECD 2010: 100). Also, the French parliament has begun to harmonize the rules for PPPs and similar methods (BEA – Bail Emphytéotique Administratifs; AOT/LOA – Autorisation d'Occupation Temporaire/Location avec Option d'Achat; BEH – Bail Emphytéotique Hospitalier). Their aim is to coordinate different procurement rules within an integrated system.

Besides the concessions (BEA) the 'Contrats de Partenariat' are the main group of contractually agreed PPPs between a public authority and a private partner. Concessions are

> long-term leases granted by a local authority to entitle a private partner proprietary rights on public land used to perform a public service. These are widely used for sizeable infrastructure projects, including toll roads and waste or water treatment facilities. Moreover, concessions cannot be used for projects with little or no user-generated revenues. (ibid.: 99)

The legal basis for the delegation of public services in the form of concessions and leasing is a law of December 2001 (also known as MURCEF). The bases for the partnership contracts are diverse and have changed since their introduction, for example, by decisions of the Constitutional Council. The legal aspects have been further clarified by a regulation of 17 June 2004 and a law of 28 July 2008. Contrats de Partenariat include, for example, leasehold contracts that are applied especially in the hospital sector (EIB 2004: 6).

However, the French Constitutional Council ruled in two decisions in June and September 2004 that the use of Contrats de Partenariat depends on particular motives of the public interest. Thus, they are only allowed if the public sector is not in a position to determine solely and in advance the technical means to meet their needs or to assess the existing financial and technical solutions available via the market (Jacob 2009: 48). The Constitutional Council's main argument is that of complexity, which by mid-2008 was also the criterion for public procurement procedures in the 'competitive dialogue'. Furthermore, an urgent need (Cas d'Urgence) should exist due to specific local circumstances. Since November 2006, these criteria have to be checked in a study (Évaluation Prealable), which also must produce a case specific public sector comparator to assess the different procurement options (ibid.: 49).

In a circular to local authorities on partnership agreements dated 29 November 2005, the government provided a cabinet decision, made on 2 August 2005, in which PPPs are to be given new impetus, especially to revitalize and increase public investment. Per the circular, the reasons for the creation of the new instrument of partnership contract (Contrat de Partenariat) are to provide local authorities with additional tools for the exercise of their public duties.

In January 2006, an important PPP law was passed that allows state-owned railways (specifically the Réseau Ferré de France, RFF) to undertake infrastructure projects according to the Contrat de Partenariat and to make payment arrangements based on demand, availability or performance. In the same year RFF announced that they were preparing four PPP projects for tendering (EPPPR 2007: 71). The focus of the French PPP activities is in the areas of transportation and social infrastructure. Besides the already mentioned standard PPP contract (Contrat de Partenariat) in the hospital sector there is the more commonly used and exclusively created model for this sector of the hospital long-term lease (BEH) (Jacob 2009).

The law of 28 July 2008 was a response to a decision of the Constitutional Council from 24 July 2008 (No. 2008-567 DC), in which parts of the regulation from 2004 were declared to be incompatible with the constitution. In the Amendment Act of July 2008, the favourability criterion compared to conventional implementation (Bilan Favorable) was added as a third criterion, in addition to the complexity and urgency.

The interpretation of the urgency criterion has been extended so that PPPs are appropriate to solve a situation that is harmful to the common good as well as a situation where unforeseen events occur (Jacob 2009: 49). Article 2 of the amended Act, for example, calls for an economic, financial, legal and administrative review of the project by an expert organization before award. The criteria for the review will be established by the Ministry of Economy. The review includes an analysis of the various options, particularly with regard to the total cost before taxes, to risk sharing and duties, and the pursuit of sustainable development. In 'unforeseen circumstances' such an assessment can also be 'short'. In Section II, Article 2 the Act regulates that partnership contracts can only be agreed if due to the complexity of the project the public body is not in a position to determine in advance the necessary technical means; the project serves an urgent public interest; or in the implementation of similar projects by the public sector there have been serious shortcomings.

8.1.3 PPP Politics

According to Table 3.2 of our study, France ranks 11 over the whole investigation period. However, it can be assumed that with the second Chirac presidency commencing in 2002, the PPP commitment increased. These developments cover a range of sectors such as transport, but also sports (stadiums) and higher education. Among the more recent large-scale deals were the €204 million Nice Eco Stadium, closed in January 2011, and the €5.4 billion Tours–Bordeaux high-speed railway, closed in mid-2011. Such large-scale contracts contributed to France's leading position in the European PPP market in these years. The EPEC found in its report that France for the first time 'overtook Spain and the UK as the largest European market by value size accounting for 57% of the overall market value' (Partnerships Bulletin/Deloitte 2012: 5). However, these comments were given on the eve of the 2012 presidential elections, which saw the socialist François Hollande become the next president with (at least initially) a much more socialist rhetoric.

Among the private players in the French PPP market are the three major construction corporations Bouygues, Vinci and Eiffage. Vinci and Eiffage have each received a privatized operator contract for roads and have won (like their Spanish neighbours) all local projects for themselves (EPPPR 2007: 70). Eiffage is owned by the Spanish Sacyr, who hold 32 per cent of the shares. The company is also trying to get a foot into the Portuguese, German and Hungarian markets. Bouygues took over the state's share of Alstrom in 2007 and formed a strategic alliance with Depfa in order to offer specific equity and debt solutions for smaller (up to €15 million) municipal projects. To promote such projects, Bouygues has created a €150 million fund. For large projects with more than €100 million of investment, Caisse d'Epargne has launched a €170 million fund. In addition to these French-run infrastructure funds, there are several pan-European funds available to the (growing) market in France (ibid.). 'In February 2009 the French Government showed its commitment to PPP by adopting a scheme aimed at facilitating private sector funding of projects as a result of which the State is permitted to guarantee up to 80% of the private sector financing required for PPP and concession projects' (PPP Forum 2009: 19).

By August 2010, 23 per cent of the 383 projects covered by the Task Force were located at the national level, 77 per cent at the local level. The largest proportion, 31 per cent, had been placed in the building sector (Bâtiment), followed by local development (Equpt urbain) with 25 per cent and energy and culture/sports with 15 per cent each. Eight per cent of the projects were agreed in the transport sector.[2] In the French hospital sector a total of 46 PPP procurement procedures had been started up to end of June 2008, of which two were terminated prematurely. Forty projects were carried out as hospital leaseholds (BEH) and six as partnership contracts (Contrat de Partenariat). Only four projects focused on completely new hospital buildings, with all others being extensions to existing facilities.

The investment volume of the projects is between €2 million and €330 million, with an average investment in restructuring measures of €20 million. Thirty hospital projects were under construction in 2009; twelve projects had already successfully transitioned to the operational phase (Jacob 2009: 56). Usually, several instruments are combined for the financing of a PPP hospital in France. The portion of equity capital is usually only 5 to 10 per cent, a project finance component contributes 10 to 15 per cent, while the majority of about 80 per cent is financed by the instrument of forfaiting with objection waiver (ibid.: 77).

It is a special feature in France that a project can be implemented by a mixture of forfaiting with objection waiver and project financing. The high proportion of forfaiting with waiver of objection, however, means only a limited risk transfer to the private sector takes place (ibid.). All services that require direct contact with the patients usually remain in the hands of the public partner. If the project is carried out as a hospital long-term lease (BEH), the promoters have to justify their decision to use this type of contract in legal, economic and financial terms through a study (Jacob 2009).

Following a pause due to the French presidential elections in the spring of 2007, the expected PPP boom has not occurred in France, partly caused by the onset of the credit crunch in the subsequent years. The global financial crisis has led the French government to implement a series of economic stimulus measures amounting to €26 billion, of which a part should be used for PPP. In response to the global credit crisis of 2008/09, the government has introduced state guarantees to facilitate the financing of PPP projects. These are intended to motivate the banks, which had hesitated during and after the credit crunch to finance PPP projects, to provide the necessary funds to finance such projects in the future.

To complement the government guarantees, in February 2004 the PPP framework law was changed and the requirements for bidders simplified by allowing them to submit their 'best and final offers' without 'letters of support' from the banks. In July 2008, the French parliament passed a law that is intended to facilitate the implementation of public projects as PPPs. Under the new law, projects deemed to be economically in the public interest are eligible for PPP. The background of this 'legislative easing' was that the French Constitutional Council had annulled a temporary regulation which would have allowed certain types of PPPs to be executed even without meeting the criterion of urgency. Due to the conditions of urgency and complexity a number of projects, which did not meet these criteria, had been delayed. As in Italy, the large number of projects that are at the preparatory or awarding stage contrasts with the much smaller number of signed deals. A written request to the MAPPP in March 2011 by the author gave the following annual amounts of investment for the Contrats de Partenariat.

Table 8.2 Number and investment volume of French Contrats de Partenariat (in € million)

Year	Total		Central level		Local level	
	Vol.	No.	Vol.	No.	Vol.	No.
2005	1	1	0	0	1	1
2006	149	6	70	1	79	5
2007	188	16	17	2	171	14
2008	791	12	330	3	461	9
2009	548	21	261	6	287	15
2010	1 958	22	1 094	4	864	18
Total	3 634	78	1 772	16	1 863	62

Sources: Compiled from MAPPP information request and www.ppp.bercy.gouv.fr.

In 2008 there was a slight decrease in the number of contracts, which then rose in 2009 above the pre-crisis levels. In terms of the volume of the contracts there was a dip in 2009, with an increase in 2010 to 3.5 times the previous year's volume. A list published by MAPPP also shows a significant proportion of procurement procedures were cancelled prior to the award since the introduction of the Contrat de Partenariat in 2004.[3]

In 2010 and 2011, the French PPP activity peaked despite (or because of) the global economic crisis. In 2011, for example, the French government was very active in terms of PPP and closed several large projects. Among them were the Tours–Bordeaux high-speed railway (€5.4 billion), the Ministry of Defence headquarters (€1.5 billion), the Bretagne–Pays de la Loire high-speed railway (€1.2 billion), the A63 motorway road extension scheme between Belin and Beliet in the south-west (40-year concession, €1.1 billion), and the Eco Taxe road charging project with a volume of €840 million (www.pppbulletin.com/news/view/22383).

The high-speed rail between Bordeaux and Paris, which includes the stretch between Tours and Bordeaux, is one of the largest railway PPPs in Europe with a volume of €7.8 billion. The project is part of the pan-European railway network, supported by the EU, to upgrade Trans-European transport links. The 50-year concession for the more than 300 km new high-speed track between Tours and Bordeaux was awarded by the rail operator RFF to a consortium led by Vinci (www.pppbulletin.com/news/view/15511). Between 2004 and 2010, the total signed PPP volume in France added up to about €3.6 billion (Table 8.2). The sharp increase in PPP activity at central level in 2010 and 2011 coincides with the second half of President Sarkozy's five year term in office, with France facing a deficit of over 6 per cent and public debts of up to 75 per cent of GDP in 2009, far beyond the criteria of the Euro stability pact.

In early 2011, a DBFO toll tax project was awarded by the Ministry of Ecology, Sustainable Development, Transport and Housing to a consortium of SFR, SNCF, Streia and Thales, led by Autostrada per Italia. In this 14-year scheme, heavy goods vehicles over 3.5 tons are charged for using the 15 000 km of national and departmental roads in France (www.pppbulletin.com/news/view/17044). Also in 2011, an already existing public investment fund, the Fonds Commun de Titrisation (FCT), was opened up to PPP project financing in order to reduce financial risks and interest rates for private financiers (www.pppbulletin.com/news/view/16992). Furthermore, a 3.3 billion Euro high-speed rail project (Brittany to Pays de la Loire) was agreed in mid-2011 by the French Ministry of Transport (AFITF), the railway company RFF, regional authorities and a private consortium, with a duration of 25 years and a total railway length of about 215 km.

For the new socialist president François Hollande, who took over from his predecessor Nicolas Sarkozy (UMP) in May 2012, PPP was not a top priority. However, he reaffirmed his government's commitment to the PPP approach. Under the Hollande presidency, risk transfer was emphasized, such as in the case of the A831 real toll road project, where the transport agency MEEDDAT (Ministry of Ecology, Sustainable Development and Energy) insisted on including the traffic risk in the contract. This same action led to a termination of negotiations on the A355 road project. However, large-scale projects discussed under the new Hollande presidency included a Metro around the city of Paris (€20 billion) and a French–Italian rail link under the Alps (€8 billion). Furthermore, at national level in the universities and the defence sector, PPP was expected to continue, as well as at the local level where already large shares of France's PPPs were signed (www.pppbulletin.com/news/view/23185).

8.2 ITALY

8.2.1 Institutional Context

One of the most striking features of the Italian governmental system is the highly fragmented party system and low government stability. Whereas in France the presidential element contributes to government stability and in Germany there is usually a relatively stable two party coalition, Italy suffers in this regard. Experiments with a change to a plurality system or a plurality component in the electoral system did not significantly contribute to increased governmental stability.

Due to the large number of parties participating in coalitions, policy coordination in the cabinet and between ministries is often quite challenging, with ministers and ministerial bureaucracy pursuing their own agendas (Nanetti 2007: 305). The influence of the prime minister depends, among others, on his ability to reconcile differences between governing parties and factions and to give some overall policy direction to the cabinet. In doing so, he or she is supported by 'the Office of the Prime Minister, a staff agency that had grown remarkably since the 1950s and that by 1980 employed about eight hundred people' (Nanetti 2007: 305). Among others, the Office of the Prime Minister controls government spending and the expenditures of public corporations and also supervises central–regional relations.

Further characteristics are a high degree of technocrats and ex-central bankers in the economic ministries or even as prime minister. For example, the 1995 Dini cabinet

> was again headed by a top official of the Bank of Italy and was composed entirely of technocrats. The Prodi cabinet of 1996–1998 was headed by a distinguished professor of economics, who had been at the helm of a giant public holding company (the Institute for Industrial Reconstruction, or IRI). It also included Ciampi as Treasury minister. In the D'Alema cabinet, appointed in October 1998, Ciampi was once again entrusted with the key Treasury portfolio. (ibid.)

Similar to in the UK, one of the prime minister's resources is his or her right to make appointments. However, it depends on the prime minister and the coalition constellation as to whether he or she is strongly constrained by the party groups in parliament or not. In some cases, such as under Prime Minister Ciampi (1993/04), parties were still consulted, but had no influence on the appointment process. The Ciampi cabinet was considered an experts or 'technical' government, bridging the crisis period after the collapse of most of the old parties such as the Democrazia Cristiana. In this extraordinary situation, parties were weakened and Ciampi refused to bargain with them at all when setting up his cabinet (ibid.). In such cases, a strong prime minister can much more easily push through his or her agenda – including the Merloni laws only one month before the election of March 1994.

In the territorial dimension, Italy is a decentralized unitary state with 20 regions, 106 provinces and about 8100 municipalities (in 2010), and can be best compared with France among the cases of our sample, despite being slightly more decentralized. Local government, provinces and some city regions have a strong historical identity, whereas in terms of nation-building Italy has been a European latecomer under the leadership of the Piedmont region in northern Italy. The regionalization had taken place in 1970 and was reinforced in 2001 with the creation of the 15 regular regional political and judicial jurisdictions. In addition, five regions have special statutes (Aosta Valley, Friuli-Venezia Giulia, Sicily, Sardinia and Trentino-South Tyrol). Expanded powers for some regions had already been set up in the post-war period in order to pacify regional separatism.

Despite this regionalization, Italy did not go as far as Spain in transforming central–regional relations into quasi-federal structures. Thus, the focus of the regions is on administrative and executive tasks rather than devolution of legislation to subnational level. However, the push for more regional autonomy or even federalization is stronger in northern parts of Italy. In contrast to the Spanish autonomous communities, the Italian regions in general were less strongly committed to the PPP approach – with some exceptions. Among the regions that tried to push PPP more intensely were the Emilia Romagna and the Piedmont regions. Compared with the French departments, the Italian regions were too autonomous to be easily coerced by central government to bolster PPP. In this regard, despite having more policy competences and even being constitutionally protected, the Italian regions are more similar to the 27 French administrative regions than to the 17 autonomous communities in Spain. Compared with the Spanish regions, fiscal stress and economic pressure were not strong enough to unleash coercive power towards PPP. Despite several debt crises in Italy commencing in the 1980s, austerity measures were unpopular and parties shied away from substantive measures. The policy support of PPP by the centre-left governments between 1996 and 2001 can partly be explain by the push to become a 'first round' member of the Eurozone and thus to pass the fiscal convergence criteria in the late 1990s.

In 2001 the respective parts of the constitution were completely revised and subnational units gained more competences. The reform was led by the idea of dual spheres of competences between the national and regional level. Prior to the reform, regional law-making was under the auspice of a central government commissioner (commissario di governo) for each region, in order to protect the 'national interest' (Köppl 2010: 129). However, the details of central–regional relations are still disputed between the centre-left and centre-right parties and sometimes the constitutional court has the final say. General competences and the internal affairs of the regions are regulated by statutes, not constitutions. Regions have their own parliaments (consiglio regionale) and since 1999 also directly elected presidents. The regions have legislative powers in all fields not restricted to the central state such as local police, industrial and economic policy making, tourism and farming (ibid.: 135).

A considerable amount of spending takes place in the regionalized health care system. Up to the end of the 1990s, regions largely depended on fiscal transfers from the federal level. In 1997, they were guaranteed small shares of some central taxes, and since 2001 they can raise own taxes and fees. However, central transfers still sum up to about half of the regional budgets. Similar to the autonomous communities in Spain, health services make up the largest share of local expenses (ibid.: 136). Contrarily to the UK, where central government paved the way for PPP/PFI in health care, Italian (and also Spanish) public health care services did not adopt PPP in similar ways than NHS had done.

8.2.2 Partisanship and Institutionalization

Among the samples used in this book, partisanship in Italy is probably the most difficult to analyse. After the crisis of the old parties and the emergence of a new party system in 1992–1994, deadlock was changed into a system of bipolar alternation, with centre-right coalitions superseding centre-left coalitions and vice versa (Cotta/Verzichelli 2007: 35, see also Table 8.3). The 1992–1994 transformation of the party system can be described as a change from polarized pluralism (Sartori 1976) to a fragmented bipolar system, with smaller parties exercising considerable influence on the bigger parties on the right and the left (Ieraci 2008). Extreme ideological distances had partly demised, partly been reshaped by the dissolution of the strong communist party (Partito Comunista d'Italia, PCI) on the left and the emergence of the new centre-right Forza

Italia under the influence of media entrepreneur Silvio Berlusconi. However, as a contested figure, Berlusconi and his Forza Italia were also in need of coalition partners in order to reach a parliamentary majority.

Table 8.3 Coalition governments in Italy, 1992–2008

Legislative term	Prime ministers	Types/phases of coalitions	Number of cabinets	Average duration of governments (weeks)
06/1992–05/1994	Amato, Ciampi	End of five party formula and technocratic government	2	40
05/1994–05/1996	Berlusconi, Dini	Centre-right attempt and technocratic government	2	44.4
05/1996–06/2001	Prodi, D'Alema, Amato	Centre-left	4	64.3
06/2001–05/2006	Berlusconi	Centre-right	2	130
05/2006–05/2008	Prodi	Centre-left	1	103.1

Source: Adapted from Cotta/Verzichelli 2007: 112.

For the introduction of PPP in Italy, this meant a reduction in the scope and influences of possible veto players and, with the emergence of Forza Italia as a vehicle of support for Berlusconi, the appearance of a more 'neoliberal' party than, for example, the Democrazia Cristiana in the period 1948–1994. Berlusconi's political project can best be described as a blend of patrimonialism, populism and neoliberalism, with each of these strains sometimes interfering with the others (Ginsborg 2005: 159). Thus, the often proclaimed rhetoric of a free market faced limitations, for example. by 'overpromising' and the resulting lack of credibility (populism) and a policy style of direct control of resources and opportunities (patrimonialism; ibid.: 160).

However, the first timid support for PPP had already been given by the centre-left coalitions commencing in 1996, on the eve of the third phase of the European economic and monetary union in 1999. The technocratic and banking orientation that took into account a more active PPP policy was especially strong in the Prodi (1996–1998) and D'Alema cabinets (1998–2000), in which the former director of the Bank of Italy, Ciampi, acted as Minister of the Treasury. 'The hegemonic role of technocratic and banking interests in Italy and the concomitant commitment to economic stability were vividly symbolized in May 1999 by the election of Ciampi as president of the republic' (Nanetti 2007: 306). In the same year, the Italian PPP Task Force (Unità Tecnica Finanza di Progetto, UTFP – see section 8.2.3) was set up by Law 144/99, Art. 7, to promote 'private finance in public infrastructure projects as well as other forms of PPP' (Allen & Overy 2010: 96). This example of a strong representation of banking interests at governmental level and the parallel setting up of the Italian PPP Task Force clearly underlines the results of our statistical part of analysis, revealing that the size (and thus the political influence) of the financial sector plays an important role in the adoption of the PPP approach.

In terms of party politics, under Massimo D'Alema in the mid-1990s, the post-communist Partito Democratico della Sinistra (PDS, succeeded by the Democratici di Sinistra, DS in 1998, which in 2007 merged into the Partito Democratico, PD) had taken a moderate-left policy stance with a focus on modernization and Euro membership. However, first, in 1996, Romano Prodi became prime minister of the Olive Tree coalition. 'After Prodi was forced to resign in October 1998, D'Alema formed a center-left cabinet that was broadened to include both the Communist Party of Italy (PCd'I) […] and the center-right Democratic Union for the Republic (UDR), headed by former president Francesco Cossiga' (Nanetti 2007: 337). Both centre-right cabinets pursued a policy of monetary stability, control of public spending, and austerity in order to qualify for the introduction of the Euro in early 1999. The instability of the centre-left cabinets is further illustrated by D'Alema's resignation after heavy losses for the governing parties in the regional elections of April 2000. D'Alema was succeeded by Treasury and budget minister Giuliano Amato (ibid.). After the change in government in 2001, the incoming Berlusconi cabinet continued to support the PPP policy. However, later in this era, the influential finance minister Giulio Tremonti was ousted because of his tendency to take unilateral decisions, surprising even his cabinet colleagues. However, his replacement Domenico Siniscalco was ousted in 2005 (and replaced by Tremonti) because he 'refused to turn a blind eye to a blatantly "electoral" budget that the cabinet insisted on passing in preparation for the 2006 parliamentary elections' (ibid.: 306).

The legal breakthrough for PPP was intended with the passing of the 'Legge Obiettivo' (Law 443/2001). The law enables a process acceleration (fast track) for investments in strategic infrastructures through reducing bureaucracy and simplifying approvals, increasing accountability of the central government while preserving the rights of the local levels, and providing provisions concerning the role of general contractors. In August 2002, further ordinances to the Legge Obiettivo were enacted, the Merloni law on public procurement from February 1994 was amended and the areas of supervision of the Bank of Italy expanded (UTFP 2009). In terms of the legal framework for PPP, the Legislative Decree 163/2006 (code of public works contracts) provides a systematization of different contractual forms, whereas the Legislative Decree 267/00 (Consolidated Act on Local Authorities) sets the legal conditions for local institutional PPPs. Allen & Overy (2010: 95) make a distinction between contractual and local institutional PPPs in Italy, with the former comprising public works concessions initiated by either private parties or public authorities, public service concessions, and sponsorship contracts and financial leases, and the latter public–private companies for a) the provision of local public services or b) urban regeneration programmes.

The incoming Berlusconi government in 2008, with its large majority, put its policy focus on such actions as abolishing the (former) property tax on the first self-occupied house. However, the Berlusconi governments clearly stood for the liberal model of a state, whereby the state minimizes its involvement in the lives of its citizens as far as possible. Similar to the model of the liberal state in the UK, the focus of the Berlusconi governments was on tax reduction, and especially avoiding tax increases. In this view it is not the state but private households who know best how to invest their money, whereas the state tends to waste the money (Orsina 2011). Given this ideological partisan affinity to liberal models, similar to the UK, it is no surprise that the more liberal Italian governments under Berlusconi pushed for a policy change in terms of PPP.

To sum up, party system fragmentation and government instability in Italy provided less favourable conditions for PPP than were found in, for example, the UK, Portugal, and Greece. Introduced by the centre-left D'Alema cabinet in 1999 with the PPP law, under subsequent governments PPP was mainly supported by Berlusconi's Forza Italia, less by the centre-left governments. Not only with regard to PPP, the multi-party cabinet under Prodi II (2006–2008) left a divided and paralyzed impression.

8.2.3 PPP Politics

As rhetoric, 'partenariato pubblico-privato' found broad support in Italian politics, especially under the Berlusconi governments. However, the output of signed PPP contracts is not as high as the political commitment and institutional adjustments would suggest. Due to the large size of the Italian economy (and respectively public investment), Italy ranked only 10 in the sample of this study (Table 3.2), ahead of France (11) but below Germany (9).

At national level, factors such as the high fragmentation of the party system and the instability of governments do not favour a rapid adoption of PPP; however, factors such as high government debt and a still centralized state structure during larger parts of our investigation period have been more supportive. The political will to use more PPP was clearly expressed from the late 1990s in various ways by several cabinets. However, Allen & Overy (2010: 95) describe the main obstacles for private partners as a scarcity 'of lenders willing to lend for sufficiently longer tenors; and (ii) the general lack of consensus about the scope and priorities for PPP projects'.

The Italian Task Force UTFP was established as early as 1999 (Law 144/1999, Article 7), initially at the Ministry of Economy and Finance as part of the Inter-Ministerial Committee for Economic Planning (CIPE), which reported directly to the prime minister (D'Alema). Three years later, the mandate of the Task Force had been extended by legislative decree (190/2002), with reference to the framework law on public infrastructure of 2001 (Act No. 443/2001, Legge Obiettivo). The Task Force was now able to execute preparatory analyses on behalf of the Ministry of Infrastructure and Transport in strategic infrastructure projects (UTFP 2009: 10).

After the transfer of CIPE and other units to the Presidency of the Council of Ministers (PCM) in 2006 (Law 223/2006 and Decree of the PCM, 2007), the Task Force was then assigned to the Department for Economic Policy Programming and Coordination of the PCM (UTFP 2009: 10). The UTFP itself can neither initiate projects nor order projects to be presented for advice or assessment. It offers the possibility of voluntary counselling with an extensive expertise in the areas of transport, network infrastructure, sports facilities, health facilities, housing construction and public parks. In 2004, UTFP set up the 4P Council to lobby for PPP in politics and in public. The UTFP itself is staffed with 15 professionals from both public and private sectors with legal, financial and technical backgrounds (OECD 2010: 104). The model for this was the British PFI Task Force. An important task at the beginning was the selection and monitoring of pilot projects at the central level as well as the evaluation and preparation of 'lessons learned', developing guidelines for future projects and the competencies of officials across the different levels of the Italian political system. Furthermore, the UTFP advises on legal questions, such as the tender process or the implementation of the Eurostat decision of 11 February 2004 on the posting of contracts with direct impact on the level of the budget deficit (or surplus) and debt in the national budget (see www.utfp.it/docs/UFP_English.pdf). Decree No. 163/2006 (Public Procurement Consolidated Text) unifies general rules on the award of public works and services and includes provisions for concessions, the competitive dialogue and the use of PPPs in specific sectors. With Law 31/2008, guidelines for the classification of Italian PPP projects were adopted (ibid.).

In the policy dimension, the Economic and Financial Planning Documents require particular mention. The document for the years 2000–2003 called the involvement of private financing, construction and operation of public infrastructure and facilities, particularly in the south of the country, a priority. The argument was that the involvement of the private sector improves planning, construction and operating services. In the Economic and Financial Planning Document 2001–2004, the government expected to implement new infrastructure totalling €9 billion through private funds.

The private sector was expected to be involved with both debt financing and equity capital. Also, the Economic and Financial Planning Documents in subsequent years put a clear emphasis on the financing of public infrastructure by the private sector (UTFP 2009). In 2004, the EIB observed that Italy had extensive experience with the financing of power plants in the context of PPPs, and similar to Portugal, had extended its PPP programme into the health sector (EIB 2004: 6). This early, intensive use of PPPs at the central level has not been slowed down by the Merloni law on public procurement of 1994. This law provides that the payment of fees to a concession holder is allowed only if the user fees for the relevant services remain regulated by the state.[4] Moreover, the compensation paid to the contractor was not allowed to exceed 50 per cent of the construction costs of the facility and the concession period not to exceed 30 years (de Pierris/Pescarini 2001). However, the 50 per cent rule has proved to be a hindrance particularly at the local level.

At local level there is also a spin-off of tasks to intermunicipal companies to achieve cost reductions and efficiency improvements. Bognetti/Robotti (2007) have calculated a share of 14 per cent of all local public utilities which are organized as a public–private company. Another 13 per cent are purely public, but intermunicipal companies (ibid.). According to Gianella et al. (2009: 232), the slow adoption of PPPs at the local level in Italy is due to frequent changes in the legal environment, uncertainty of demand for such services, financial constraints in interim financing and construction companies and the lack of competence centres at regional level. However, in six regions (such as Lombardy and Lazio) advisory services for local project funding have been established, following the model of the central PPP unit. Gianella et al. (2009: 233) see the year 2002 as a turning point in the dissemination and use of alternative project financing such as SPVs and PPP models such as BOT and BOO (Build, Own, Operate).

The initiative for the majority of PPP projects at national level comes from the public company ANAS SpA (Azienda Autonoma Nazionale delle Strade, see www.stradeanas.it), which is responsible for the operation of the roads, as well as from Rete Ferroviaria Italiana (RFI), which is responsible for the maintenance and expansion of railway infrastructure (16 720 km of track and 2260 stations, see www.rfi.it). Besides ANAS and other central public utilities, provincial and municipal governments, water authorities and local health authorities are involved in PPP procurement. 'Some regions have incorporated special companies to act as awarding authorities for public–private partnerships in place of other local authorities (e.g. Lombardy)' (OECD 2010: 104).

De Pierris/Pescarini (2001) provide a good overview of the distribution of early projects by sector and region. By volume, 54 per cent of the investments up to 2001 were made in the central regions, 25 per cent in the south and 21 per cent in the north. Based on the number of projects, 37 per cent were signed in the north, 35 per cent in the centre and 28 per cent in the south. Seventy-two per cent of the investment volume was dedicated to the transport sector, 13 per cent to water supply, 12 per cent to other infrastructure and 1 per cent to environmental and recreational facilities (ibid.: 76f). The reasons for the early adoption of PPP in Italy despite adverse factors such as the Merloni law can be seen in the low level of infrastructure spending compared to the EU average and high public debt levels at the various levels of government.

However, it seems the Italian PPP market has stagnated in the second half of the last decade. EPPPR (2007: 3) explains this with the stalling of the Messina Bridge, the merger of Autostrada and Abertis and the change of government to the centre-left coalition led by Romano Prodi in April 2006. With the incoming Prodi government the support for PPP cooled down, but 'there is little hard evidence yet (apart from the high profile Messina bridge casualty) that regional and municipal governments will stop developing new PPP projects' (ibid.).

The prestigious project of a bridge over the strait between Calabria and Sicily would create the longest suspension bridge in the world (over 3 km), but is politically highly controversial. Under the Prodi government the project was suspended in 2006; however, it was resumed in 2008 by the Berlusconi government. The original estimation of almost €4 billion has doubled since, and project start has been delayed again and again. The incoming Prodi government viewed the project 'as an extreme example of a system which promises a large pipeline (in excess of what the public purse can afford) and then fails to deliver' (EPPPR 2007: 100).

EPPPR (2009) mentions enormous frustration among Italian market participants about the lack of progress in the preparation of PPP. A recent report by a management school had found that between 2005 and 2008 up to 88 per cent of local initiatives in the areas of parking, sports facilities, public buildings and cemeteries have been cancelled or failed because of a change in political will or organizational deficits in the public sector. Large projects involving more than €100 million had been hardly completed between 2007 and 2009 (ibid.: 63). However, following the change of government in 2008 (Berlusconi IV), there was more support for PPP. For instance, a new definition of PPP was introduced in an amendment of the Public Contracts Code (Terzo Decreto Correttivo), and project financing in procurement was amended in September 2008 in favour of PPP procurement procedures (ibid.).

In general, Italian politics seemed to be using PPP primarily as a means to reduce the perceived gap between the scope and quality of Italy's infrastructure compared to that in other EU countries and to stimulate the economy after the global credit crisis. However, the number of projects that were awarded or actually completed was still sparse (ibid.: 64f). The PPP Forum (2009: 19) reports that by 2009, only 20 projects had been signed with a total investment of about €3.6 billion similar to France until 2010 (see above).

Although PPPs in Italy should have benefited from an infrastructure plan announced in March 2009, with a volume of €17.8 billion, illustrating political commitment, the outcome was often very limited. The quantitative extent of Italian PPP activities is best monitored by UTFP and NPFO (National Project Financing Observatory, http:infopieffe.it). NPFO was founded under the leadership of the Ministry of Economy and the CIPE Technical Project Support Unit, Unioncamere[5] as well as Rome Chamber of Commerce in cooperation with CRESME (Centro Ricerche Economiche Sociali di Mercato per l'Edilizia e il Territorio).[6] The NPFO database contains information on project proposals, market and background analyses, and other information in relation to Italian PPP.

At regional level, SIOP Emilia Romagna (Sisteme Informativo sulle Opportunità di PPP; www.sioper.it) and SIOP Lazio (www.siop-lazio.it) are two examples of information offices of the regional industry and chambers of commerce, which in collaboration with CRESME as a service for institutions, municipalities, corporations, individuals and financial experts, regularly update reports on events and information on PPPs in the regions and at the national level.

From 2000 to 2007, UTFP advised over 330 PPP projects, of which 110 were advised between June 2004 and December 2006. Demand for project advice came mostly from the local governments (84 per cent), with 9 per cent from regional administrations, and only 7 per cent from the national level (de Calboli 2007: 19). The following table summarizes the main PPP activities of Italian governments during our investigation period.

Table 8.4 Italian governments and their major PPP activities

Years	Cabinet	Action
02/1994	Ciampi	Merloni law on public procurement (amended 1998 and 2002)
1996–1998	Prodi	–
1999	D'Alema I (DS)	Set up of the Project Finance Technical Unit (UTFP, www.utfp.it)
2000–2001	Amato	–
2001	Berlusconi II (FI)	Infrastructure law Legge Obiettivo
08/2002	Berlusconi II (FI)	Decree law to the infrastructure law and changing of the Merloni law
2003	Berlusconi II (FI)	Code of Works, Services and Supplies Public Contracts
2004	Berlusconi II (FI)	4P Council set up
04/2006	Berlusconi III (FI)	Decree for unification of public works Guidelines for statistical treatment of PPP projects
03/2008 09/2008	Berlusconi IV (FI/ PdL)	Changing of the Public Contracts Code NPFO set up
03/2009	Berlusconi IV (FI/ PdL)	Implementation of measure to (among others) support infrastructure investment and public–private collaboration

Note: FI = Forza Italia, PdL = Il Popolo della Libertà (The People of Freedom).

Source: Own compilation.

8.3 CASE COMPARISON

Due to the overall size of their economies and the absence of large or mega projects such as the London Underground PPPs under New Labour and the Toll Collect system under the red–green coalition in Germany, France and Italy ranked in the lower midfield of our sample as number 10 (Italy) and 11 (France), followed only by the group of the Nordic countries (section 3.2). While at first sight some institutional features may appear similar in both cases, a closer look reveals important differences in the details. In total numbers, the French PPP market is considerably bigger than the Italian one, but taking into account the size of the economy and public investment, Italy ranks slightly better than France.

Despite their low ranking within our sample, in both countries PPP played an important role over the course of the investigation period. However, different emphases can be observed. Whereas in France PPP could build on a long tradition of concessions and public–private collaboration, in Italy the stimulus came more from the outside. In particular, the policy blueprint of the UK and the Maastricht criteria for membership of the Eurozone have played an important role in the process of adopting the PPP approach. Italy followed more the 'copy and paste' mode in the policy transfer from the UK, for example in the setting up of the PPP Task Force, the UTFP, while France developed more its own style in the adoption of the PPP approach. The setting up of the well-staffed Italian UTFP was guided by the blueprint of the UK Treasury Task Force, later PUK.

Furthermore, in both the UK and Italy the Treasury was among the biggest supporters of the PPP approach at governmental level. Similar not only to the UK but also Spain, the PPP approach in Italy was already set on the agenda at the end of the 1990s. In France, political support came mainly from the neo-Gaullists, first under President Chirac and later with a strong emphasis under Sarkozy. Furthermore, in Italy in the late 1990s the centre-left cabinets supported the PPP approach with an eye on the Maastricht criteria, while later it was Berlusconi and his cabinets, especially under finance minister Giulio Tremonti, who continued to support this approach with conviction. However, while policy support in Italy was high (at least at the rhetorical level), and while institutional revisions had been addressed, the project output remained rather small. Large and symbolic projects such as the Messina bridge that were promoted by some private and political actors as perfect cases for PPP, did not obtain sufficient political support, at least among the centre-left parties. While the Berlusconi governments were more supportive, administrative hurdles led to a standstill and eventually burying of the Messina bridge project. In this context, two institutional features of the Italian polity have contributed to stop a more successful PPP policy in Italy under the Berlusconi cabinets: the need for consensus in large coalition governments and – compared to the semi-presidential system of France – the weaker position of the Italian prime minister.

On the other hand, France was the only country in our sample that faced serious problems with constitutional rigidity while trying to adopt the PPP approach. Even Portugal, where privatization was prohibited under the early constitution (later abolished) and where the constitutional court cancelled some of the reform laws passed by parliament in 2012/13, constitutional matters were no problem for introducing PPP in the 1990s. In France, the Constitutional Council asked for a more sophisticated justification for each project, until in 2008 under the Sarkozy presidency, some clarifications had been issued by parliament. Despite these higher legal requirements for a PPP in France, the country did issue some large-scale projects especially under the Sarkozy presidency.

Another factor coming into influence towards the end of our investigation period is the impact of the global financial crisis commencing in 2008. The French (similarly to the Belgian and Dutch) banking sector was more severely hit by the global financial crisis than the Italian one, needing reconstruction and bailout. Due to the absence of a real estate bubble, the relatively low debt level of private households as well as the focus of Italian banks on traditional credit business has helped the Italian financial sector to pass relatively untroubled through the crisis. Thus, the Italian state did not have to launch spectacular bailout programmes as, for example, in Ireland, Portugal or Greece. However, sovereign debt provided some problems, due to the downgrading of the Italian credit rating and decreasing revenues. In these troubled economies, private credit not only for PPP was much harder to get in the years following 2008. In this time, state guarantees for operational and planned PPPs were discussed, but did not find much political support (see section 3.3.1).

NOTES

1. Grimsey/Lewis (2005b: xiii) point at the long history of concessions contracts, with the first being 'awarded for the financing and construction of the "Canal de Briare" in 1638 and "Canal du Midi" in 1666. Later, in the second half of the nineteenth century, France extensively used PPPs to finance its infrastructure, and railways, water, electricity and

tramways were all designed, constructed, financed and operated by private enterprises and banks. [...] This system was then generalized to numerous activities considered in France as "commercial public services" such as water supply and sanitation, waste management or urban transportation'.
2. www.ppp.bercy.gouv.fr/liste_projets_extract_boamp.pdf [23 September 2010].
3. www.ppp.bercy.gouv.fr/liste_projets_extract_boamp.pdf [23 September 2010].
4. The Merloni law was somehow comparable to the British Ryrie rules of the 1980s.
5. Founded in 1901, Unioncamere is the central interest group of the Italian chambers of commerce and represents Italian interests in Eurochambres, the European Association of chambers of industry and commerce. Typically for a SPV, it gained functional autonomy for its area of regulation in February 2010.
6. CRESME Research Centre was founded in 1982 as a non-profit organization of the construction industry with a focus on interdisciplinary studies in the construction and civil engineering sector (www.cresme.it).

9. The Iberian Peninsula and Greece

9.1 PORTUGAL

9.1.1 Institutional Context

The Portuguese political system is still highly centralized despite a constitutional norm of administrative decentralization and EU pressure for decentralization (Rodrigues/Madureira 2010). It is a unitary state with two autonomous regions (Madeira and the Azores), local autonomy and a directly elected president who scrutinizes legislation and symbolizes stability rather than having executive functions (similar to the directly elected Austrian president). However, in some cases of 'cohabitation', presidents have also used their right to veto government legislation. For instance, in 2004 President Sampaio (Partido Socialista, PS) vetoed extensively against the Lopes cabinet (Partido Social Democrata, PSD), which was going to break with the consolidation policy of its predecessor, the Barroso cabinet (PSD). Finally, the president decided to dissolve the unicameral parliament at the end of 2004 (Fonseca 2009: 774).

Another institutional feature is the frequent alternation of minority cabinets, single party cabinets and two or three party coalitions. However, this does not seem to weaken 'governability' in Portugal. To avoid inertia by fragmentation or polarization, the constitution allows parliament to transfer certain non-restricted powers to the government. Thus, cabinets can try to gain legislative powers, enabling them to govern in certain fields by decree laws. Such 'authorizations' of governments by parliament are a common feature in southern European political systems; however, Portugal has maybe the most far reaching opportunities in this regard.

Policy making is still mainly undertaken by central government and the centralized parties, leaving nearly no latitude for other levels of government or actors to independently choose different policy options than those pre-set at central level. The strong tendency to steer policy making from the centre is a feature of the political system that survived the democratic transformation following the 1974 revolution. In terms of social cleavages, the north/south divide as well as coastal/inland and urban/rural antagonism support the centralization of power and administrative units in the capital, limiting the range of policy options. For example, distributive issues of the welfare state or issues of further democratization of political structures have been systematically kept off the agenda (Rodrigues/Madureira 2010: 255f.). Contrarily, once convinced of a policy change as for instance in the case of PPP, the core executive has a huge capacity to push its ideas through easily. Powerful, institutional veto players are rare in Portugal.

In terms of vertical differentiation, municipalities are the only actors at regional level with some clout. However, in financial terms they heavily rely on central grants and subsidies. Thus, Portugal has not followed trends such as in neighbouring Spain, the UK or Italy to devolve administrative, executive or even legislative functions to newly established regional bodies. Even mere administrative regions were not created, due to lack of demand from lower levels and to central resistance towards regionalization (ibid.: 255). However, there are some administrative structures above the municipality level, comprising supra-municipal bodies and deconcentrated regional institutions such as the Regional Coordination and Development Commissions (ibid.).

At municipal level itself, the executive body (Câmara Municipal) is directly elected by PR (d'Hondt). Executive bodies across the country range from having 5 to 17 members. Each executive is presided over by the candidate who got the most votes on the winners list. At local and municipal level, these câmaras are the decisive institutions, involved in a lot of management tasks as well as more political functions such as drafting the annual budget, issuing public construction works, licensing and supporting parishes (ibid.).

The deliberative body at municipal level is the 'Assembleia Municipal', consisting of the presidents of the parishes' executives as well as elected members from each parish and from all resident voters. It is, among others, responsible for the monitoring and controlling of the executive, as well as for approving regulations and the budget, land-use management plans, and changes to the number of municipal staff. It is also responsible for 'the creation and participation in public-owned corporations, establishing municipal taxes and approving capital loans' (ibid.: 255f.). With regard to PPP, municipalities were similarly as 'influenceable' by central government policy changes as local governments in the UK. In contrast to Spain and also to France, more or less directly elected regional jurisdictions do not exist. In the Portuguese case central government best 'enjoys' the amenities of almost direct influence on local policy making.

9.1.2 Socioeconomic Background

To understand Portugal's socioeconomic (as well as some political) challenges, one has to recall its peripheral location on the continent, with Spain as the only neighbour by land. Similar to the Nordic countries, regional proximity led to close economic relations and a high density of policy coordination. Both Portugal and Spain share a long history of authoritarian rule, leading to social and economic backwardness being one of the reasons for the overthrow of the rulers in the mid-1970s and the introduction of a process of democratization (transition). In both countries democracy and a market economy soon took deep roots, with Portugal being more challenging due to the long history of authoritarian corporatism (estado novo) under António de Oliveira Salazar.

Compared to Spain, Portugal is also more challenged because of the small size of its economy and its peripheral location on the continent, the latter making transport of goods by land to trading partners other than Spain more difficult, a situation that cannot even be rudimentarily offset by sea trade with the former American colonies. From the perspective of critical theory, the challenges for small-sized, relatively poor and underdeveloped peripheral economies have been characterized as 'peripheral capitalism', more or less oppressed and exploited by the modernized capitalist 'core'. While this perspective of a 'world system theory' initially was developed using the example of the globalized economy (Wallerstein 2004), interpretation patterns of asymmetrical central/periphery relations have also been used to analyse European relations from within (Rodrigues/Reis 2012).

During and after its accession to the EU in 1986 (together with Spain), Portugal remained one of the poorest countries in the Community. Thus, it received significant subsidies from the European structural and cohesion funds. In the first 25 years (1986–2011) it is estimated that Portugal received about €81 billion from European funds, which was mainly invested in infrastructure (Wieland 2013: 19). In the course of the banking crisis of 2011, a further €78 billion followed from European rescue facilities to stabilize the Portuguese banking system and to prevent the crisis spreading further across the endangered countries.

In general, the effects of the European subsidies remained uncertain. On the one hand, roads, railways, airports, bridges, and school and hospital facilities were modernized and expanded. On the other hand, these investments did not leverage industrial and agricultural production and had little impact on the structure and competitiveness of the producing (and service delivery) sector in general. If it happens at all, growth is very moderate. After the EU Eastern enlargement in 2004, the low paid industrial sector partially moved its production eastwards.

Joining the Euro in the first round in 1999 has been a consensual and prestigious project for Portugal, which even today resolutely clings to Euro membership. While support for the Euro is still high among the people, the austerity measures enforced by the 'troika', as well as the lack of opportunity for external devaluation, limits the options of monetary policy. As external devaluation to stimulate productivity and competitiveness was ruled out, internal devaluation, such as through wage adjustment, has been considered, partially limited by constitutional law (i.e. the constitutional court) and challenges from the unions.

With the decline of domestic demand in Portugal as well as in Spain since the start of the financial crisis in 2008, the export sectors have become more important to avoid an even deeper slide into recession. With a share of about 30 per cent of GDP, the export sector in Portugal is slightly bigger relative to GDP than the one in Spain. The use of PPPs, however, which primarily focuses on domestic sectors such as construction and service delivery, is less likely to be driven by the export sector. Here, domestically driven growth would be more important to, for example, stimulate the use of infrastructure such as (toll) highways.

Similar to other (southern) European countries, trade union influence on the labour market has been diminished in the last decades, thus reducing the unions' capabilities to mobilize or even veto liberalization of the labour market or privatization of public entities (Rodrigues/Madureira 2010: 261). Unions try to counteract this diminution of power through mergers of smaller unions, for example. In Portugal, the two largest unions are the General Confederation of Portuguese Workers (CGTP-InterSindical) and the General Union of Workers (UGT) (ibid.). However, for the implementation of PPP not only low organizational membership density but also the overall pluralistic structure of interest groups has played an important role.

9.1.3 PPP Politics

Against this background of the small-sized Portuguese economy and the peripheral location, Portugal turned out to be among the most active PPP countries in this study (see Chapter 3). Portugal had experience with PPPs as early as the mid-1990s and is characterized as one of the most active countries in the use of PPP across Europe (EPPPR 2009: 83). The initial justification for the intense use of PPP was to overcome budget constraints and to improve the quality of services in the road, rail and sea port sectors (Macário et al. 2013: 143). Similar to the consensus on the

Euro accession policy, the strong support of PPP was consensual between the two large parties, the Socialists and the Social Democrats. Opposition against the use of PPP as a means of public policy has not been reported at a significant level. Political considerations in election years as well as the aim of bypassing excessive bureaucracy have further contributed to the popularity of PPP among Portuguese policy makers. The electoral system favours the two big parties and has reduced the need to search for coalition partners when a change of government takes place (Colomer 2008). This means that PPP has not become subject to bargaining deals during coalition talks.

As in other countries, primarily infrastructure projects, especially highways, were planned via PPP. As in neighbouring Spain, concession models were a preferred means of public–private collaboration in Portugal. However, concessions in a strict sense are not PPP. Sarmento/Renneboog (2014: 10) counted a total of 35 projects at national level between 1995 and 2010 with a volume over €25 million. Among these, roads counted for 22 projects, health ten, railways two and security one. The total amount of investment in the 22 road sector projects was €18.8 billion, the two railway projects amounted to €502 million, the ten health projects €623 million and the security sector €126 million. In total, Sarmento/Renneboog (2014: 19) calculated €20.08 billion of central government signed PPP investment volume between 1995 and 2010. In the road sector, most operating companies were licensed for around 30 years and obliged to build additional traffic lanes if a certain traffic volume was reached. Compensation of operators is managed either by a direct or a shadow toll. The latter was introduced by the Guterres government in the late 1990s as a so-called 'SCUT model',[1] in which the state, depending on the volume of traffic, pays a fee to the operator (Legislative Decree 267/97 of October 1997). However, since late 2011 SCUT highways have also been directly tolled as a result of the effect of the global financial crisis on the public budget.

The major operating companies include the former state monopolists Brisa[2] and Estradas de Portugal (EP).[3] New highways are planned centrally by the Ministry of Transport and Public Works. An example of an early PPP project is the 17 km Vasco da Gama Bridge in Lisbon, which was completed within a tight schedule for the World Exhibition 1998. The PPP policy has been supported by a number of governments of different partisan composition, though with different focuses. Monteiro (2005: 73) observed a broad consensus in Portuguese politics that PPP should continue to be used and developed, not only in the infrastructure sector.

Such an extension was made, for example, for the health sector (EIB 2004: 6). Compared to other EU countries, as a share of GDP PPP investment is very high (Monteiro 2005: 73). 'Related to this is that compared to countries with a higher per capita income – such as the United Kingdom – PPPs in Portugal often imply a major extension of infrastructure assets rather than small additions to the existing infrastructure' (ibid.).

Some legal adjustments were carried out in the process of institutionalization of PPP. For example, the budget law now provides several PPP assessment procedures. The decision for or against PPP and the respective model has to be based on a public sector comparator and must be made with the participation of experts from the Ministry of Finance. All tenders initiated after 30 July 2008 have to apply a new Public Contracts Code which harmonized the various previously existing procurement rules across different statutes. Also, the competitive dialogue procedure was introduced. The high-speed link from Poceirão to Caia was the first one to be procured under the new Public Contracts Code (EPPPR 2009: 83).

Furthermore, the proposal of a PPP was now expected to include an assessment of long-term budgetary implications to streamline the decision-making process (Monteiro 2005). A number of legal provisions for PPP were laid down in 2003, including the financial evaluation of projects, the support of the Ministry of Finance through 'Parpública' (the privatization unit) and the supervision and control of PPPs. In 2006, a modifying decree was adopted followed by a decree law on public contract procedures in 2008 (Decree 18/2008, 29 January 2008).[4]

Set up in 2003, the Portuguese PPP unit is assigned to Parpública SA, a public holding company. A predecessor was founded in 2001 as a PPP Task Force in the health sector. Parpública itself (Participações Públicas) already existed in the year 2000 as a public administration and investment company for privatization. Its tasks comprise the monitoring and development of privatization processes in the context of government guidelines, the restructuring of public enterprises, the control of public shares in privatized companies, the management of public real estate assets, the support of the Treasury in financial supervision of public enterprises and the promotion of PPP (www.parpublicasgps.com). Thus, Parpública is a multi-purpose public entity and completely owned by the Ministry of Finance (OECD 2010: 108). It is responsible for the review of public–private collaboration; the collection, analysis and dissemination of information on PPP; and for advising the ministries. Furthermore, it evaluates projects, advises on procurement procedures and gets involved in negotiations with private interests. It has no own decision-making powers, but can make recommendations about the feasibility and efficiency of projects to the Ministry of Finance.

The PPP unit within Parpública is staffed with seven full-time employees, 'most on long-term secondment from government audit bodies such as the Inspectorate-General of Finance (Inspecção-Geral de Finanças)' (ibid.). It reports directly to Parpública's chief executive officer and is financed by the government. It also is involved in the management and renegotiation of the refinancing of current contracts (ibid.). Besides Parpública, some ministries have their own PPP units for the development and maintenance of specific PPP programmes, for example in the health sector. Such health sector programmes are developed and managed by 'Parcerias Saúde', the PPP unit in the Ministry of Health, and supported by Parpública (Monteiro 2005: 80). However, the output of PPP hospitals is so far scarce (Simões et al. 2010).

In the road sector, Estradas de Portugal (EP) is the executing agency in charge (equivalent to e.g. ASFINAG in Austria). In 2007, EP was transformed into a commercial company by decree law (374/2007) and it was granted a 75-year concession for the operation of the national roads. This concession model for EP also involves 'smaller sub-concessions structured in PPP projects whereby the private partner is responsible for financing, constructing, operating and maintaining the awarded roads or highways against availability payments' (EPPPR 2009: 84).The organization of EP as a private law company has, for example, the consequence that the company can go bankrupt, which complicates the loan procurement for new PPPs in the road sector (ibid.). Another challenge for EP is (according to the EPPPR) the monitoring of sub-licensees as the payment of the charges depends on the actual availability. Besides infrastructure and the health sector, PPP has also been used for prisons, schools and public buildings (EPPPR 2007: 116).

In contrast to in Germany and Austria, PPP in the Portuguese health care sector gained some attention in the early 2000s, when the then government set up a PPP construction programme for hospitals. However, the vast majority of PPP investments in Portugal were done in the road sector, followed at some distance by rail and then other sectors such as schools and hospitals. Compared to the larger Spanish market, the Portuguese one has been characterized as less commercialized with a stronger focus on 'best practice' (ibid.). In 2012, through a further amendment of the PPP law, the influence of the Ministry of Finance on the PPP procurement process was strengthened. Also, a high number of contract renegotiations, not only during the course of the financial crisis (Sarmento/Renneboog 2014), indicates a more 'proactive' policy of the central government.

Macário et al. (2013: 160) have listed some points in relation to Portuguese PPP policy that have been criticized. Among others, risk sharing between public and private partners has been characterized as inappropriate. Furthermore, policy makers were often biased towards new projects instead of optimizing old ones; regulation was regarded as weak and lacking pressure for performance, leading to non-efficient delivery and delays; and last but not least, instruments such as a public sector comparator were either missing or underdeveloped.

Table 9.1 Portuguese cabinets and their main PPP activities

Years	Cabinet	Party	PPP action
10/1991–10/1995	Cavaco Silva III	PSD	No PPP action
19/1995–10/1999	Guterres I	PS (minority government)	1995: First PPP signed by national government Shadow toll (SCUT model) for highway concession operators
10/1999–04/2002	Guterres II	PS (minority government)	2000: Parpública established (www.parpublica.pt)
04/2002–07/2004	Barroso	PSD/CDS–PP	2001: First PPP Task Force set up 04/2003: First PPP law passed, set up of the PPP unit within Parpública
07/2004–03/2005	Lopes	PSD/CDS–PP	No major PPP action
03/2005–09/2009	Sócrates I	PS	2006: PPP law amended
10/2009–06/2011	Sócrates II	PS	2009: Opposition criticized PPP 2009: Pausing and review of PPP politics and contracts
06/2011	Coelho	PSD	Contract review and renegotiating continued

Note: CDS–PP = Centro Democrático e Social – Partido Popular.

Source: Own compilation.

9.1.4 Impact of the Financial Crisis

Portugal was severely hit by the global financial crisis commencing in 2008. Similarly to Ireland and the UK, politicians started questioning their governments' PPP policy. In Portugal, prior to the 2009 parliamentary elections, the large PPP programme of the government had been criticized by the then PSD opposition. This signalled an erosion of the implicit PPP consensus among the two main parties. However, the socialist government, re-elected in September 2009, had promised extensive public investment in infrastructure as a means to combat the economic crisis, which partly should be done using the PPP approach. On the other hand, the financial crisis has led to the cancellation or the halting of some major PPP under preparation (EPPPR 2009: 84). Among these, the new Lisbon Airport and a high-speed rail line were the most prestigious.

With the financial crisis of 2008, a reassessment of the government's PPP policy slowly emerged. While in September 2010 a new PPP hospital contract worth €434 million (Vila Franca de Xira) had been signed, the government announced some months later that it would re-evaluate all of its PPPs, including the new Lisbon Airport project. The tendering of PPPs had been stalled and a working group had been set up to re-evaluate all projects that were either under preparation but not yet signed or still under construction. 'The move is being seen as part of a deal struck with Portugal's main opposition party – PSD – to get the government's budget approved' (www.pppbulletin.com/news/view/16287). Pressure on the PPP programme was also exercised by the IMF in spring 2011 in the course of the negotiations on the €78 billion EU and IMF bailout programme. Government and opposition parties were urged to sign a memorandum of understanding concerning a 'review of the government's financial obligations' including its PPP programme. The review was a condition of the €78 billion EU and IMF bailout programme outlined in a signed agreement by Portugal's government and opposition parties.

After two periods in office under José Sócrates, the Socialists (PS) lost the election of June 2011. Since the mid-1990s, the two main parties have always alternated after two terms in office. The new government under Pedro Passos Coelho (PSD) announced in its government manifesto the cancellation of a planned PPP high-speed rail project in the Lisbon area. Furthermore, the contracts review process continued. As a result, in August 2012, a first contract was successfully renegotiated by EP, which should lead to savings of about €500 million over the whole contract time of the Pinhal Interior highway in central Portugal (www.pppbulletin.com/news/view/24221). The prime minister announced a further cut to Portugal's PPP obligations by 30 percent in the next 30 years.

> Total future PPP costs for the state have been estimated at €26bn, but the government is obligated to enact structural reforms mandated under the €78bn bailout from the European Union and International Monetary Fund. Many experts have said the government used over-optimistic projections for traffic volumes and profitability when PPPs such as the €1.2bn Pinhal project were first signed. (ibid.)

9.2 SPAIN

9.2.1 Institutional Context

After the transition to full democracy in 1978, the opportunity given in the new constitution to establish 'autonomous communities' based on several provinces, and confirmed in a regional referendum (and/or by the national parliament, Cortes Generales), was soon used extensively. Whereas initially two different levels of competencies between the autonomous communities were introduced, in the course of the 1990s their competencies became more and more alike. For some observers the political system became 'federalized', thus marking a departure from Portugal's much more centralized model of transition (Garcia-Milà/McGuire 2007).

However, some crucial features of federalism are still missing. Three quarters of the second chamber (Senado) is elected at the level of the provinces; only one quarter is elected by the parliaments of the autonomous communities. Furthermore, autonomous communities do not have their own constitution. Their respective statutes (and any change or amendment) have to be negotiated with central government and approved by the community as well as by the Cortes Generales. Formally, these statutes are central government laws. Horizontal policy coordination between the communities is weak; much more important are (bilateral) vertical negotiations. Inspired by the German basic law, the administration is judicially regulated to a high degree. The traditional tendency to clientelism (or nepotism) in public offices is intended to be limited by Article 103 of the Spanish constitution, aiming at a professional, meritocratic and politically neutral bureaucracy (Barrios 2009: 728).

The constitution allows some of the autonomous communities to enjoy special rights, for example in areas such as language and fiscal matters. Thus, an asymmetrical relationship between the communities is established. The constitution also provides a list of competences that may be devolved (Articles 148, 149), while all others have to remain in the hands of the central state. In terms of public spending, meanwhile, little more than half is determined by central government, one third by the autonomous communities and the rest by local government. A huge share of community spending is dedicated to the school and education sector as well as the health sector (Nagel 2010: 157). Compared to Portugal and Greece, this level of policy making is unique in Spain and allows for a variety of additional actors and institutions interested in the PPP approach. The autonomous communities have mostly welcomed the PPP approach and utilized it in their public policies.

Some more institutional features of the Spanish political system have helped the utilization of PPP at national, regional and local level. First, like in the UK, a two party system has minimized the influence of possible partisan veto players at government level. The de facto two party system is established by relatively small multi-member constituencies (with 3 per cent threshold, see Barrios 2009: 736), with similar disproportionality and regionalization effects as a plurality system. On the other hand, this PR system frequently produces minority governments, supported by small regional parties in exchange for larger influence on specific government policies. Regional parties with strong cultural identities have sometimes been needed to create majorities at national level, and in such cases these parties have usually been quite successful in negotiating additional benefits for their region or clienteles. However, such additional regional subsidies were in general compatible with PPP procurement, so that this political bargaining was not a substantial obstacle towards the PPP approach in Spain. Furthermore, similar to the UK and Portugal, the pluralistic structure of interest groups provided a supportive environment for the implementation of PPP in Spain. Similarly to Portugal and Greece, Spain never adopted the northern and central European style of tripartite policy making in the fields of social and economic policy (see section 9.2.3).

At the level of the cabinet, inter-ministerial committees (Comisiones Delegados del Gobierno) can be set up to address specific topics (similar to Ireland and Greece). Additionally, informal meetings between the prime minister and a limited number of ministers can be arranged – also inter-ministerial committees at the level of senior officials (Barrios 2009: 727). In contrast to Greece, an inter-ministerial PPP committee has not been established, illustrating that the Spanish governments never embraced the PPP approach as actively as the Greek or UK governments.

9.2.2 Socioeconomic Background

Spain's economy has proven to be more dynamic than that of Portugal and experienced a long period of growth during the investigation period, driven mainly by a real estate boom and cheap labour resulting from immigration. The foundations for the construction boom were already laid with the European Community accession in 1986 and the subsequent infrastructure investments financed by European funds. Following the accession, large European companies (e.g. in the automotive sector) transferred production sites to the Iberian peninsula because of lower labour costs. In the construction and transport sector, ACS/Hochtief, Abertis, Ferrovial-Cintra, OHL and Sacyr became big players in the Spanish and international market (Acerete et al. 2011). Besides construction and infrastructure development, tourism and consumer spending contributed to an economic growth period from the mid-1990s to the outbreak of the banking crisis in 2008.

Additionally, joining the Eurozone in 1999 led to a period of 'cheap money' owing to low refinancing rates, leading to an extension of the credit-based economy, for example the property market and high-quality consumer goods. In the construction sector, an informal 'agreement' between domestic companies and politics has led to a relatively closed market, enabling mid-sized firms to grow to national champions. Similar patterns of protective (or 'mercantilist') politics have been observed for the banking sector, nurturing, for example, Banco Santander to become a global player. The Spanish PPP market has strongly benefited from this development.

However, the banking and financial crisis in 2008 has led to a stiff decline in many sectors, raising unemployment rates as well as deficit and debt levels to new heights. Also, the banking crisis has severely affected the balance between the regions. The most prosperous regions, Catalonia and Madrid, complained about the fiscal transfers to the poorer regions, while these strongly depend on such transfers to fulfil their tasks in the areas of education, health and social services. For 2012, the Rajoy government employed a deficit ceiling of 1.5 per cent of GDP for the regions; for 2013 even 0.7 per cent (Derichsweiler 2012: 7). Given the chronic scarcity of money, some of the regions applied PPP (concessions) intensely to avoid running further into debt. The high indebted costal Mediterranean regions Valencia and Catalonia, in particular, as well as Murcia, intensely used PPP as a means of infrastructure procurement.

In terms of industrial relations, the density of union membership is among the lowest in Europe. Furthermore, Spanish unions are notoriously short of money and indebted, due to low membership fees and payment motivation. Thus, services offered for members remain sparse, compared to French and German standards (Barrios 2009: 743). Similar to the UK, the ties between unions such as UGT and the Workers' Commissions (CC.OO – Confederación Sindical de Comisiones Obreras) and their affiliated parties PSOE (Partido Socialista Obrero Español or Spanish Socialist Party) or the communist PCE (Partido Comunista de España or Communist Party of Spain), respectively, have been weakened in the last decades; automatic party membership of union members was abolished in the 1980s; however, a high rate of cross-membership still exists (ibid.). On the employers' side, the main association is the CEOE (Confederación Española de Organizaciones Empresariales). In the field of PPP, SEOPAN, founded in 1956, is a most influential association. It represents over 30 large companies from the construction and concession sector. While its main task is to provide services for its export-oriented members, it has also supported the use of concessions (or PPP) inside Spain. Among these services, SEOPAN provides good quantitative data about the annual number and volume of Spanish infrastructure concessions across the different levels of government.

Similar to Ireland, the politics of social pacts (or partnerships) was very popular in Spain up to the Gonzales government in the mid-1990s. The politics of social pacts was a successor of the authoritarian corporatism under the Franco regime. The politics of social pacts was abolished in the 1990s, after the (socialist) government and the unions split up over issues of restructuring shipyards and heavy industry. However, in the course of the financial crisis in 2008, which ended the immense growth period, the Zapatero government remembered this tradition of social pacts in Spain. The real estate bubble and the subsequent global financial crisis have led to major restructuring in the financial sector. Especially 'cajas', smaller, regional saving banks, which had focused on mortgages, were hit hardly and forced into mergers by the Spanish state. Thus, the number of cajas was reduced from 45 to below 10 by 2013, the remaining cajas including the troubled – and finally, in 2012, bailed-out and nationalized – 'Bankia'. This bankruptcy led to a request for European assistance by the Spanish government, leading to a credit line of €40 billion for the banking sector and the setting up of a 'bad bank' for subprime credits and mortgages. The heavily hit construction and financial sectors also led to a slump of PPP in Spain. For example, concessioners of toll highways were forced by the decline of traffic volume (as well as the surplus of road infrastructure) to ask for bailouts or face insolvency.

9.2.3 PPP Politics

Similar to France, the implementation of the PPP approach in Spain could build upon a long tradition of concessions for procurement and service delivery. Since the mid-1960s, there has been a legal framework for infrastructure concessions. In the 1990s it had become clear that it was possible to respond to increasing infrastructure investment requirements with concession models. The financial sector has supported PPP projects to a growing extent, and the Spanish banks have adjusted their financing instruments to these new developments. In light of historical experience with private participation in public tasks, according to Allard/Trabant (2008: 3) it seemed consistent that the conservative government under José María Aznar (Partido Popular or People's Party, PP) after taking office in 1996 with a focus on deregulation and privatization, also harnessed the PPP approach. There was a rapid increase in the number of projects up to the new millennium, especially in the area of road construction.

After the first (positive) experiences in the 1990s in the road/construction sector, PPPs were also transferred to other sectors such as health. However, as in the health sector the autonomous communities had meanwhile gained important responsibilities, it was only to be expected that the 17 regions also started to join in PPP more or less intensely. Thus, the contracting authorities expanded from the central to the regional (and later also to the local) level of government. Besides health (hospitals and health care), waste disposal and the construction and maintenance of public buildings were further emphases at regional and local level. Thus, in the early 2000s, Spain emerged as a leading PPP market in Europe, in terms of both project volume and diversification of policies, becoming one of the biggest markets in Europe in terms of project volume between 2003 and 2005 (ibid.).

The preference for PPP endured the change of government in 2004 (incoming cabinet Zapatero I). In 2005, the PSOE government announced in an infrastructure plan that it would finance up to 40 per cent of total investment for new and improved roads, railways, airports, ports and other infrastructure in 2020 with the help of the private sector. This would represent about 0.5 per cent of Spanish GDP and make Spain a 'market leader' in Europe in the field of PPP project financing (ibid.). Thus, as an incoming government the PSOE took over most of the policies developed by the Spanish People's Party (PP), which had ruled the country at the central level from 1996 to 2003 as well as in many of the regions. They sympathized with the view that efficiencies and high-quality public services can best be achieved through the involvement of private actors (ibid.: 8). Moreover, the Zapatero government even intensified the use of PPP at the national level. In the public debate only the benefits of additional private financing for public investment were discussed. The rush for Eurozone membership in the late 1990s, with its Maastricht criteria of convergence and its demand for fiscal restraint, and the EU Eastern enlargement in 2004, along with the (expected) shift of EU structural and cohesion money towards the poorer Eastern countries, provided major rationales for the intensive use of private financing for public tasks.

Thus, Spain and Portugal were in the early 2000s in a similar situation to Ireland (Reeves 2003). In these cases (add Greece as another example), among the most important conditions that have driven PPP have been budget problems and a high demand for infrastructure investments in the face of reduced EU funding. Understandably, this has led in these countries to a search for alternative financing models. 'This exclusive emphasis on financing has conditioned the Spanish approach to managing PPP' (ibid.).

While there are some contextual similarities to other countries like Portugal, Ireland or Greece, the Spanish approach to PPP has also been described as a 'hands off' search for private financing, distinguishing it from the other cases. Existing policy and political support for PPP through legislation and competence centres is – unique in Europe for a country with such a high commitment – barely recognizable. In contrast to this more 'self-organized' approach in Spain, the British approach with stronger planning and control elements is characterized as a 'hands on' approach by Allard/Trabant (2008). For example, except for the Infrastructure Act 2003, which also regulated privately funded projects, virtually no PPP-specific regulation emanated from the various cabinets at central level.

Also, PPP units similar to Portugal or the UK did not exist and model contracts or a public sector comparator were not developed by central government. Unlike the other countries, the Spanish 'Centro Español de Excelencia y Conocimiento de la Colaboración Público Privada' (CECOPP) was founded not by government, but by private initiative. It is an association of interest groups and non-profit organizations that increases the participation of private investors in the financing and administration of public services. The tasks of the Centre of Excellence are the consultation and dissemination of information, the streamlining of procedures, the review of projects under approval and the role of an arbitrator.

The statutes of the Centre stipulate in Article 6 that its main purpose is to improve the satisfaction of the general (or public) interest through the development and management of infrastructure and the provision of public services through concessions and public–private cooperation. Thus, its operational task is to support regional and local authorities with appropriate knowledge, to organize seminars and training sessions, to promote scientific studies, propose legislative changes, and to report about experiences and 'best practice' (http://cecopp.com, 17 October 2011). Thus, a lot of aspects were left to the respective contracting ministries and public authorities to decide. Also, a public database of projects such as found in many other countries does not exist. However, SEOPAN and CECOPP do monitor project activities and also provide aggregate data on specific sector activity.

In Spain there is a legal framework that governs the award of public contracts (public works). These requirements are part of the law regulating the concession of public works as one of the standard procurement procedures in public administration. This law is well prepared and enables the application of concessions in different fields of procurement. The provisions of this Act have been successively adopted and applied by the lower levels of the political and administrative system. The statutory provisions for the awarding of concessions for roads were updated in May 2003 (Law 13/2003) in order to create an incentive for more private investment in this area. A PPP programme was initiated in the hospital sector (EIB 2004: 6). Regional airports were another political focus of PPP.

Sanz-Menéndez (2003: 10) sees the rapid spread of PPP in Spain in the context of path dependency (concessions),

> but also in functional terms due to the benefits and gains that they bring to innovation policies. [. . .] PP/Ps result from a more politically-oriented process, with the initiative being taken either by government or from below, and aim at consensus and compromise. The new approaches make STI [science–technology–innovation] policy implementation more efficient but also, if well designed and implemented, provide policy with support and legitimation. (ibid.)

The Spanish PPP market was initially, and still is, partly dominated by domestic firms. Foreign companies, but also non-profit organizations, have a hard time in the beginning. 'The non-Spanish businesses gaining a toehold have something unique to offer in terms of product or sector skills. Meanwhile the domestic market players have the strength and skill to globalise rapidly' (EPPPR 2007: 124).

9.2.4 Cross-Level Distribution

With the autonomous communities becoming more empowered since the 1990s, it is no wonder that they have contributed significantly to the overall level of PPP activity. Furthermore, the local governments are also allowed to use concessions (Table 9.2). For institutional PPP at the local level, the government often reserves the key positions and resources in the joint corporation, while the private partner remains entirely focused on the operational aspects of the business. In contrast with contracting out, this allows for lower monitoring and transaction costs. 'In many cases, the local government holds a majority of the shares. Mixed public–private firms play a significant role in the delivery of local services in Spain' (Bel/Fageda 2010: 130).

As mentioned above, the Spanish regions had their first experiences of PPP in the fields of infrastructure and health. At local and regional level, in the field of technology and innovation, PPP was the preferred choice. At central level the Ministry of Public Works (Ministerio de Fomento) supported the application of PPP to road enhancement schemes. In the pre-crisis year of 2007 it had prepared 16 such schemes to be tendered, 'with a total value of around € 5 bn' (ibid.). Table 9.2 provides a survey of concessions closed between 2003 and 2010, based on data from SEOPAN, the trade association of the Spanish construction industry.[5]

Table 9.2 Annually signed concessions (volume in € million and percentage of total)

	2003	2004	2005	2006	2007	2008	2009	2010
Central level	3 501.43 61.5%	–	641.31 9.3%	954.59 21.1%	5 648.51 58.3%	–	51.96 1.1%	13.33 0.2%
Regional level	1 835.28 32.2%	2 597.27 93.4%	4 280.61 62.0%	2 353.14 51.9%	3 327.87 34.4%	3 805.70 75.8%	4 135.53 85.8%	7 983.24 97.1%
Local level	356.71 6.3%	183.61 6.6%	1 986.28 28.7%	1 225.30 27.0%	706.61 7.3%	1 214.34 24.2%	633.87 13.1%	222.78 2.7%
Total	5 693.42	2 780.88	6 908.20	4 533.02	9 682.99	5 020.04	4 821.36	8 219.35

Sources: SEOPAN 2010, answer from 2 February 2011 to an information request of the author, percentage share own calculation; up to 10 October 2010.

The total volume of the signed contracts varies greatly. The highest amounts were signed in 2007 with nearly €9.7 billion. At central level the ups and downs are most remarkable, with significant cuts in the crisis years of 2008 and 2009, but also a rapid recovery in 2010. The total subscribed volume almost reached pre-Lehman levels (until October 2010).

Furthermore, a continuous increase at regional level since 2006 can be observed, which also slowed down because of the financial crisis. In contrast, at the local level the capital invested since 2005 almost continuously decreased, with an exception for 2007. At the level of regions (autonomous communities) Catalonia is the most active, as measured by the cumulative investment from 2003 to 2010, followed by Aragón, Valencia and Madrid (SEOPAN 2010). Table 9.3 breaks down the total number of concessions for the levels of government. Looking at the aggregate number of projects, the figures are falling since 2005. Given very high amounts of investment in 2007 and 2010, this means that there is a trend towards fewer but more capital-intensive projects.

Table 9.3 Signed concessions in Spain (number of projects and percentage share)

	2003	2004	2005	2006	2007	2008	2009	2010	Total
Central level	10 22.2%	–	4 4%	8 9.8%	13 22.8%	–	2 4.6%	1 3.0%	38 8.4%
Regional level	20 44.4%	18 62.1%	42 41.6%	26 31.7%	17 29.8%	21 35.0%	11 25.6%	15 45.5%	170 37.7%
Local level	15 33.3%	11 37.9%	55 54.4%	48 58.5%	27 47.4%	39 65.0%	30 69.8%	17 51.5%	242 53.7%
Total	45	29	101	82	57	60	43	33	450

Sources: Adapted from SEOPAN 2010, answer from 2 February 2011 to an information request, percentage share own calculation; up to 10 October 2010.

In order to assess whether and to what extent their debt share motivates the regions to use PPP concessions in the awarding of public contracts, hereinafter, the debt ratio of the regions of 2007 is correlated with aggregated project volume and the number of projects from 2003 to 2010 (Table 9.4). As the debt levels of the regions were not available for the entire period of 2003 to 2010, a single year – 2007 – has been selected that is approximately in the middle of the period.

The results show that there is a significant correlation between the level of debt and both the project value and the project number (2003–2010). The Pearson correlation between the debt ratio in 2007 and project volume from 2003 to 2010 is .518, significant at a level of .033 (Spearman's rho: .556*, N = 17). Furthermore, the Pearson correlation between the debt ratio in 2007 and aggregated project number of regions is even more evident. The coefficient is .612, the significance .009 (Spearman's rho: .493*, N = 17). Thus, in a bivariate correlation there is strong evidence that the regional debt level acts as an important driver of a region's inclination to PPP and concessions.

Table 9.4 Public debt and PPP concession value in Spanish regions

	Public debt (% of GDP)		PPP concessions 2003–2010	
Region	Mean 1995–2006	2007	Volume (€ m)	No.
Valencia	9.5	11.6	6 153.2	65
Galicia	8.5	6.9	1 500.9	22
Catalonia	8.5	7.5	10 642.2	80
Andalusia	7.6	5.0	1 620.7	59
Navarra	6.4	3.6	443.1	5
Extremadura	5.9	4.5	17.6	2
Madrid	5.2	5.4	5 903.4	53
Pais Vasco	4.8	1.0	231.0	17
Aragón	4.6	3.5	8 492.8	38
Asturias	4.3	3.2	99.0	9
Murcia	4.1	2.4	1 407.5	12
Baleares	4.0	6.9	2 389.5	15
Canarias	4.0	3.7	240.8	11
Castilla y León	3.3	3.3	2 355.8	32
Cantabria	3.3	3.3	269.3	5
Castilla – La Mancha	3.2	5.1	5 383.9	22
La Rioja	3.1	3.6	28.0	2
Mean	5.3	4.7	2 775.2	26

Sources: Adapted from http://politikon.es/entredatos/2011/12/14/cinco-graficas-sobre-la-deuda-de-comunidades-autonomas-y-ayuntamientos/ [10 February 2012]; SEOPAN 2010, up to October 2010.

9.3 GREECE

9.3.1 Institutional Context

Despite minor reforms, many aspects of the Greek political system resemble those of the UK (such as the strong position of the prime minister), thus providing a favourable institutional context for the implementation of the PPP approach. Despite a PR electoral system, the pre-crisis party system was dominated by a centre-left (Panhellenic Socialist Movement, PASOK) and a centre-right (Nea Dimokratia, ND) party, a constellation similar to Spain, with a PR system and small electoral districts. Institutional centralization is still high, especially in the field of public finances, despite Article 101 of the constitution which prescribes 'the principle of decentralization' for the public administration. Regional and local jurisdictions heavily depend on central subsidies, which in theory enable government institutions in Athens to financially steer from the centre. In practice the capacity for steering from the centre is limited due to some public sector pathologies such as weak performances of the bureaucracy and a high level of clientelism and corruption.

Similarly to in the UK, government and parliamentary majority are strongly intertwined. Constitutionally, a parliamentary mandate and a government position are not only compatible, but also frequently used. Extensive cross-memberships of parliamentarians with party and government positions are typical; about one third of the parliamentarians of the governing party hold permanent government positions. Articles 56 and 57 of the constitution enumerate a list of incompatibilities for members of parliament, but remain silent upon government positions. By such double and triple memberships, the government tries to control the parliamentary behaviour of the majority party by opening up (or closing) career opportunities (Zervakis/Auernheimer 2009: 830). Similar to the UK, the power of appointments is a strong disciplinary instrument in the hand of the government, especially in those of the prime minister.

The cabinet (ministerial council) is dominated by the prime minister. Whereas constitutionally the cabinet should act 'collegially', in practice powers of the prime minister such as the setting of guidelines for cabinet decision making and the right to 'hire and fire' ministers have contributed to the predominance of the prime minister in cabinet. Similar to the UK, the cabinet is usually not the central decision-making body, rather it has to legitimize the decisions drawn beforehand by the prime minister (and special cabinet committees) ,or settle conflicts between ministries. Much more important for decision making are the subject-related cabinet committees, comprising the prime minister and a few ministers with their leading officials (ibid.: 834).

As in the UK, the transfer of decision making from cabinet as a whole to more specialized subcommittees can enhance the potential for policy changes. It reduces the potential veto power from other actors and thus strengthens the capability of the prime minister within his or her cabinet to shift policies. Once the prime minister or a minister has made up his or her mind in favour of a policy change and got it through the cabinet committee, he or she does not have to fear much resistance – neither from the whole cabinet nor from the parliamentary majority, which is usually closely tied to the government. Furthermore, on the basis of a transfer of 'executive' competences from parliament to government, the Greek government is allowed to pass encompassing statutory orders without assent of parliament. Thus, this 'Westminster style' of government–parliament relations in Greece can (in theory) contribute to quick policy changes – as for instance the adoption of the PPP approach.

In contrast to the compatibility of parliamentary and governmental positions, there are strict regulations on the incompatibility of public offices (such as mayors and heads of public utilities) with a parliamentary mandate. This led to a high share of self-employed professionals such as lawyers, doctors and engineers in parliament. In contrast to Germany with its guaranteed right of civil servants to return to civil service after their mandate expired, the share of officials in the Greek parliament has been much lower. However, in 2001 a constitutional reform expanded the incompatibility rules also to the private sector, now banning every kind of professional double or side activities. This made a parliamentary mandate on the one hand less attractive, especially for the self-employed professionals who used to privately gain from the synergies of their mandate, leading on the other hand to a drive towards parliamentary professionalization with better pay and more staff and resources (ibid.: 826).

The high share of self-employed from the private sector in the Greek parliament also is a contrast to parliaments in France and Germany, which have a higher share of public sector employees (maybe with a classical 'public sector ethos'). Differences in the professional structure of these parliaments might also be a supportive factor for contested policies such as PPP. Parliaments with a lower share of public sector employees might be easier to 'convince' by the PPP proponents. Whereas the judicial political culture in Germany provides an example of a parliament strongly recruited from the public sector, Greece and also the Anglo-Saxon countries provide examples of parliaments where a greater proportion of the parliamentarians have been recruited from the private sector. Furthermore, tax evasion has always been a problem, especially among the high share (about 25 per cent) of self-employed. With the courts being chronically overburdened, legal security and law enforcement have been typically weak.

In contrast to the other southern European crisis states, consensus among the different party elites in order to overcome the difficulties was reached very late and only under massive international pressure for domestic reforms. Typical for a 'Westminster style' of political culture, policy making usually was adversarial and regarded as a zero-sum game by the political elites. Gains for one side were seen as losses for the other. Seeking cross-party cooperation even on fundamental issues was rather uncommon. Given this confrontational style of policy making in the 'old' party system, it was very difficult to reach necessary majorities for austerity measures and crisis management in general. In the course of the political crisis, trust in the 'old' parties and elites eroded and new, more radical (sounding) parties gained large support.

9.3.2 Socioeconomic Background

Much could be said about the socioeconomic conditions in Greece in the last decade. However, with the focus on the 1990s up to 2009 in this study, the later monetary turbulences cannot be covered in detail. In general, the socioeconomic dynamic can be characterized as a struggle between a traditional culture of securing the (individual) status quo and a pressure for modernization, quite often induced by European integration in relation to European and international institutions. Much of the 'social closure' in socioeconomic relations and the reluctance towards higher levels of competition can be explained by historical experiences such as the military rule from 1967 to 1974 and the location as a country on the European periphery. In contrast to Portugal and Spain with a similar context, clientelist relations remained very influential and undermined the professionalism of the political, administrative and economic elites. Additionally, up to the mid-1990s, politics was strongly influenced by 'charismatic' leadership such as that of Konstantinos Karamanlis (ND) or Andreas Papandreou (PASOK) (Auernheimer 2003).

Due to lack of professionalism, administrative capacity has hardly been used for reforming the economy; political and economic elites (and their decision making) were tightly intertwined. A need for a privatization policy and a reduction of the huge public sector was (and still is) hardly acknowledged. Instead, the oversized public sector provided lots of opportunities for party elites from both sides for 'networking' and clientelism. Public corporations were highly open to political influence due to such networks and could not operate efficiently according to European standards. Impulses for structural reforms did not emerge through 'intrinsic motivation' within the political elites, but only from outside stimuli such as the European Community membership in 1981 and the push for Eurozone membership (realized in 2001). 'Europeanization' (as well as efficiency arguments) was also used to characterize the two waves of local government reform, namely the 'amalgamations' of municipalities in 1998 and 2008–2009 (Hlepas 2010).

Part of the problem that had to be addressed in the course of the financial crisis commencing in 2008 was the unreliability of statistical data used as a basis of Greek and EU decision making. Only in

2010–2011 was this problem addressed, by setting up an independent statistical agency (Elstat) headed by a former Greek IMF official. However, this measure was imposed by the EU and IMF as a condition of the €110 billion bailout in 2009. The new Elstat head was heavily criticized by Elstat's union and its board of directors for their loss of influence. According to a former statistical official, 'It seems that board members wanted to go back to the old days when officials from the finance ministry and the central bank got together to produce figures that served the national interest, regardless of accuracy' (Financial Times 2011: 7).

Among these statistical figures, long-term public debt and annual budget deficit have drawn most attention since the global financial crisis. The 15 per cent deficit figure of 2009 in particular pushed Greece's political elites to seek an EU/IMF bailout. A factor that contributed to low GDP and competitiveness has been the large share of 'closed professions' such as taxi drivers, welders and speech therapists (Fuster 2011b). Protective mechanisms such as closed professions were initially aimed at enabling the self-employed more security, especially in their older years. In fact, they raised wages and lowered competition and productivity in the respective sectors and thus contributed to the economic malaise.

Consequently, the troikas' austerity and reform packages (especially in February 2012) aimed at achieving higher flexibility in the labour market, reducing labour costs and thus improving the competitiveness of the Greek economy. Among other measures, monthly minimum wages were cut by 22 per cent to €568 and the right to free collective bargaining was suspended. Depending on the sector, in 2012 wages were cut between 10 and 20 per cent. However, while labour costs had been significantly reduced, firms were still reluctant to take on new staff.

9.3.3 PPP Politics

Given the small size of the economy, Greece has been one of the big players in the field of PPP in Western Europe. In terms of the approaches of the different government parties, the PASOK approach until their loss of power in 2004 can be characterized as pragmatic with regard to EU funding, while the ND approach after 2005 is best characterized as substantive support for PPP similar to that under the Sarkozy presidency in France. While already experimenting in the late 1990s with PPP to bypass deficient state bureaucracy and more efficiently adopt EU programmes for local and regional needs, the institutional breakthrough came in 2005 with a PPP law and the setting up of an inter-ministerial committee along with a special secretariat by the Karamanlis (ND) cabinet. As shown in Chapter 3, Greece's PPP investment volume in relation to the size of its public sector investments ranked 3 (behind Portugal and in front of Spain) among the 14 countries investigated.

As early as the beginning of the 1990s, public–private cooperation had been used in Greece as a tool of economic development. This took place in the context of the Community Support Framework (CSF) programmes in regional policy, which commenced in 1989. Under the CSF, EU Structural and Cohesion Funds were used in national programmes, this being supported by the preference to improve the poor conditions of infrastructure in the country compared to other cohesion countries such as Ireland and Portugal, which were doing, or had already done, more (Paraskevopoulos et al. 2009: 237).

In practice, the impression was that the first CSF funds, which had been split up into many small, local projects across the country, may have had greater impact if they were concentrated in large infrastructure projects. Nevertheless, in the second and in the third round of the CSF the issues of transparency and efficiency gained decisively more influence in the planning and implementation processes (ibid.). In fact, the funding priorities shifted towards larger projects, which should achieve clearly visible results in improving the infrastructure. This was accompanied by a recentralization of the policy making in the Ministry of National Economy and its associated agencies.

In the second and third rounds of the CSF (from 1994 and 2000 onwards) a general increase in private sector participation in the projects and, at the national level, an enlargement of the projects themselves had been achieved (ibid.: 238). In the course of the CSF, a joint steering committee in the Ministry of Economics was founded (in 1995), which in particular was in charge of promoting PPP (ibid.: 240).

Major infrastructure projects such as Athens International Airport in Spata, the Rion–Antirion bridge and the Essi highway (Athens ring road) were performed on a PPP basis. The Greek PPP programme was subsequently expanded and included, in 2004, the expansion of the motorway network with the help of PPP-type financial instruments (EIB 2004: 6). A year later, in September 2005, a PPP law was passed that implemented the relevant EU directives on public procurement (including Directives 2000/52/EC and 2004/18/EC) (EPPPR 2007: 138).

The Greek PPP law was passed in the same month as the German PPP Acceleration Law. Chamakou (2011) has compared the differences between the German and the Greek PPP law. For example, the German law is merely an 'omnibus law', changing paragraphs in a range of existing laws to remove obstacles and ambiguities concerning PPPs. The

Greek law, however, is a general law, which introduces a legal definition of PPP. The Greek PPP law aimed to establish a comprehensive framework for PPP, eliminate existing legal uncertainties and further promote the development of PPP in Greece (ibid.: 213).

However, the Greek law only covers contract-based models, not permanent, institutional collaboration, something that Chamakou (2011: 179) interpreted as a shortcoming. Another Greek limitation is given in Article 2 with the restriction of the act to projects with maximum costs of €200 million (excluding VAT). Thus, a lot of large-scale projects were directly ruled by government legislation. Regarding the tendering process, a task force, the Special Secretariat in the Ministry of Economy and Finance, can choose between the four common variants: the open and the restricted procedure, the competitive dialogue and negotiated procedures. According to EPPPR (2009: 56), only the restricted procedure has been used so far. In selecting the private partner, characteristics such as reliability, performance and expertise (Chamakou 2011: 181) are to be considered. Both the invitations to tender and project agreements are highly standardized (EPPPR 2009: 56).

Furthermore, the Greek public law cannot be applied to the contract after contracting (Article 17 of the PPP law). It merely allows applying the contractual provisions themselves and the Code Civil. In other words, after contracting, certain obligations and bonds of public administration arising from the public law cannot be applied any longer (Chamakou 2011: 183). To avoid gaps, the contract must cover certain minimum requirements of the partnership, such as contract duration, payment and financing issues, risk issues and control rights. Another special feature of the law is the exclusion of the Greek public jurisdiction and its replacement by arbitration in disputes. This is legitimized by the long duration of ordinary trials and by the lack of expertise of the judges in the often complex issues. In particular, the often very long process time would deter private investors from a PPP (ibid.: 186).

According to Article 31 of the Greek PPP law, the contract has to list all necessary elements regarding the conduct of the arbitration proceedings, such as the appointment of arbitrators, the applicable arbitration rules, the place of arbitration, the remuneration of the referee and the language to be used (ibid.: 187). In addition to these procedural regulations it is also likely that tax regulations contribute to the attractiveness of PPPs to Greek politics and private investors. Thus, the PPP entities are free from corporate tax on accrued interest collected from the start of the operational phase. Furthermore, the financial contributions of the public partner for project financing are completely exempt (ibid.: 191). However, the Act does not include provisions for efficiency studies (public sector comparator) and regulations to secure the influence and oversight of the public partner. According to Chamakou (2011: 215), the law should stipulate that the public sector must have sufficient influence, steering and control rights with regard to the fulfilment of the public tasks.

The Greek Special Secretariat resembles the structure and functions of other European task forces. Its overall mission is to support the Inter-Ministerial PPP Committee in the development of appropriate policies and public institutions in the use of PPPs. More specifically, its job is to identify tasks and services that are eligible for execution as a PPP, and to generally promote works and services through partnership models. Proposals of public institutions for projects viable as PPPs will be evaluated in advance and then forwarded to the Inter-Ministerial PPP Committee. Other tasks include the support of public institutions in procurement procedures and in the selection of private partners under the Law 3389/2005, as well as monitoring the implementation of partnership agreements (www.sdit.mnec.gr/en/sdit/sdit).

Article 3 of the PPP law regulates the composition and duties of the Joint Ministerial Committee. Its overall mission is to implement the government's policy on the participation of private capital for public works and services. The committee is composed of the Minister of Economy and Finance, the Minister of Development and the Minister for Environment, Planning and Public Works as full members and those ministers responsible for the participating public institution as special members. The Minister of Economic and Finance chairs the meetings and forwards the assessed proposals of the Special Secretariat to the Committee. The Committee then makes the final decision on the proposed project. 'Since March 2006, 34 public private partnership projects worth EUR 4 billion have been approved' (OECD 2010: 101).

While many of the small- and medium-scale projects such as parking facilities or marinas were subject to the PPP law, large-scale projects (especially in the transport sector) were directly regulated by a government act. Roumboutsos (2013: 112) distinguished two waves of large-scale projects, with the first including Athens International Airport, the Athens ring road (Attica tollway) and the Rion–Antirion bridge, all tendered in the late 1990s. The second wave of projects was awarded between 2007 and 2008 and 'included the so called "axis of development" motorways. These were the Maliakos–Kleidi Motorway (Aegean Motorways); the Elefsina–Corinth–Patra–Tsakona Motorway (Olympia Odos); the Antirio–Ioannina Motorway (Ionia Odos); the Central Greece Motorway (E65 motorway) and the Corinth–Tripoli–Kalamata Motorway (Moreas)' as well as the port of Piraeus transhipment terminal concession. Some planned projects in this period also failed, for example the Thessaloniki Metro, the port of Thessaloniki container terminal and the tunnel of Maliakos. 'In short, most large-scale transport projects in Greece over the last two decades have been delivered through a PPP-type model', meaning that PPPs in Greece constitute a significant share of the GDP (ibid.).

In 2008 the government proposed a PPP programme mainly for the development of social infrastructures, with a value of over €5 billion. The first project in this programme (fire stations) was signed in April 2009. Two more reached the stage of preferred bidder up to mid-2009. The Special Secretariat is said to have gained considerable credibility and experience and had a lot of projects 'in the pipeline'. As part of the favourable conditions in Greece, PPPs have not yet suffered from legal actions regarding the procurement procedure, although issues at courts due to procurement decisions in conventional procedures are not uncommon (EPPPR 2009: 55).

In terms of partisanship, both big parties supported PPP, but with different slants. Konstantinos Simitis (who studied law in Germany) began the restructuring of PASOK after he took over leadership in 1996. His ambition was to modernize the party's organization and programme and open it to centre(-left) policy positions, inspired by similar strategies pursued by New Labour in the UK and the Social Democrats in Germany. As a reference to New Labour, the modernizers around Simitis called themselves 'New PASOK' (Georgiadou 2002: 597). Prior to the general election of September 1996, Simitis had been regarded within the party as the only candidate who could yield a victory for PASOK. Eventually, he was elected party leader, despite lacking the support of left-wingers. Simitis was elected as prime minister twice with support of the middle class. Electoral losses of support from the working class in 1996 had been rebalanced in 2000.

Table 9.5 summarizes PPP activities and government majorities. As can easily be seen, PPP had already been used by the PASOK Papandreou III cabinet. Both Simitis cabinets intensified their support for infrastructure PPP, but without setting new incentives. In these early stages, the main motives were to mediate and efficiently distribute EU funds to infrastructure projects at local and regional level. This corresponded with the policy priority of both Simitis cabinets to push for Greek integration into the Eurozone (ibid.). At the organizational level the party had been much more sluggish: some modernizing reforms after 1996 soon lost support and Simitis had to return to an 'anti-right-wing rhetoric' in order to appease the left-wingers in his party (ibid.: 604). Thus, contrarily to New Labour in the UK, Simitis lost much of the middle class support during his second term as prime minister.

After a change in government in 2004, the new Karamanlis (ND) cabinet started a new phase of the PPP approach by, for example, introducing the PPP law, which was passed by parliament in September 2005. This indicates that PPP now not only reached its highest level of support but also found broader, more systematic support at government level. Furthermore, after the global financial crisis of 2008, the use of PPP soon gained pace again. Thus, it can be said that there has been cross-party support for the PPP policy during the investigation period. While under the Simitis cabinets the policy was transferred and applied at national level, especially in the context of EU projects, the conservative Karamanlis cabinet institutionally broadened their approach by passing the PPP law, which set up the Inter-Ministerial PPP Committee and the Special Secretariat, and by initiating the 'second wave' of large-scale projects.

Table 9.5 Greek governments and PPP actions 1990–2009

Years	Cabinet	Party	PPP action
04/1990–10/1993	Mitsotakis	ND	–
10/1993–01/1996	Papandreou III	PASOK	1994: CSF adopted PPP 1995: Joint steering committee founded to promote PPP
01/1996–04/2000	Simitis I	PASOK	Intensified use of PPP for EU cofounded infrastructure projects
04/2000–03/2004	Simitis II	PASOK	Intensified use of PPP for EU cofounded infrastructure projects
03/2004–09/2007	Karamanlis I	ND	09/2005: PPP law passed; set up of Task Force (Special Secretariat) and Inter-Ministerial PPP Committee
09/2007–10/2009	Karamanlis II	ND	Political support for the use of PPP 'Second wave' (2007–2008) of large-scale PPP projects

Source: Own compilation.

9.4 CASE COMPARISON

9.4.1 General Characteristics

Portugal, Spain and Greece are three highly active PPP states with some similarities, but also having different pathways and motivations. Portugal and Spain have deployed different styles of PPP policy, but both have developed high levels of activity. Whereas the Portuguese government was convinced of the PPP approach in public procurement and service delivery as early as the mid-1990s, the Spanish government was more of a latecomer. Furthermore, while Portugal centrally pushed its PPP politics, Spain preferred a 'hands off' approach, relying on private initiative and interest groups to start PPP activity. Consequently, Spain is the only case in this group without a public PPP unit at central level. Also, a standard contract and a PPP law do not exist.

In both Spain and Portugal, PPP played a major role in modernizing road infrastructure and supporting the construction sector. However, there are also differences. In Portugal, bypassing budget constraints and improving service quality were major motivations of policy makers at the early stages of implementing PPP. In Greece, in the late 1990s, besides budgetary concerns, the implementation of EU funds into local and regional projects was a major motivation. In contrast, the more 'passive' approach in Spain at central level suggests that budgetary concerns (Eurozone membership) have been less important. Instead, the PPP approach was seen as an instrument supporting the domestic construction sector. This is understandable against the background of an economic boom driven by the real estate sector and immigration, only stopped by the global financial crisis in 2008. In other words, due to its economic success up to 2007, Spanish governments did not have the need to actively push for higher levels of private capital involvement. Most of the supporting measures that we found for Portugal and Greece (but also in a lot of other cases like UK, France and Italy) were not practices in Spain. With these features of a high level of PPP activity despite a lack of active institutionalization, Spain is a unique case in our sample of 14.

Regarding institutional features, all three political systems have a tendency towards a two party system and a low number of partisan veto players at government level. Similar to the UK before 2010, small parties as coalition partners were usually not needed and therefore had no power over a change of government policy. Despite the two major parties regularly alternating in office, the support of PPP was continuously given and a fundamental consensus on PPP has always been in place. In Spain, party politics was the most neutral towards PPP, whereas in Portugal the Socialists (PS) in government and in Greece the conservatives (ND) had a more supportive policy towards PPP. A pluralistic system of interest groups, as found in all three cases, has proved to be supportive, too. Particularly in Portugal and Greece, clientelism between politicians and local and regional companies is widespread and has for instance important functions for party financing. In Portugal in particular, as with ordinary procurement contracts, PPPs were utilized as a means of strengthening local and regional 'support' (in a wider sense) for government parties. There, the absence of a public sector comparator and other *ex ante* evaluation tools contributed to the popularity of PPP as a means of political clientelism.

Portugal and Greece share some institutional features and socio-economic backgrounds which can be seen as very supportive for the PPP approach. Similar to the UK, they have a highly centralized administration with Lisbon and Athens being what 'London' is for UK politics. Once policy makers are convinced of a new policy, it is easy to implement it in such strongly centralized systems. In terms of fiscal centralization, Portugal and Greece even top the UK. Thus, central government has all the financial means to set incentives or even to use some forms of soft coercion to 'convince' regional and local policy makers of the advantages of a policy change.

Furthermore, all three countries have similar economic problems, with low international competitiveness and a relatively inflexible labour market. As a consequence, unemployment rates are high, especially for the younger people. Whereas Spain has been most severely hit by, for example, unemployment, but has managed to tackle its economic problems, in Greece economic and financial problems are intertwined with an ineffective and oversized public sector.

In terms of administrative and legislative centralization, the case of Spain is different. With 17 autonomous communities, Spain is a strongly decentralized unitary state; some even call it a federal state. In this regard, the Spanish polity resembles more the German case than the British one. Consequently, in terms of policy making, governments in Madrid less actively supported the use of the PPP approach than those in Porto and Athens. They preferred a 'bottom-up' approach, with the initiative left to the private sector or the regional and local governments, while central government preferred to adjust some legal frameworks. As a share of investment volumes, regional and local governments were predominant.

The structure of Greece's political institutions resembles that of the UK. Once a decision for a policy change is made, the centralized state structure in theory offers good opportunities for implementation. In contrast to the UK, the low-efficiency Greek bureaucracy has to be considered a limiting factor. At executive level, PPP was also seen as an opportunity to bypass inefficient administrative structures (without a need to initiate major administrative reforms) by incorporating the competences and expertise of the private sector. In Greece, politicians also regarded PPP as a tool to bypass inefficient bureaucratic structures, for example in implementing EU (co-)financed projects. Against this background of a significantly oversized and semi-qualified public administration, Greece politicians were keen to 'bypass' public line management, especially in prestigious projects such as the Olympic Games of 2004. In this case the authorities did not rely on established, time-honoured line management, but successfully set up new management structures.

Furthermore, given the high level of public debts and deficits, PPP also appears a promising way of bypassing budget constraints imposed by the EU with the aim of attaining Eurozone membership in the late 1990s. As tested in Chapter 3, it is not the overall debt level as a share of GDP that correlates with higher PPP activity but the annual budget deficit. This openness for the 'creative' use of complex financial instruments has also been applied in other cases in the context of the Greek Eurozone accession in 2001. Together with Goldman Sachs, the Greek government constructed special currency swaps that enabled a billion Euro credit to be kept out of deficit statistics (FAZ 2012: 14). In general, a high degree of fiscal centralization, as found in Greece, can be helpful in implementing a policy change at local level. Also, the high level of clientelism and corruption may have contributed to the popularity of PPP among Greek and Portuguese policy makers. For entering the Eurozone, financial instruments that helped to camouflage the real situation were popular, aiming to redress budget data by, for example, disguising credits as currency swaps – not a nice environment for the PPP approach.

9.4.2 Impact of the Global Financial Crisis

With the exception of Ireland, this group samples the countries that suffered most under the global financial crisis. Factors such as the squeeze on liquidity in the banking sector were especially acute in the smaller, low-income countries of the southern periphery (as well are in Ireland despite its healthy pre-crisis public finances). Together with the private (and public) financial liquidity needed for a PPP, the trust in the instrument in general had suffered. Private banks were more selective and reluctant to support PPP projects due to financial and political insecurities, and politicians were more sceptical due to higher risks for successful project management. In addition, operational PPPs came under pressure from several sides. At the political level, a change in government such as in the UK in 2010, Germany in 2009, Italy in 2011, Portugal in 2011, Greece in 2009 and Spain in 2011 led to shifting priorities and reduced support. Pro-PPP governments such as the Sócrates administration in Portugal, ND in Greece, New Labour in the UK and the Social Democrats in Germany lost power and offices.

Furthermore, while the interest rates for private borrowing soared tremendously, government (or public) borrowing was still relatively cheap. In combination with a preference of many governments for more direct steering, this led to the revival of classical economic stimulus programmes such as for instance the car scrapping scheme in the UK and Germany. PPP still had some government support, but the priorities clearly shifted. With the exception of some cases under the Sarkozy presidency in France, government support for large-scale projects belonged to the past. This was particularly noticeable in the roads and railways sectors, where high investment volumes are easily reached.

At the street level, toll roads in Spain and Portugal, but also in France, came under pressure, as car users were more reluctant to spend their money for road use. Other models based on user fees faced similar problems. This brought trouble for the concessioners, as the toll revenues stayed far below the expected level. Against this background, private companies and lobby groups were pressing for 'state guarantees', but with limited success (see section 2.3). Additionally, private lenders became reluctant to finance new projects based on user fees. In Greece, four of the five motorways awarded in 2007 and 2008 were obliged to stop works and enter into a period of renegotiation with the government after lenders imposed a 'drawstop'. 'In April 2013, the government announced the terms of agreement which included an increase of public financial contribution, a decrease in scope, and the payment of claims' (Roumboutsos 2013: 114). Furthermore, the crisis accelerated the 'brain drain' of engineers and other specialized workers to other, less affected regions or countries. In Greece, but also in Spain and Portugal, the construction sector had to cope with such losses. In Greece, from 2009 no new projects had been added to the 'pipeline' of PPP projects with a construction budget of less than €200 million (as managed by the Special Secretariat under the PPP law of 2005) (ibid.).

Compared to Greece and Spain, Portugal was the most compliant and inconspicuous among the troubled peripheral countries, being

> not mendacious and profligate like Greece; it did not recklessly run a low-tax economic model off the rails like Ireland; it has not lived off dodgy Russian

> money like Cyprus; and it did not permit a runaway property boom like Spain. Instead Portugal was a chronic underachiever, suffering from years of low growth. (Economist 2013: 30)

In this context of low growth and a relative inflexible economy it can also be compared with Italy, but lacking the Italian 'self-indulgent public debt and bunga-bunga parties. And since its rescue, Portugal has been most devout in repentance. Both the ruling centre-right party [...] and the opposition Socialists embraced salvation through austerity and structural reforms' (ibid.).

The problem of austerity had been on the agenda at least since the Euro accession sought by all three governments. After accession in 1998/99 (Greece in 2001), the 'golden decade' from 1998 to 2008 is characterized by relatively comfortable refinancing conditions. The 2008 crisis raised again questions of creditors' confidence, banking solvency, structural reforms and austerity measures. The policies of coping with these challenges are not under investigation in this study; however, it is obvious that Portugal and Ireland have adapted best to the new circumstances, whereas Greece's problems have evolved slowly into a 'never ending story'.

The Greek private banking sector is, comparatively, not very integrated into the global financial system, which reduced its vulnerability during the course of the global financial crisis. However, on the other side of the coin, the high amount of Greek bonds in the banks' portfolios made them much more vulnerable to a possible state insolvency. Furthermore, Greek banks acted carefully with regard to the new products of investment banking. Consequently, the level of 'toxic credits' at the beginning of the crisis in 2008 was relatively low. With the high amount of Greek bonds in the portfolio, the main problem for Greek banks was the possible insolvency of the state.

Thus, the development of the banks became closely intertwined with those of the state. The refinancing of the banking sector shifted completely from the interbank market to the ECB and emergency mechanisms of the Greek Central Bank. Among others, such as the withdrawal of private money from the Greek banks, a major consequence has been a pressure for mergers across the banking system (Fuster 2011a: 8). With regard to PPP, the main consequence of the crisis has been the drying up of private money for PPP projects. And with the melting away of acceptable securities, public lenders such as the EIB became more reluctant, too.

The 2008 crisis and its aftermath have had a severe impact on Portugal's and Greece's PPP policy, less on the Spanish one. More rigid, the new Portuguese Coelho cabinet announced and conducted a complete overhaul of its PPP projects and tried to reduce costs by renegotiation. A similar policy was deployed in the UK after the Conservative–Liberal Democrat coalition took over in 2010 and rebranded PFI as PF2. In our sample of 14, Portugal and the UK are not only among the most active PPP countries, both are also the only ones who announced a fundamental review of the government's PPP programme and of already operational as well planned projects, in both cases initiated by centre-right governments.

In contrast to the renegotiation approach of the Coelho government, the incoming Spanish Rajoy cabinet opted for a 'hands off' approach, which led to the bankruptcy of several toll road highway concessionaires in 2012 as the government refused to offer a bailout. This reluctance can be explained by the austerity measures imposed on Spain and the government's ambition to rely on the European rescue fund only for its banks, thus avoiding further downgrading its international credit ratings. Furthermore, the Rajoy cabinet initiated a policy transfer of economic policies applied in Germany. 'From the moment the Rajoy government took office in late 2011, it has made a conscious effort to replicate some of the strategies that helped Germany overcome its own recession a decade ago, including labour market reform and a strong focus on export growth and competitiveness' (Buck 2013: 3)

In Greece, the social and political support for PPP has been high until recently, even following changes in governments. 'For example, both waves of transport PPPs have been implemented under changing government offices. In addition, any opposition registered to date focused on environmental or similar social stakeholder issues, which are independent of the procurement method or model' (Roumboutsos 2013: 112). It is only recently, in the face of rising transportation costs, that protest movements formed to signal the unwillingness 'to pay tolls and other contributions to social services' (ibid.). This contrasts sharply to the level of acceptance of PPP in the Nordic countries, leading up to the construction of regional patterns of PPP scepticism in the north and PPP support in the south of Europe. However, the prevalence of PPP in the south should not be seen as a driver of the fiscal crisis; rather, both have similar causes such as inefficient bureaucracies and a tendency to avoid austerity or profound reform measures. Furthermore, the historical use of concessions in Spain and Portugal (as well as in France) can contribute to explain the prevalence of PPP in the south-east and south-west of the continent.

NOTES

1. SCUT means 'sem cobrança ao utilizador' (without direct user costs).
2. Brisa operates 11 highways with a length totaling around 1100 km. The company was founded in 1972 with the task to build and operate toll motorways. In a first concession contract it was agreed that until the end of 1981 around 390 km of highway should be built. However, up to 1986 the first highway, the A1 between Lisbon and Porto, still was not finished (see Schumann 2004: 2). In 1983 Brisa operated 158 km of highway, in 2002 1000 km (www.brisa.pt [12 October 2012]).
3. See www.estradasdeportugal.pt. EP is a shareholder company owned by the government and supervised by the Ministry of Finance. Its task is financing, maintenance, operation and widening of existing roads was well as conception, planning, construction and financing of new roads. These tasks were transferred to EP in November 2007 through a concession contract for 75 years on the legal basis of Decreto-law No. 380/2007 from 13 November. EP is a successor of the agency for road administration.
4. www.parpublicasgps.com/index.php?option=com_content&view=article&id=100&Itemid=97 [18 July 2012].
5. The group sees one of its main tasks as assisting the Spanish construction industry abroad and as attracting foreign orders (http://www.seopan.es/quienes-somos.php?Opcion=0 [15 October 2015].)

10. Conclusion

10.1 COMPARING SOCIOECONOMIC FACTORS

In this section, the focus is on some concluding remarks regarding the tested socioeconomic variables. It would be too easy as a conclusion to simply point at the results of the empirical third chapter and emphasize the role of interest groups pluralism (also an institutional factor) and the size of the financial sector. However, the size of the financial sector and probably also the size of the construction sector do play a role in the adoption of a high level of PPP activity in a national economy (together with the structure of interest groups). However, these tested variables are only a small part of a broader range of factors that might influence a policy change in favour of PPP. And from the perspective of political economy (Hare 2013), the roles of the financial and the construction sector are among the ones intensely debated.

Other factors such as the efficiency or effectiveness ('value for money') of PPPs were not taken into consideration in this study, as this would require a completely different research design. From the perspective of comparative public policy, this would, for instance, require an examination of how PPP is capable of delivering government objectives and public services in different areas, such as transport infrastructure, health or prisons, across international borders. The positive result for the financial sector in Chapter 3 suggests that such policy-specific differences are less crucial for the adoption of PPP than the size of the financial sector.

The impact of the global financial crisis on PPP has been analysed in two chapters: first in general in Chapter 2 (section 2.3), then specifically for the cases of Portugal, Spain and Greece in Chapter 9 (section 9.4.2). The impact of the lack of liquidity on the use of PPP in these countries was severe. This illustrates the crucial role of what is probably the most important private resource: money. Without sufficient provision of short-term private money, no project is going to reach 'financial close'. From the perspective of the private sector, it is basically money that matters (and from the perspective of the public purse, too). Focusing on the impact of the global financial crisis is instructive also in other regards: it shows changing patterns in the sharing of risks between the public and private partner; and it shows different kinds of reactions of governments, from a 'no-bailout' policy to a subtle accommodation of the problems of the private corporations, as can be seen in Spain and Portugal. For instance, the initially toll free SCUT highways in Portugal have been chargeable since 2011.

As could be shown in the chapters above, for the concrete adoption of the PPP approach, socioeconomic factors did matter in a range of countries. However, they have to be seen in a broader context of political and institutional factors. As we have seen among the tested variables in Chapter 3, the structure of interest groups highly correlates with the level of PPP activity. In contrast to the size of the financial sector, the influence of the annual (average) budget deficit (or surplus) turned out to play a much weaker role, if at all. This is somewhat surprising, as in the theoretical literature, avoiding running further into debt is discussed as one of the major motivations for the political actions of PPP supporters. Also, the GDP per capita as an indicator of wealth turned out to be not relevant in this sample of 14. This is partly due to the role of the UK (and also Ireland), which has both a high GDP and a high level of PPP/PFI activity. However, a bigger sample or a different case selection might lead to a 'better' result for the GDP variable.

10.2 COMPARING POLITICAL AND INSTITUTIONAL FACTORS

Politics matters, but though this appears obvious at first sight, it is not that easy. According to Chapter 3, the number of partisan veto players at cabinet level is the most influential variable in the case of a policy change favouring PPP. This is quite understandable, as with each additional coalition partner, the potential for bargaining, compromises and even blackmailing, at least theoretically, rises. The institutional analysis done in Chapter 3 only focused on one aspect of the veto player theory as designed by Tsebelis (2002): the number of government parties; in the case studies, the internal cohesion of parties has also been focused on to a certain degree as we were looking for opposition towards PPP, too. Surprisingly, in cases of highly active countries like Greece, Portugal, and to a certain degree, the UK, there was no or only weak opposition against the use of PPP as a public policy tool.

In terms of party politics, there is no obvious left–right pattern of support or opposition across our sample. The UK and Germany are examples where (modernizing) centre-left parties have been committed to

PPP; however, Social Democrats in the Nordic countries shied away from this policy tool. In contrast, in southern Europe it was more the conservative or centre-right parties that demonstrated stronger support for PPP. In contrast to Germany, Austria was the 'first' southern case (from a northern perspective) where a People's Party (Schüssel cabinets) became supportive of PPP. In most countries of the southern periphery, conservative (i.e. centre-right) parties supported PPP most strongly, examples being the Berlusconi cabinets in Italy and the Karamanlis cabinets in Greece. However, in Portugal under Socrates (2005–2011) and in Spain under Zapatero (2001–2008), centre-left governments supported PPP at national level. Taking into consideration also the British and the German experiences, PPP seems to be rather 'neutral' in terms of partisanship. Thus, in contrast to the number of veto players at governmental level, partisanship does not significantly contribute to a high level PPP activity across the whole sample. However, it seems that in some cases (the UK, Germany, the Netherlands, Portugal) modernizing centre-left cabinets were more supportive of PPP, while in some southern European cases centre-right cabinets were more supportive (Austria, France, Italy, Greece). Table 10.1 tries to summarize the governments, as well as their formats, with the most active PPP policy.

Table 10.2 goes more into detail as to what cabinets have done to institutionally support the use of PPP. Again, we link the action and time with the specific cabinet in the respective country. The focus is only on institutionalization, such as the passing of a PPP law or the setting up of a task force or specialized unit, not on the support of individual, large-scale projects. The scope of institutional activity should, however, not be used as an indicator of the PPP activity in general. For example, in Greece the only major step of institutionalization was the passing of the PPP law in 2005 (which also set up the Special Secretariat and the Inter-Ministerial Committee), but this helped Greece to become one of the 'big players' in terms of PPP in the following years up to the global financial crisis. A similar situation of low institutionalization activity and high PPP project outcome is found in Spain and Portugal. In contrast, in the UK a high level of institutionalization is found in combination with a high level of project outcome. These contrasting patterns again illustrate the shortcomings of focusing only on a single factor such as 'institutionalization' in order to explain the level of project outcome.

Table 10.1 Central governments with strongest support for PPP politics

Country	Government	Government format(s)	Parties	Years
AT	Schüssel	Two party coalition	ÖVP/BZÖ ÖVP/FPÖ	2000–2006
DE	Schröder	Two party coalition	SPD/B'90 & Greens	1998–2002 2002–2005
EL	Karamalis	Single party	Nea Dimokratia	2004–2008
ES	Aznar Zapatero	Single party	PP PSOE	1996–2000 2001–2008
FI	Vanhanen	Four and five party coalitions	Centrum et al.	2003–2011
FR	Sarkozy/ Fillon	Single party	UMP	2009–2011
IE	Ahern	Single party minority and two-party coalitions	Fianna Fáil et al.	1997–2008
IT	Berlusconi	Two- and multi-party coalitions	Forza Italia et al.	2001–2008
PT	Barroso Socrates	Two party coalition Single party	PSD/CDS-PP PS	2002–2004 2005–2011
SE	Bildt Reinfeldt	Minority government Four party coalition	Moderates et al. Moderates et al.	1993–1994 2006–2010
UK	Blair Brown	Single party Single party	New Labour New Labour	1997–2008 2008–2010

Source: Own compilation.

Table 10.2 Comparison of institutionalization of PPP in Western Europe

	Year	Act/measure	Government
AT	2006	Planned competence centre not realized	Schüssel II (ÖVP)
BE	07/2002	Flemish PPP competence centre	Flem. Gov. (Dewael, VLD)
	06/2003	Flemish PPP Act	Flem. Gov. (Dewael, VLD)
	11/2007	Governmental Policy Paper on PPP	Flem. Gov. (Peeters I, CV&D)
DE	2002	Steering committee	Schröder II (SPD)
	2004	PPP Task Force	Schröder II (SPD)
	2005	PPP Acceleration Law	Schröder II (SPD)
	11/2008	ÖPP Deutschland AG (successor of Task Force)	Merkel I (CDU)
DK	2006	ÖPP Unit in the Danish Enterprise and Construction Authority (2009 disbanded) www.deaca.dk/publicprivatepartnership	A.F. Rasmussen II (Liberals and Conservatives)
EL	09/2005	PPP Act, establishing of the Task Force (Special Secretariat) and Inter-Ministerial PPP Committee	Karamanlis I (Nea Dimokratia)
ES	2003	Public Works Law amended	Aznar II (PP)
	2008	Competence centre CECOPP (established by private initiative)	Zapatero II (PSOE)
FI		No PPP law in Finland	
FR	12/2001	Act about concessions and leasing (MURCEF)	Jospin (PS)/Chirac (RPR/UMP)
	06/2004	Decree law on Contrats de Partenariat	Raffarin/Chirac (RPR/UMP)
	05/2005	Task Force MAPPP	de Villepin/Chirac (RPR/UMP)
	01/2006	Deregulation of public railways	Fillon/Sarkozy (UMP)
	07/2008	Amendment of Contrats de Partenariat Law	

	Year	Act/measure	Government
IE	2001	The Transport (Railway Infrastructure) Act	Ahern I (FF)
	03/2002	State Authority (PPP Arrangements) Act	Ahern I (FF)
	01/2003	NDFA Act	Ahern II (FF)
	2007	NDFA (Amendment) Act	Ahern III (FF)
		Central PPP Policy Unit: www.ppp.gov.ie/	
IT	1999	Project Finance Technical Unit (UTFP) http://www.utfp.it	D'Alema I (DS)
	2001	Infrastructure framework law 'Legge Obiettivo'	Berlusconi II (FI)
	08/2002	Decree to the infrastructure law and amendment of the Merloni law	Berlusconi II (FI)
	2004	4P Council established	Berlusconi II (FI)
	04/2006	Act to unify public works regulation, guidelines for statistical treatment of projects	Berlusconi III (FI)
	03/2008	Amendment of the Public Contracts Code	Berlusconi IV (FI/ PdL)
	09/2008	NPFO	
NL	1999	PPP Knowledge Centre	Kok II (PvdA)
	2006	PPP Asset Management (formerly PPP Knowledge Centre)	Balkenende II (CDA)
PT	2000	Parpública SA: www.parpublica.pt	de Oliveira Guterres (SP)
	2003	PPP unit set up in Parpública	de Oliveira Guterres (SP)
SE		No legislative action; however, first PPP project in 1993	Bildt (Moderate Party)
UK	1992	PFI enabling legislation	Major I (Con)
	1997	PPP Task Force	Blair I (Lab)
	2000	PUK	Blair I (Lab)
	2006	OTF	Blair III (Lab)
	2006	PRG	Blair III (Lab)
	2009	IUK	Brown (Lab)
	2012	PF2 (revision of the PFI policy)	Cameron/Clegg (Con/ LibDem)

Note: PvdA = Partij van de Arbeid (Labour Party), CDA = Christian Democratic Appeal.

Source: Own compilation.

10.3 COMPARING POLICY DIFFUSION

For the analysis of policy change, certain approaches have gained particular prominence. One of them is the veto player approach, which is less an instrument of comparative public policy and more a theory of institutional analysis. To a certain degree, this approach has helped to structure the proceedings in this book. Turning to more qualitative approaches, the design and diffusion of specific policies is certainly of interest for comparative policy analysis. However, these qualitative approaches have also been mediated by the more encompassing (and thus vaguer) concept of governance. Whereas in the governance paradigm since the 1990s the focus was more on institutional and procedural arrangements and their impact on policy decisions and outcomes, policy analysis tried to conceptualize policy change more at the actor level (i.e. the micro- and meso-level) of the policy process. With the governance approach being often derived from normative concepts of 'good governance' in international and developmental politics, the tools of policy analysis appear to be normatively less demanding. On the other hand, the governance approach might offer some useful pointers concerning the societal context of the development of PPP politics. A broad understanding of the governance concept 'suggests that the principles of modern society, with its division of labour between state, market and civil society, is under siege and, in particular, hierarchical state–society relations are being replaced by other forms of interrelationships, which often imply some "co"-action between public and private' (Bogason 2006: 107). While these approaches might offer an appropriate conceptual framing for the analysis of PPP policies, they also often lack more precise tools and terms for sound analysis. There is no 'one size fit all' approach; for example, the concept of policy diffusion (or transfer) has been criticized for offering 'only a limited explanation to the broader question of policy change' (Peters/Pierre 2006: 3) and thus lacks sound causal explanations.

In the remainder of this section we apply some basic tenets of comparative policy analysis (in an overall governance context) to the development of PPP policies in Western Europe. Firstly, it is obvious that there are policy forerunners and latecomers in terms of PPP. Among the forerunners (or entrepreneurs, pioneers), different attitudes towards PPP can be observed. In the UK, a strong 'mission' was connected with the introduction of PPP under the New Labour government after 1997. The policy was designed clearly in general support of the PPP/PFI approach, which had been characterized as 'the only game in town' (Bidgood 2012). The character of PPP as a policy mission also becomes clear with regard to policy transfer (or diffusion), where UK policy claimed a world leading role (HM Treasury 2008, Sack 2009). In contrast to the UK, Portugal, as another forerunner in using the PPP approach, took on a much more pragmatic policy stance. In Portugal, socioeconomic factors such as an underdeveloped infrastructure, tight budgets and political ambitions to join the Euro-group in the first round despite high debt levels led to a positive but pragmatic policy stance towards the PPP approach. Similar overall patterns can be observed for Spain, with its much greater confidence in (economic and societal) interest groups and local and regional actors to pursue their own ways in the context of the PPP approach. In line with the idea of a decentralized 'state of autonomous communities', the Spanish way was more driven 'bottom-up', while in Portugal, with its weak regional and local autonomy, hierarchical steering was used to push policy goals via the PPP route. Similar to Portugal, the Irish central government set out on the PPP route in the late 1990s by using hierarchical steering tools, but without reaching such significant levels of PPP activity as in the UK or the Iberian peninsula.

At the other end of the scale there were the latecomers. In our sample of 14 countries, this group is clearly represented by the three Nordic states. While in Sweden and Finland at least a few larger projects were initiated at central level, Denmark held back from even doing that. A first large-scale project in Sweden under the conservative Bildt government was not followed up after a change in government. This constellation in Sweden resembles the one in Austria in the early 2000s under the Schüssel government. In terms of policy coordination or 'diffusion', the PPP policy in this northern group appeared rather homogeneous. This contrasts somehow to the policy diffusion at the Iberian peninsula, where PPP policy differences between Portugal and Spain appeared to be more significant. However, we have to keep in mind that with the devolution in Spain the institutional setting of policy making has become more heterogeneous than in the still unitary (though decentralized) Nordic countries. Policy support in favour of PPP at the highest political level in a system with a low number of partisan veto players is still a very good predictor for a high PPP commitment. More detailed analysis of policy making can accompany such explanations, but not substitute them. Thus, in terms of comparative policy analysis, we may infer from such findings that institutional variables count even more than regional (and cultural) proximity as predictors for policy diffusion between states. Methodologically, it is often already a valuable result to accurately describe detailed patterns of policy diffusion across states. However, if at all possible, the perspective of causal explanations should be made as strong as possible.

10.4 PRIVATIZED KEYNESIANISM?

In this final section we try to explore the concept of 'privatized Keynesianism' as an explanation for the intensified use of PPP/PFI in some of the countries under investigation. Firstly, let's remember that in the empirical part at the beginning of the book we did not find a correlation between the level of privatization proceeds and the level of PPP activity. Thus, it seems justified not to place PPP in the context of privatization policies. The clear lack of a correlation suggests that PPP is not a continuation of privatization policies by other means or a form of 'privatization light'. From a theoretical perspective this raises the question of whether there is a different, suitable 'policy regime' to explain these country-specific differences. Thus, in this section we ask if the concept of 'privatized Keynesianism' (coined by Colin Crouch) is more appropriate for explaining the diffusion of PPP across Europe from a theoretical point of view.

Usually politicians like to announce goodies and spending more than austerity measures and spending cuts (at least outside the UK). Thus, it is not surprising that Keynesian ideas gained more support among politicians than under economists. Already in one of Europe's pioneering governments in PFI, the British Major government (1992–1997), a Keynesian moment was admitted later by John Major: 'I followed Keynesian politics. If I had not let government spending increase, unemployment would have been much higher' (quoted in Seldon 1997: 743). PFI was introduced by Major and Norman Lamont in a pragmatic and 'undoctrinaire' style of policy making. Across a range of policy issues, Major avoided ideologically derived policy making and preferred a more pragmatic style.

> Instead of, like the right, wishing that the public sector would go away or, like much of the centre-left of his party, considering it sacrosanct, he took a case-by-case approach to reform. The same applies to privatisation: rail privatisation and the Private Finance Initiative have involved innovative ways of mixing public and private sector. (ibid.)

The pragmatic approach to policy making of New Labour in combination with a Keynesian embedding of the British PPP/PFI has been observed by Hellowell (2012: 308), who discovered a 'distinctly Keynesian flavour' in an early New Labour policy paper (Brown et al. 1994).

However, classical Keynesianism was meanwhile politically difficult to 'sell' due to its well-known side effects on the public budget. In order to avoid these side effects, politicians and economists in some Anglo-Saxon countries developed some variations that were later labelled as privatized Keynesianism by the British economist Colin Crouch. According to Crouch (2008, 2009, 2011) these policies were developed in the 1990s, in the US under the Clinton administration and the UK under the governments of Major and Blair, to close certain gaps in the neoliberal growth model. In his analysis, Crouch applies an interpretive model that had already been applied for the interpretation of the 'Keynesian revolution' in economic policy making: Keynesianism as an attempt to save the system of free markets in the face of economic and political crisis of liberalism (Skidelsky 2006: 169).

One of Keynes's concerns was the belief that capitalism was the best system despite its imperfections that humans had devised to realize a civilized economy. Regarding its imperfections, he tried to address two major faults of capitalism: first the problem of providing full employment and second a random and unbalanced allocation of income and wealth. 'Until these faults were corrected, Keynes argued, the capitalist system could be extremely unstable and therefore subject to periods of economic booms that could often lead to catastrophic collapses' (Davidson 2009: 6). In order to address these flaws, governments have to design proper policies 'that cooperate and augment private initiatives' to 'develop a stable, fully employed capitalist economy that would still enjoy the advantages of a market-oriented entrepreneurial system' (ibid.).

Under the impact of the world economic crisis, Keynes assumed in his 'General Theory of Employment, Interest and Money' (1936/1973) (also labelled as classical Keynesianism) that wage cuts are not always the best cure for unemployment, as previously adopted by neoclassical economics. Instead, Keynes shifted his focus from wages to investment and from the supply side to the demand side. This can be illustrated by his rejection of classical Say's theorem, according to which each supply (of work) also creates a demand, so that with sufficient wage flexibility full employment should prevail. According to Keynes's shift of paradigm in the wake of the global economic crisis in the early 1930s, wage cuts and high savings rates can withdraw demand from the economy. On the issue of a (too) high savings rate, politics can react with a moderate inflation, which at the same time reduces the debt level. The goal of strengthening demand with macroeconomic imbalances should, according to the 'classical' Keynesianism, be achieved by, for example, lowering interest rates and increasing government spending, particularly through public investment.

However, large-scale public investment also leads to immediate effects on the deficit and, in the medium term, on the debt level. More public investment usually also forces the government to either raise taxes or increase its borrowing. From this point of view, PPP/PFI is an opportunity to 'pump up the market demand' by having additional expenditures, without running immediately deeper into deficit. In privatized Keynesianism, this is an improvement on classical and post Keynesianism, which neglected the aspect of the size of the public deficit needed to achieve full employment. 'Neoclassical Keynesians, who professed that neoclassical principles underlie their macroeconomic analysis are therefore forced, if they are to be logically consistent, to view government deficits as an ultimate evil' (Davidson 1991: 78).

To sum up, the variants of Keynesian theory have encouraged the development and application of a range of policy instruments, which have been used internationally in fighting the housing bubble crisis cycle commencing in 2008. Under 'privatized Keynesianism' demand stimulation at least partially was privately financed and therefore exercised less (short-term) strain on public budgets. In this perspective, the banking crisis following the real estate bubble is the private equivalent of a public debt crisis. Table 10.3 summarizes some key points of varieties of Keynesianism.

In the remainder of this section, we go deeper into this concept. Crouch (2009) locates the emergence of what he described as privatized Keynesianism in the 1990s in the Anglo-Saxon countries, particularly in the US under the Clinton presidency. The crisis of Keynesianism in the 1980s, expressed in monetarist concepts (Friedman 1962) and neoliberal policies (Ronald Reagan, Margaret Thatcher), led to new, pragmatic forms of Keynesian 'demand management' in the 1990s, trying to obviate the negative consequences of classic Keynesianism.

The innovation of this economic policy regime is to shift borrowing (and thus 'debt management') from the public to the private sector in order to stimulate both private and public demand. PPP/PFI is only one element to this policy; others encompass, for example, conditions for mortgages and credit cards. Politics changed legal conditions so that private households had significantly more incentive for 'deficit spending'. Lower-income households in particular responded positively to such measures and piled on additional debt; among others, this laid the basis of the so-called 'subprime crisis'. The facilitating of private deficit spending was aimed particularly at the mortgage and housing markets and the market for condominiums. The mortgage debt in the Anglo-American economies reached a significantly higher level than in continental European countries, where the number of credit cards as well as the turnover was considerably lower (Crouch 2009: 391).

Table 10.3 Varieties of Keynesianism

	Basic concepts	Instruments
Classical Keynesianism	Critique of equilibrium assumptions of (neo)classical theory Effective demand as a key variable of employment level Aim of public policy is stimulating demand in order to reach full employment	Public stimulus and investment programmes to push up private demand Public deficit spending Moderate inflation is helpful to push up private consumption and investment
Post Keynesianism and neoclassic synthesis	Acting under uncertainty and instability of market orders Reduction of deficit can be counterproductive, depending on the general economic and employment situation	Low interest rates by central banks Intervention and global steering Control of movement of capital, nationalization of banks and industries
Privatized Keynesianism	Financing of demand stimulus measures is transferred from the pubic to the private sector Combination of (short-term) public austerity with impulses for growth	Deficit spending by private households, for instance by credit cards, leasing and mortgage contracts Public housing and infrastructure programmes as useful stimulus, but best financed off-balance-sheet PPP/PFI Low interest rates and quantitative easing by central banks

Sources: Own compilation from Cezanne 2008, Crouch 2009 and Keynes 1973.

Anglo-Saxon financial markets were much more receptive to such instruments; for instance, they developed a much larger segment for risk bonds and risk credits, which eventually contributed to the collapse of the credit bubble in 2008 (Crouch 2008: 476). 'Under privatized Keynesianism vast quantities of totally fictitious cake were produced, on the basis of the notional values of which even vaster quantities of such cake were leveraged. Bad debts were funding bad debts, and so on in an exponentially growing mountain' (Crouch 2009: 393). A loss of confidence in the prospective solvency of the loan and mortgage holders was accompanied by the refusal of the US government to provide guarantees for the ailing banks (e.g. Lehman Brothers in September 2008). According to Crouch, this refusal ushered in the beginning of the end of the policy of privatized Keynesianism.

The basis for this crisis was already laid by two developments since the 1990s, which had originally provided for very successful economic growth: 'the growth of credit markets for poor and middle-income people, and of derivatives and futures markets among the very wealthy' (ibid.: 390). This initially rather incidental combination laid the basis for a policy that was later labelled by Crouch as privatized Keynesianism. Although labelled by Crouch as case of 'market entrepreneurship', it subsequently became a most important matter for public policy. 'Instead of governments taking on debt to stimulate the economy, individuals did so' (ibid.).

In contrast to classical Keynesianism with the state as the main borrower and the risk of inflation as an unwanted side effect in the absence of corporatist embedding, in the privatized Keynesianism since the 1990s a loss of confidence in the creditworthiness or credit rating of private borrowers has been the unsought side effect. The policy of privatized Keynesianism (and its crisis) especially affected Anglo-Saxon countries, less so continental European ones such as Germany and France. The export-oriented German economy model is less dependent on domestic demand (and its variation). For such export economies, the crucial parameters are less open to influence from domestic politics. In such cases, the policy of the government is less focused on increasing domestic demand than keeping prices low (or quality high) to support the export of goods.

In contrast, stimulating domestic demand for domestic goods can be achieved by promoting the housing and real estate sector, whereas export strategies rely more on corporatist wage agreements and fighting inflation by supporting respective policies pursued by the ECB: '[c]ontinental European, Japanese and now a wide range of new producers, were dependent on US and to a lesser extent UK consumers buying their goods. But what would enable these consumers to do so? This is where the debt model became so important' (ibid.: 391). According to Crouch, particularly the British government has taken up the idea of privatized Keynesianism in their public policy making. Besides PPP/PFI, the mortgage/housing market was another priority of the government. For the functioning of the model it was important that house prices remained at relatively high levels, as these constitute the security of mortgages. A slump in house price finally undermined the confidence in the security of the loans.

With the countercyclical intervention strategy already promoted by classic Keynesianism still in place, its result in privatized Keynesianism was that the majority of mortgage and consumer loans were only weakly secured. Otherwise sufficient demand stimulation would not have been possible. This resembles the sometimes very optimistic assumptions of user fee or shadow toll revenues in PPPs especially in Spain and Portugal. Once the global economic situation changed in 2008, both private households and corporations suffered heavily or even went bankrupt. Thus, the situation of low- and moderate-income households was somehow similar to the low GDP–high PPP countries in the southern periphery. 'The possibility of prolonged, widespread unsecured debt was in turn made possible through innovations that had taken place in financial markets, innovations which for a long time had seemed to be an excellent example of how, left to themselves, market actors find creative solutions' (ibid.: 392).

To sum up, the approach of privatized Keynesianism provides a theoretically convincing framework of interpretation for the invention and the rise of the PPP policy in a range of European states. Its core assumption is a shift of deficit spending from the public to the private sector in order to stimulate private (and public) demand. However, if this is an adequate description of the development, it should also be expressed in the deficit and debt statistics of the respective countries. Finding only a weak correlation of the deficit and the PPP figures in Chapter 3 is in line with this interpretation, as higher PPP commitment should lead to lower or only moderately rising public deficits.

However, the private debt statistics of the Anglo-Saxon countries are less clear. The levels of gross debt of private households in Anglo-Saxon countries presented in the IMF Global Financial Stability Report from September 2011 can be seen as a confirmation of the hypothesis, but this is not the case for net debt (IMF 2011: 5). Unlike with gross debt, in the net debt the short-term-available liquid assets such as bank accounts and securities holdings are deducted. In terms of gross household debt, Ireland reached the highest value with an average of 123 per cent of GDP from 1990 to 2009 in the IMF sample, followed by Portugal with 106 per cent, the UK with 101 per cent and the US with 92 per cent of GDP. The average value of the Eurozone is 70 per cent; the figure for Germany is 60 per cent. The net debt of households gives a different picture. Belgium comes in with a value of 195 per cent of GDP (the highest among our sample of 14), the UK with 184 per cent and Italy with 178 per cent. The Eurozone mean is 126 per cent of GDP (IMF 2011: 5). Leaders in the IMF compilation are Japan and the US with a net household debt of about 230 per cent of GDP. In countries with high net debt the liabilities of private households are balanced by substantial liquid assets, which can be distributed, though quite unevenly, across the different sections of society. In the gross debt of the financial sector (financial institutions' gross debt) Ireland comes first with 689 per cent of GDP, followed by the

UK with 547 per cent, compared with an average in the Eurozone of 143 per cent and Germany with 98 per cent of the GDP (ibid.).These remarks can provide only some general ideas. In order to really empirically test the concept of privatized Keynesianism and the place PPP has in it, much more would be needed.

References

Acerete, Basilio, Anne Stafford and Pamela Stapleton (2011), 'Spanish healthcare Public Private Partnerships: The "Alzira model"', *Critical Perspectives on Accounting*, 22 (6), 533–49.

Adshead, Maura and Jonathan Tonge (2009), *Politics in Ireland*, Basingstoke: Palgrave.

Allard, Gayle and Amanda Trabant (2008), 'Public–Private Partnerships in Spain: Lessons and opportunities', *International Business and Economics Research Journal*, 7 (2), 1–24.

Allen & Overy (2010), *Global Guide to Public–Private Partnerships*, March 2010, London: Allen & Overy LLP.

Angerer, Dieter J. and Gerhard Hammerschmid (2005), 'Public Private Partnership between euphoria and disillusionment. Recent experiences from Austria and implications for countries in transformation', *Romanian Journal of Political Science*, 5 (1), 129–59.

Auernheimer, Gustav (2003), 'Das politische System Griechenlands. Zäsuren und Funktionsprobleme einer europäischen Demokratie', *Zeitschrift für Politikwissenschaft*, 13 (4), 1933–60.

Ball, R., M. Heafey and D. King (2000), 'Private finance initiative – a good deal for the public purse or a drain on future generations?', *Policy and Politics*, 29 (1), 95–108.

Barlow, James and Martina Köberle-Gaiser (2008), 'The Private Finance Initiative, project form and design innovation: The UK's hospitals programme', *Research Policy*, 37 (8), 1392–1402.

Barrios, Harald (2009), 'Das politische System Spaniens', in Wolfgang Ismayr (ed.), *Die politischen Systeme Westeuropas*, Wiesbaden: VS, pp. 713–64.

Bayrischer Oberster Rechnungshof (2006), *Jahresbericht 2006*, Munich, accessed 3 September 2012 at www.orh.bayern.de/files/Jahresberichte/2006/JB-Zusammenfassung2006.pdf.

Bel, Germà and Xavier Fageda (2010), 'Partial privatisation in local services delivery: An empirical analysis of the choice of mixed firms', *Local Government Studies*, 36 (1), 129–49.

Belke, Ansgar and Friedrich Schneider (2006), 'Privatization in Austria: Some theoretical reasons and performance measures', in Marko

Köthenbürger, Hans-Werner Sinn and John Whalley (eds.), *Privatisation Experiences in the European Union*, Cambridge, MA: MIT Press (CESifo seminar series), pp. 89–115.

Berg-Schlosser, Dirk (2005), 'Makro-qualitative vergleichende Methoden', in Sabine Kropp and Michael Minkenberg (eds.), *Vergleichen in der Politikwissenschaft*, Wiesbaden: VS, pp. 170–79.

Berg-Schlosser, Dirk and Lasse Cronqvist (2012), *Aktuelle Methoden der Vergleichenden Politikwissenschaft*, Opladen: B. Budrich.

Berne, Michel and Gérard Pogorel (2006), 'Privatization experiences in France', in Marko Köthenbürger, Hans-Werner Sinn and John Whalley (eds.), *Privatization Experiences in the European Union*, Cambridge, MA: MIT Press (CESifo seminar series), pp. 163–98.

Bezançon, Xavier, François Bergère, Guillaume Goulard, Marc Fornacciari and Laurent Deruy (2009), *Le guide opérationnel des PPP. Conditions du recours au partenariat public-privé, Passation du contrat, Risques et matrices des risques, Questions fiscales et comptables*, Paris: Le Moniteur Editions.

Bidgood, Elliot (2012), *PFI: Still the Only Game in Town?*, London: Civitas Institute for the Study of Civil Society, accessed 13 June 2012 at www.civitas.org.uk/nhs/PFIDec2012.pdf.

Blanc-Brude, Frédéric, Hugh Goldsmith and Timo Välilä (2007), *Public–Private Partnerships in Europe: An Update*, Economic and Financial Reports no. 2007/03, European Investment Bank, accessed 29 November 2011 at http://hdl.handle.net/10419/45292.

Bogason, Peter (2006), 'Network and bargaining in policy analysis', in B. Guy Peters and Jon Pierre (eds.), *Handbook of Public Policy*, London: Sage, pp. 97–113.

Bognetti, G. and L. Robotti (2007), 'The provision of local public services through mixed enterprises. The Italian case', *Annals of Public and Cooperative Economics*, 78 (3), 415–37.

Broadbent, Jane and Richard Laughlin (2003), 'Control and legitimation in government accountability processes: The Private Finance Initiative in the UK', *Critical Perspectives on Accounting*, 14, 23–48.

Broadbent, Jane and Richard Laughlin (2004), 'Striving for excellence in public service delivery: Experiences from an analysis of the Private Finance Initiative', *Public Policy and Administration*, 19 (4), 82–99.

Brown, Gordon, R. Cook and John Prescott (1994), *Financing Infrastructure Investment: Promoting a Partnership between Public and Private Finance*, London: The Labour Party.

Buck, Tobias (2013), 'Austerity fuels Spanish irritation with Germany', *Financial Times*, 24 June 2013, p. 3.

Bundesministerium für Verkehr, Bau und Stadtentwicklung (BMVBS) (2007), *Erfahrungsbericht- Öffentlich-Private-Partnerschaften in Deutschland*, Berlin: BMVBS.

Bundesministerium für Verkehr, Innovation und Technologie and Bundesministerium für Finanzen (BMVIT/BMF) (2008), *Ergebnisbericht über die PPP-Projekte der Bundesministerien sowie der ausgegliederten Bundesgesellschaften*, Wien: BMVIT/BMF, accessed 8 May 2011 at https://www.bmf.gv.at/Budget/BesondereBudgetthemen/Ergebnisbericht-080403.pdf.

Burger, Philippe and Ian Hawkesworth (2011), 'How to attain value for money: Comparing PPP and traditional infrastructure public procurement', *OECD Journal on Budgeting*, 1, accessed 18 November 2013 at http://www.oecd.org/gov/budgeting/49070709.pdf.

Cezanne, Wolfgang (2008), 'Postkeynesianische (Analyse) Theorie', in Artur Woll (ed.), *Wirtschaftslexikon*, München: Oldenbourg, S. 612–14.

Chamakou, Kalliopi (2011), *Die Öffentlich-Private Partnerschaft als neues Handlungsinstrument zwischen öffentlichem Recht und Zivilrecht*, Hamburg: Dr. Kovač.

Christoffersen, Henrik and Martin Paldam (2006), 'Privatization in Denmark, 1980–2002', in Marko Köthenbürger, Hans-Werner Sinn and John Whalley (eds.), *Privatization Experiences in the European Union*, Cambridge, MA: MIT Press (CESifo seminar series), pp. 117–40.

Circular IPPP 01/02 (2002), *State Authorities (PPP Arrangements) Act 2002*, accessed 24 April 2012 at http://www.environ.ie/en/Publications/DevelopmentandHousing/PPP/.

Circular IPPP 04/04 (2004), *PPP Fund for Local Authorities*, accessed 24 April 2012 at http://www.environ.ie/en/ Publications/Development and Housing/PPP/.

Clark, Gordon L. and Amanda Root (1999), 'Infrastructure shortfall in the United Kingdom: The Private Finance Initiative and government policy', *Political Geography*, 18, 341–65.

Coalition Agreement CDU/CSU–SPD (2005), *Gemeinsam für Deutschland. Mit Mut und Menschlichkeit. Koalitionsvertrag von CDU, CSU und SPD*, Berlin.

Coalition Agreement SPD – Bündnis90/Die Grünen (2002), *Erneuerung – Gerechtigkeit – Nachhaltigkeit*, Berlin.

Collin, Sven-Olof (1998), 'In the twilight zone: A survey of Public–Private Partnerships in Sweden', *Public Productivity and Management Review*, 21 (3), 272–83.

Colomer, Josep M. (2008), 'Spain and Portugal: Rule by party leadership', in Josep M. Colomer (ed.), *Comparative European Politics*, London: Routledge, pp. 174–208.

Commission of the European Communities (1987), *Towards a Dynamic Economy. Green Paper on the Development of the Common Market for Telecommunications Services and Equipment*, Com(87) 290 final, Brussels: European Commission.

Conor, David (2005), 'The United Kingdom Private Finance Initiative: The challenge of allocating risk', in Graeme Hodge and Carsten Greve (eds.), *The Challenge of Public–Private Partnerships: Learning from International Experience*, Cheltenham, UK and Northampton, MA, USA: Edward Elgar Publishing, pp. 44–61.

Conservative Party (2008), *Plan for Change*, London.

Cotta, Maurizio and Luca Verzichelli (2007), *Political Institutions in Italy*, Oxford: OUP.

Cronqvist, Lasse (2007), *Introduction to Multi-value Qualitative Comparative Analysis (MVQCA)*, accessed 20 November 2010 at http://www.tosmana.net.

Crouch, Colin (2008), 'What will follow the demise of privatised Keynesianism?', *Political Quarterly*, 79 (4), 476–87.

Crouch, Colin (2009), 'Privatised Keynesianism: An unacknowledged policy regime', *British Journal of Politics and International Relations*, 11 (3), 382–99.

Crouch, Colin (2011), *The Strange Non-death of Neoliberalism*, Cambridge: Polity.

Cuttaree, Vickram and Cledan Mandri-Perrott (2011), *Public–Private Partnerships in Europe and Central Asia*, Washington, DC: The World Bank.

Dachs, Herbert, Peter Gerlich, Herbert Gottweis et al. (eds.) (2006), *Politik in Österreich: Das Handbuch*, Vienna: Manz.

Database of Political Institutions (DPI) (2009), edited by Philip Keefer et al. for Development Research Group, The World Bank, accessed 11 February 2011 at http://econ.worldbank.org/WBSITE/EXTERNAL/EXTDEC/EXTRESEARCH/0,,contentMDK:20649465~pagePK:64214825~piPK:64214943~theSitePK:469382,00.html.

Davidson, Paul (1991), *Controversies in Post Keynesian Economics*, Aldershot, UK and Brookfield, VT, USA: Edward Elgar Publishing.

Davidson, Paul (2009), *The Keynes Solution: The Path to Global Economic Prosperity*, Basingstoke: Palgrave Macmillan.

De Calboli, Manfredo Paulucci (2007), 'Strategies and instruments for PPP development', Rome (working paper).

De Pierris, Luigi and Gabriele Pescarini (2001), 'Italian PPP at a glance', *Project Finance International*, 217, 73–7.

Deloitte (2009), *Benchmark PPS in Vlaanderen: Wat kunnen we leren uit het buitenland*, Brussels.

Derichsweiler, Cornelia (2012), 'Spaniens Regionen bringen Madrid zusehends in Bedrängnis', *Neue Zürcher Zeitung*, 25 July 2012, p. 7.

Deutsches Institut für Urbanistik (DIFU) (2009), 'PPP-Projekte in Deutschland 2009. Erfahrungen, Verbreitung, Perspektiven', Berlin: DIFU.

Dirninger, Christian (2013), 'Mehr Markt und weniger Staat', in Robert Kriechbaumer and Franz Schausberger (eds.), *Die umstrittene Wende. Österreich 2000–2006*, Vienna: Böhlau, pp. 211–70.

Duffield, Colin F. (2010), 'Different delivery models', in Graeme A. Hodge, Carsten Greve and Anthony E. Boardman (eds.), *International Handbook on Public–Private Partnerships*, Cheltenham, UK and Northampton, MA, USA: Edward Elgar Publishing, pp. 187–215.

Dye, Thomas R. (1976), *Policy Analysis*, Tuscaloosa, AL: University of Alabama Press.

Dyton, Richard and Raj Bavishi (2008), 'England and Wales', in Maurice Button (ed.), *A Practical Guide to PPP in Europe*, London: City & Financial Publishing, pp. 527–62.

Economist, The (2004), 'Road tolls in Germany: Trucking hell', 21 February, p. 74

Economist, The (2013), 'Euro wobbles: Portugal's constitutional court creates new problems for the euro', 13 April, p. 30

Edel, Friederike and Birgit Grüb (2011), 'Partial privatization of prisons in Germany – state of the art', in Thomas M. Lenk, Martina Kuntze, Matthias Redlich and Oliver Rottmann (eds.), 'Public–Private Partnership: An appropriate institutional arrangement for public services?', *ZögU (Journal for Public and Nonprofit Services)*, Supplement 41, 34–46.

Edwards, Pam, Jean Shaoul, Anne Stafford and Lorna Arblaster (2004), *Evaluating the Operation of PFI in Roads and Hospitals*, Association of Chartered Certified Accountants (ACCA) Research Report No. 84. Glasgow.

Ejersbo, Niels and Carsten Greve (2005), 'Public–Private Partnerships for infrastructure in Denmark: From local to global partnering?', in Graeme Hodge and Carsten Greve (eds.), *The Challenge of Public–Private Partnerships. Learning from International Experience*, Cheltenham, UK and Northampton, MA, USA: Edward Elgar Publishing, pp. 257–68.

European Commission (2004), *Green Paper on Public–Private Partnerships and Community Law on Public Contracts and Concessions*, COM(2004) 327 final, Brussels: Commission of the European Communities, accessed 7 January 2010 at http://eur-lex.europa.eu/legal-content/EN/TXT/PDF/?uri=CELEX:52004DC0327&from=EN.

European Investment Bank (EIB) (2004), *The EIB's Role in Public–Private Partnerships*, Luxemburg.

European PPP Expertise Centre (EPEC) (2011a), *The Guide to Guidance: How to Prepare, Procure and Deliver PPP Projects*, Luxembourg: European PPP Expertise Centre.

European PPP Expertise Centre (EPEC) (2011b), *State Guarantees in PPPs: A Guide to Better Evaluation, Design, Implementation and Management*, Luxembourg: European PPP Expertise Centre.

European PPP Expertise Centre (EPEC) (2011c), *Market Update – 2010: Review of the European PPP Market*, accessed 21 October 2012 at http://www.eib.org/epec/library/index.htm#Market_Updates.

European PPP Expertise Centre (EPEC) (2012a), *Belgium – Wallonia: PPP Units and Related Institutional Framework*, October 2012, Luxembourg: European PPP Expertise Centre.

European PPP Expertise Centre (EPEC) (2012b), *Market Update – 2011: Review of the European PPP Market*, accessed 21 August 2013 at www.eib.org/epec/library/index.htm#Market_Updates.

European PPP Expertise Centre (EPEC) (2014), *PPPs Financed by the European Investment Bank from 1990 to 2013*, March, Luxembourg: EPEC.

European PPP Report (EPPPR) (2007), *European PPP Report 2007*, London: DLA Piper.

European PPP Report (EPPPR) (2009), *European PPP Report 2009*, London: DLA Piper.

Financial Times (2011), 'A history of statistics that failed to add up', 1 October, p. 7.

Fischer, Katrin, Andrea Jungbecker and H.W. Alfen (2006), 'The emergence of PPP task forces and their influence on project delivery in Germany', *International Journal of Project Management*, 24, 539–47.

Fleischer, Thorsten and Günter Halbritter (2004), 'Toll Collect: Panne von Industrie und Politik', *Internationales Verkehrswesen*, 56, 363–6.

Flinders, Matthew (2005), 'The politics of Public–Private Partnerships', *British Journal of Politics and International Relations*, 7 (2), 215–39.

Fonseca, Sara Claro da (2009), 'Das politische System Portugals', in Wolfgang Ismayr (ed.), *Die politischen Systeme Westeuropas*, Wiesbaden: VS, pp. 765–818.

Frankfurter Allgemeine Zeitung (FAZ) (2004), *Toll Collect erwägt Maut-Einführung in zwei Stufen*, 15 January, p. 12.

Frankfurter Allgemeine Zeitung (FAZ) (2012), 'EZB will brisante Griechen-Berichte nicht offenlegen', 14 December, p. 14.

Frankfurter Allgemeine Zeitung (FAZ) (2013), 'Milliardengrab Bankenrettung', 16 August, p. 12.

Friedman, Milton (1962), *Capitalism and Freedom*, Chicago, IL: University of Chicago Press.
Froud, Julie (2003), 'The Private Finance Initiative: Risk, uncertainty and the state', *Accounting, Organizations and Society*, 28 (6), 567–89.
Fuster, Thomas (2011a), 'Griechische Banken in fataler Seilschaft', *Neue Zürcher Zeitung*, 10 October, p. 8.
Fuster, Thomas (2011b), 'Politikversagen in Griechenland', *Neue Zürcher Zeitung*, 7 November, p. 11.
Garcia-Milà, Teresa and Therese J. McGuire (2007), 'Fiscal decentralization in Spain: An asymmetric transition to democracy', in Richard M. Bird and Robert D. Ebel (eds.), *Fiscal Fragmentation in Decentralized Countries*, Cheltenham, UK and Northampton, MA, USA: Edward Elgar Publishing, pp. 208–25.
Gee, Graham, Robert Hazell, Kate Malleson and Patrick O'Brien (2015), *The Politics of Judicial Independence in the UK's Changing Constitution*, Oxford: OUP.
Georgiadou, Vassiliki (2002), 'Parteireform in Griechenland. Am Beispiel der Panhellenischen Sozialistischen Bewegung (PASOK)', *Zeitschrift für Politikwissenschaft*, 12 (2), 585–609.
Gianella, Tobiolo, Marco Meneguzzo and Josef Bernhart (2009), 'Öffentlich-Private Partnerschaften. Eine erste Gegenüberstellung der aktuellen Erfahrungen in Italien und der Schweiz', in Harald Pechlaner, Wolf von Holzschuher and Monika Bachinger (eds.), *Unternehmertum und Public Private Partnership. Wissenschaftliche Konzepte und praktische Erfahrungen*, Wiesbaden: Gabler, pp. 223–44.
Ginsborg, Paul (2005), *Silvio Berlusconi: Television, Power and Patrimony*, London: Verso.
Greenaway, John, Brian Salter and Stella Hart (2004), 'The evolution of a "meta-policy": The case of the Private Finance Initiative and the health sector', *British Journal of Politics and International Relations*, 6 (4), 507–26.
Greiling, Dorothea and Eveline Häusler (2011), 'Public–Private Partnership in the health care sector – a comparative analysis', in Thomas M. Lenk, Martina Kuntze, Matthias Redlich and Oliver Rottmann (eds.), 'Public–Private Partnership: An appropriate institutional arrangement for public services?', *ZögU (Journal for Public and Nonprofit Services)*, Supplement 41, Baden-Baden: Nomos, 162–80.
Greve, Carsten (2003), 'Public–Private Partnerships in Scandinavia', *International Public Management Review*, 4 (2), 59–68.
Greve, Carsten and Ulrika Mörth (2012), 'Public–Private Partnership: The Scandinavian experience', in Graeme A. Hodge, Carsten Greve and Anthony E. Boardman (eds.), *International Handbook of*

Public–Private Partnerships, Cheltenham, UK and Northampton, MA, USA: Edward Elgar Publishing, pp. 439–55.

Grimsey, Darrin and Mervyn K. Lewis (eds.) (2005a), *The Economics of Public Private Partnerships*, Cheltenham, UK and Northampton, MA, USA: Edward Elgar Publishing.

Grimsey, Darrin and Mervyn K. Lewis (2005b), 'Introduction', in Darrin Grimsey and Mervyn K. Lewis (eds.), *The Economics of Public Private Partnerships*, Cheltenham, UK and Northampton, MA, USA: Edward Elgar Publishing, pp. xiii–xl.

Grimsey, Darrin and Mervyn K. Lewis (2005c), *Public Private Partnerships: The Worldwide Revolution in Infrastructure Provision and Project Finance*, Cheltenham, UK and Northampton, MA, USA: Edward Elgar Publishing.

Grout, Paul A. (1997), 'The economics of the Private Finance Initiative', *Oxford Review of Economic Policy*, 13 (4), 53–66.

Haensch, Peter and Everhard Holtmann (2008), 'Die öffentliche Verwaltung der EU-Staaten', in Oskar W. Gabriel and Sabine Kropp (eds.), *Die EU-Staaten im Vergleich*, Wiesbaden: VS, pp. 606–30.

Hague, Rod and Martin Harrop (2010), *Comparative Government and Politics*, Basingstoke: Palgrave Macmillan.

Hammami, Mona, Jean-Francois Ruhashyankiko and Etienne B. Yehoue (2006), 'Determinants of Public–Private Partnerships in infrastructure', IMF Working Paper 06/99, Washington, DC: International Monetary Fund.

Hancock, M. Donald (2007), 'Sweden', in M. Donald Hancock et al. (eds.), *Politics in Europe*, Washington, DC: CQ Press, pp. 393–449.

Hare, Paul (2013), 'PPP and PFI: The political economy of building public infrastructure and delivering services', *Oxford Review of Economic Policy*, 29 (1): 95–112. doi: 10.1093/oxrep/grt007.

Hellowell, Mark (2012), 'The UK's Private Finance Initiative: History, evaluation, prospects', in Graeme A. Hodge, Carsten Greve and Anthony E. Boardman (eds.), *International Handbook on Public–Private Partnerships*, Cheltenham, UK and Northampton, MA, USA: Edward Elgar Publishing, pp. 307–32.

Helm, Toby and Philipp Inman (2009), 'We'll bring a new model PFI', *The Observer*, 15 November 2009.

Hlepas, Nikolaos-K. (2010), 'Incomplete Greek territorial consolidation: From the first (1998) to the second (2008–08) wave of reforms', *Local Government Studies*, 36 (2), 223–49.

HM Government (2010), *The Coalition: Our Programme for Government: Freedom, Fairness, Responsibility*, London: Cabinet Office.

HM Treasury (2003), *PFI: Meeting the Investment Challenge*, London: HM Treasury.

HM Treasury (2006a), *Value for Money: Assessment Guidance*, London: HM Treasury.

HM Treasury (2006b), *PFI: Strengthening Long-Term Partnerships*, London: HM Treasury.

HM Treasury (2008), *Infrastructure Procurement: Delivering Long-Term Value*, London: HM Treasury.

House of Commons (2012), *London Underground after the PPP, 2007–*, London: House of Commons Library Standard Note SN01746, accessed 12 June 2014 at www.parliament.uk/briefing-papers/SN01746/london-underground-after-the-ppp-2007.

Huomo, Laura (2008), 'Finland', in Maurice Button (ed.), *A Practical Guide to PPP in Europe*, London: City & Financial Publishing, pp. 439–50.

Ieraci, Giuseppe (2008), *Governments and Parties in Italy: Parliamentary Debates, Investiture Votes and Policy Positions (1994–2006)*, Leicester: Troubador Publishing.

International Monetary Fund (IMF) (2011), *Global Financial Stability Report: Grappling with Crisis Legacies*, World Economic and Financial Surveys, Sept. 2011, Washington, DC: IMF.

Jacob, Dieter (2009), *Endbericht zum Forschungsprojekt 'PPP – Krankenhäuser: Qualitative und quantitative Risikoverteilung und die Lösung von Schnittstellenproblemen bei der Umstrukturierung von Kliniken'*, Freiberg: TU Bergakademie Freiberg.

Jahn, Detlef (2009), 'Das politische System Schwedens', in Wolfgang Ismayr (ed.), *Die politischen Systeme Westeuropas*, Wiesbaden: VS, pp. 107–49.

Kappeler, Andreas and Mathieu Nemoz (2010), 'Public–Private Partnerships in Europe – before and during the recent financial crisis', Economic and Financial Report 2010/04, EIB, accessed 8 May 2011 at www.eib.org/epec/resources/efr_epec_ppp_report.pdf.

Katzenstein, Peter J. (1985), *Small States in World Markets: Industrial Policy in Europe*, Ithaca, New York, NY: Cornell University Press.

Keeler, John T.S. (1987), *The Politics of Neo-corporatism in France*, New York, NY: OUP.

Keman, Hans and Jaap Woldendorp (2010), 'The Netherlands: Centralized – more than less!', in Roland Sturm and Jürgen Dieringer (eds.), *Regional Governance in EU-Staaten*, Opladen: Budrich, pp. 269–85.

Keynes, John Maynard (1973/1936), *The General Theory of Employment Interest and Money*, London: Macmillan.

Koppenjan, Joop F.M. (2005), 'The formation of Public–Private Partnerships: Lessons from nine transport infrastructure projects in the Netherlands', *Public Administration*, 83 (1), 135–57.

Köppl, Stefan (2010), 'Italien – asymmetrischer Regionalismus im Wandel', in Roland Sturm and Jürgen Dieringer (eds.), *Regional Governance in EU-Staaten*, Opladen: Budrich, pp. 127–48.
Köthenbürger, Marko (2006), 'Introduction', in Marko Köthenbürger, Hans-Werner Sinn and John Whalley (eds.), *Privatization Experiences in the European Union*, Cambridge, MA: MIT Press (CESifo seminar series), pp. ix–ixx.
Krampe, Thomas (2010), *Nutzerzufriedenheit Bundeswehr/BWI IT. Ergebnisse der Befragung der Anwender und Anwenderinnen 2010*, Strausberg: Sozialwissenschaftliches Institut der Bundeswehr.
Krumm, Thomas (2011), 'Die irische Parlamentswahl vom 25. Februar 2011: Ende des dominierten Parteiensystems?', *Zeitschrift für Parlamentsfragen*, 42 (3), 604–19.
Krumm, Thomas (2013), *Das politische System der Schweiz. Ein internationaler Vergleich*, Munich: Oldenbourg.
Krumm, Thomas (2013b), 'Parlamentarische Kontrolle von ÖPP', Der moderne Staat (dms), 6 (2), 393–410.
Krumm, Thomas (2014), 'Vetospieler als Prädiktor für Policy-Wandel? Ein Test anhand von öffentlich-privaten Partnerschaften im internationalen Vergleich', *Politische Vierteljahresschrift*, 55 (3), 445–71.
Krumm, Thomas (2015), *Föderale Staaten im Vergleich*, Wiesbaden: Springer VS.
Lenk, Thomas and Manfred Röber (2011), 'Public–Private Partnership as part of public-sector modernisation', in Thomas M. Lenk, Martina Kuntze, Matthias Redlich and Oliver Rottmann (eds.), 'Public–Private Partnership: An appropriate institutional arrangement for public services?', *ZögU (Journal for Public and Nonprofit Services)*, Supplement 41, Baden-Baden: Nomos, pp. 1–6.
Leväinen, Kari I. and Willem Korthals Altes (2005), 'Public Private Partnership in land development contracts. A comparative study in Finland and in the Netherlands', *Nordic Journal of Surveying and Real Estate Research*, 2 (1), 137–48.
Leviäkangas, Pekka (2013), 'Finland', in Koen Verhoest, Nunzia Carbonara, Veiko Lember, Ole Helby Petersen, Walter Scherrer and Martijn van den Hurk (eds.), *Public Private Partnerships in Transport: Trends and Theory P3T3*, 2013 Discussion Papers. Part I Country Profiles, Brussels: COST, pp. 218–31.
Lichère, François, Boris Martor, Gilles Pédini and Sébastien Thouvenot (2009), *Pratique des partenariats public-privé. Choisir, évaluer, monter et suivre son PPP*, Paris: Lexis Nexis.
Lijphart, Arend (1989), 'From the politics of accommodation to adversarial politics in the Netherlands: A reassessment', *West European Politics*, 12 (1), 139–53.

Lijphart, Arend (1999), *Patterns of Democracy. Government Forms and Performance in Thirty-Six Countries*, New Haven, CT: Yale University Press.

Linder, Stephen H. (1999), 'Coming to terms with the Public–Private Partnership: A grammar of multiple meanings', *American Behavioural Scientist*, 43 (1), 35–51.

Lowi, Theodore J. (1964), 'American business, public policy, case studies and political theory', *World Politics*, 16 (4), 677–715.

Lowi, Theodore J. (1972), 'Four systems of policy, politics, and choice', *Public Administration Review*, 32 (4), 298–310.

Maass, Gero (2002), *Public Private Partnership – Königsweg oder Mythos? Die britischen Gewerkschaften nicht nur hier im Streit mit der Blair-Regierung*, London: Friedrich-Ebert-Stiftung.

Macário, Rosário, Rui Couchinho and Joana Ribeiro (2013), 'Portugal', in Koen Verhoest, Nunzia Carbonara, Veiko Lember, Ole Helby Petersen, Walter Scherrer and Martijn van den Hurk (eds.), *Public Private Partnerships in Transport: Trends and Theory P3T3*, 2013 Discussion Papers. Part I Country Profiles, Brussels: COST, pp. 142–62.

Marriage, Madison (2013), 'Europe courts long-term investment', *Financial Times*, 1 July 2013, p. 9.

Mause, Karsten and Thomas Krumm (2011), 'Public–Private Partnershipping as a tool of government: Exploring its determinants across German states', *German Politics*, 20 (4), 527–44.

Monteiro, Rui Sousa (2005), 'Public–Private Partnerships: Some lessons from Portugal', *EIB Papers*, 10 (2), 72–81.

Nagel, Klaus-Jürgen (2010), 'Spanien – auf den Weg zum Föderalismus?', in Roland Sturm and Jürgen Dieringer (eds.), *Regional Governance in EU-Staaten*, Opladen: Budrich, pp. 149–70.

Nanetti, Rafaella Y. (2007), 'Italy', in Marion Donald Hancock et al. (eds.), *Politics in Europe*, Washington, DC: CQ Press, pp. 279–389.

Nannestad, Peter (2009), 'Das politische System Dänemarks', in Wolfgang Ismayr (ed.), *Die politischen Systeme Westeuropas*, Wiesbaden: VS, pp. 65–106.

National Audit Office (2003), *PFI: Construction Performance*, Report by the Comptroller and Auditor General HC 371 Session 2002–2003: 5 February 2003, London: NAO.

National Audit Office (2008), *Protecting Staff in PPP/PFI Deals*, London: NAO.

Neue Zürcher Zeitung (NZZ) (2011), *Wenn Privatinvestoren den Staat prellen*, 22 August 2011, p. 9.

Niedermayer, Oskar (2006), 'Das Parteiensystem Deutschlands', in Oskar Niedermayer, Richard Stöss and Melanie Haas (eds.), *Die Parteiensysteme Westeuropas*, Wiesbaden: VS, pp. 109–33.

Oosterwaal, Annemarije and René Torenvlied (2010), 'Politics divided from society? Three explanations for trends in societal and political polarization in the Netherlands', *West European Politics*, 33 (2), 258–79.

ÖPP Deutschland AG (2011), *Öffentlich-Private Partnerschaften in Deutschland 2010*, Berlin: ÖPP Deutschland AG.

Organisation for Economic Co-operation and Development (OECD) (2003), *OECD e-Government Studies: Finland 2003*, Written by Edward Lau; with the assistance of Marco Daglio and Stine Dragsted, Paris: OECD Publishing. doi: 10.1787/9789264102613-en.

Organisation for Economic Co-operation and Development (OECD) (2007), *OECD e-Government Studies: Netherlands 2007*, Paris: OECD Publishing. doi: 10.1787/9789264030299-en.

Organisation for Economic Co-operation and Development (OECD) (2008a), *OECD e-Government Studies: Belgium 2008*, Paris: OECD Publishing. doi: 10.1787/9789264055810-en.

Organisation for Economic Co-operation and Development (OECD) (2008b), *Public–Private Partnerships: In Pursuit of Risk Sharing and Value for Money*, Paris: OECD Publishing.

Organisation for Economic Co-operation and Development (OECD) (2010), *Dedicated Public–Private Partnership Units: A Survey of Institutional and Governance Structures*, Paris: OECD Publishing.

Orsina, Giovanni (2011), *Partiti e sistemi di partito in Italia e in Europa nel secondo Dopoguerra*, Soveria Mannelli: Rubbettino.

Osborne, David and Ted Gaebler (1992), *Reinventing Government: How the Entrepreneurial Spirit Is Transforming the Public Sector*, Reading, MA: Addison-Wesley.

Osborne, Stephen P. (2007), 'Introduction', in Stephen P. Osborne (ed.), *Public–Private Partnership: Theory and Practice in International Perspective*, London: Routledge, pp. 1–5.

Palan, Ronen, Richard Murphy and Christian Chavagneux (2010), *Tax Havens: How Globalization Really Works*, Ithaca, NY: Cornell University Press.

Pällmann-Kommission Verkehrsinfrastrukturfinanzierung (2000), 'Schlussbericht', accessed 3 September 2011 at www.bmvbs.de/Anlage/original_5991/Bericht-der-Paellmann-Kommission.pdf.

Paraskevopoulos, Christos J., Panagiotis Getimis and Leeda Demetropoulou (2009), 'Griechenland als Gegenstand europäischer Kohäsionspolitik im Rahmen der EU-Strukturfonds', in Björn Egner and

Georgios Terizakis (eds.), *Das politische System Griechenlands*, Nomos: Baden-Baden, pp. 229–46.

Parker, David (2006), 'The United Kingdom's privatization experiment: The passage of time permits a sober assessment', in Marko Köthenbürger, Hans-Werner Sinn and John Whalley (eds.), *Privatization Experiences in the European Union*, Cambridge, MA: MIT Press (CESifo seminar series), pp. 365–98.

Partnerships Bulletin and Deloitte (2012), *The Global PPP Market 2012*, accessed 6 March 2013 at www.deloitte.com/view/en_GB/uk/industries/infrastructure-and-capital-projects/95d514e0e9c97310VgnVCM3000001c56f00aRCRD.htm.

Pasquino, Gianfranco (2008), 'Italy. The never-ending transition of a democratic regime', in Josep M. Colomer (ed.), *Comparative European Politics*, London: Routledge, pp. 135–73.

Pelinka, Anton and Sieglinde Rosenberger (2007), *Österreichische Politik. Grundlagen, Strukturen, Trends*, Wien: facultas wuv.

Peters, B. Guy and Jon Pierre (2006), 'Introduction', in B. Guy Peters and Jon Pierre (eds.), *Handbook of Public Policy*, London: Sage, pp. 1–9.

Petersen, Ole Helby (2011), 'Public–Private Partnerships as converging or diverging trends in public management? A comparative analysis of PPP policy and regulation in Denmark and Ireland', *International Public Management Review*, 12 (2), 1–37.

Petersen, Ole Helby (2013), 'Denmark', in Koen Verhoest, Nunzia Carbonara, Veiko Lember, Ole Helby Petersen, Walter Scherrer and Martijn van den Hurk (eds.), *Public Private Partnerships in Transport: Trends and Theory P3T3*, 2013 Discussion Papers. Part I Country Profiles, Brussels: COST, pp. 180–96.

Pichler, Christian (2009), *Österreich, ein besseres Deutschland?*, Marburg: Tectum.

Pignon-Xardel, Sophie, Stéphane Manoukian and Laurent Vitse (2009), *Le financement des partenariats public-privé. Problématiques juridiques et financières, pratiques et enjeux*, Paris: Le Moniteur Editions.

Powell, Jonathan (2010), *The New Machiavelli*, London: Vintage.

PPP Forum (2009), *Annual Review 2009*, London.

Privatization Barometer (2011), Database provided by the Fondazione Eni Enrico Mattei (FEEM), accessed 16 February 2011 at http://www.privatizationbarometer.net/index.php.

Quinn, Brid (2010), 'Ireland – rather local than regional', in Roland Sturm and Jürgen Dieringer (eds.), *Regional Governance in EU-Staaten*, Opladen: Budrich, pp. 239–54.

Ragin, Charles (1987), *The Comparative Method: Moving beyond Qualitative and Quantitative Strategies*, Berkeley, CA: University of California Press.
Ragin, Charles (2000), *Fuzzy-Set Social Sciences*, Chicago, IL: University of Chicago Press.
Ragin, Charles (2006), 'Set relations in social research: Evaluating their consistency and coverage', *Political Analysis*, 14, 291–310.
Rásony, Peter (2014), 'Der subventionierte Haustraum. Noch mehr staatliche Kredithilfen für die britische Immobilienbranche', *Neue Zürcher Zeitung*, 20 March 2014, p. 10.
Reeves, Eoin (2003), 'Public–Private Partnerships in Ireland: Policy and practice', *Public Money and Management*, 23 (3), 163–70.
Rekenhof (2009), *Publiek–private samenwerking bij de Vlaamse overhead*, No. Stuk 37-A (2008–2009) – Nr. 1, Brussels.
Reuterskiöld, Gustaf and Malin Cope (2008), 'Sweden', in Maurice Button (ed.), *A Practical Guide to PPP in Europe*, London: City & Financial Publishing, pp. 463–72.
Ribault, Anne (2005), 'Lessons from the French experience in Public and Private Partnership', in Darrin Grimsey and Mervyn K. Lewis (eds.), *The Economics of Public Private Partnerships*, Cheltenham, UK and Northampton, MA, USA: Edward Elgar Publishing, pp. 510–21.
Rodrigues, João and José Reis (2012), 'The asymmetries of European integration and the crisis of capitalism in Portugal', *Competition and Change*, 16 (3), 188–205.
Rodrigues, Miguel and César Madureira (2010), 'Portugal – highly centralised despite European pressures', in Roland Sturm and Jürgen Dieringer (eds.), *Regional Governance in EU-Staaten*, Opladen: Budrich, pp. 255–68.
Roumboutsos, Athena (2013), 'Greece', in Koen Verhoest, Nunzia Carbonara, Veiko Lember, Ole Helby Petersen, Walter Scherrer and Martijn van den Hurk (eds.), *Public Private Partnerships in Transport: Trends and Theory P3T3*, 2013 Discussion Papers. Part I Country Profiles, Brussels: COST, pp. 107–25.
Rügemer, Werner (2008), *'Heuschreckenim' öffentlichen Raum*, Bielefeld: Transcript.
Saalfeld, Thomas (2005), 'Political parties', in Simon Green and William E. Paterson (eds.), *Governance in Contemporary Germany: The Semisovereign State Revisited*, Cambridge: CUP, pp. 46–77.
Sack, Detlef (2009), *Governance und Politics. Die Institutionalisierung öffentlich-privater Partnerschaften in Deutschland*, Baden-Baden: Nomos.
Sadka, Efraim (2007), 'Public–Private Partnerships. A public economics perspective', *CESifo Economic Studies*, 53 (3), 466–90.

Sanz-Menéndez, Luis (2003), 'Public/Private Partnerships and innovation policy: The Spanish experience', Working Paper 03-01, Unidad de Políticas Comparadas (CSIC).

Sarmento, Joaquim Miranda and Luc Renneboog (2014), 'The Portuguese experience with Public–Private Partnership', CentER Discussion Paper Series No. 2014-005, accessed 12 January 2015 at http://ssrn.com/abstract=2378720 and http://dx.doi.org/10.2139/ssrn.2378720.

Sartori, Giovanni (1976), *Parties and Party Systems: A Framework for Analysis*, Cambridge: CUP.

Sawyer, Malcolm (2005), 'The Private Finance Initiative: The UK experience', *Research in Transportation Economics*, 15, 231–45.

Schedler, Kuno and Isabella Proeller (2011), *New Public Management*, Berne: Haupt

Scheidges, Rüdiger (2010), 'Milliarden-IT-Projekt "Herkules" wird zum Debakel', *Handelblatt*, 27 April 2010, accessed 30 August 2011 at www.handelsblatt.com/politik/deutschland/milliarden-it-projekt-herkules-wird-zum-debakel/3421532.html.

Scherrer, Walter (2013), 'Austria', in Koen Verhoest, Nunzia Carbonara, Veiko Lember, Ole Helby Petersen, Walter Scherrer and Martijn van den Hurk (eds.), *Public Private Partnerships in Transport: Trends and Theory P3T3*, 2013 Discussion Papers. Part I Country Profiles, Brussels: COST, pp. 2–17.

Schild, Joachim and Henrik Uterwedde (2006), *Frankreich*, Wiesbaden: VS.

Schneider, Carsten Q. and Claudius Wagemann (2007), *Qualitative Comparative Analysis* (QCA) und Fuzzy Sets, Opladen: Leske & Budrich.

Schumann, Alexander (2004), *Das Verhältnis Portugals zu Europa zwischen Abkehr und Affirmation: ein Beispiel für den Einfluß informeller Institutionen auf den Systemwandel*, Marburg: Tectum.

Scottish Government (2011), *Infrastructure Investment Plan 2011*, Edinburgh: The Scottish Government, accessed at 17 September 2013 at www.scotland.gov.uk/Resource/Doc/364225/0123778.pdf.

Seldon, Anthony (1997), *Major. A Political Life*, London: Phoenix.

SEOPAN (2010), *Distribución de las Licitaciones de Consesiones*, accessed 20 March 2012 at http://www.seopan.es/.

Shaoul, Jean (2005), 'A critical financial analysis of the Private Finance Initiative: Selecting a financing method or allocating economic wealth?', *Critical Perspectives on Accounting*, 16, 441–71.

Shaoul, Jean (2012), 'A review of transport Public–Private Partnerships in the UK', in Graeme A. Hodge, Carsten Greve and Anthony E.

Boardman (eds.), *International Handbook on Public–Private Partnerships*, Cheltenham, UK and Northampton, MA, USA: Edward Elgar Publishing, pp. 548–67.

Shaw, E. (2003), 'Privatization by stealth? The Blair government and Public–Private Partnerships in the National Health Service', *Contemporary Politics*, 9 (3), 277–92.

Siaroff, Alan (1999), 'Corporatism in 24 industrial democracies: Meaning and measurement', *European Journal of Political Research*, 36 (2), 175–205.

Simões, Jorge, Petro Pita Barros and Marta Temido (2010), 'Public–Private Partnerships in the Portuguese health sector', *World Hospital Health Service*, 46 (1), 6–9.

Skidelsky, Robert (2006), 'Gegen die Krise des Liberalismus', in Michael Hüther (ed.), *Klassiker der Ökonomie*, Bonn: BzpB, pp. 169–72.

Spackman, Michael (2002), 'Public–Private Partnerships: Lessons from the British approach', *Economic Systems*, 26, 283–301.

Tálos, Emmerich (1997), 'Sozialpartnerschaft. Kooperation, Konzertierung, politische Regulierung', in Herbert Dachs, Peter Gerlich and Herbert Gottweis (eds.), *Handbuch des politischen Systems Österreichs*, Wien: Manz, pp. 432–51.

Tsebelis, George (2002), *Veto Players: How Political Institutions Work*, Princeton: PUP.

UN Public Administration Network (UNPAN) (2012), *E-Government Survey 2012*, New York, NY: UN, accessed 15 October 2015 at www.unpan.org/e-government.

Unison Scotland (2011), 'PPP/PFI projects in Scotland', Policy Briefing No. 16, Dec. 2011, accessed 27 February 2013 at www.unison-scotland.org.uk/briefings/b016_PolicyBrief_PPPPFIinScotland_December11.pdf.

Unita Tecnica Finanza Di Progetto (UTFP) (2009), *100 Questions and Answers*, accessed 9 May 2011 at www.utfp.it/docs/100 Questions and Answers_2009.pdf.

Uterwedde, Henrik (2009), 'Der unvollendete Wandel der Wirtschaftspolitik', in Joachim Schild and Henrik Utterwedde (eds.), *Die verunsicherte Französiche Republik*, Baden-Baden: Nomos, pp. 87–116.

Van den Hurk, Martijn and Koen Verhoest (2013), 'Flanders, Belgium', in Koen Verhoest, Nunzia Carbonara, Veiko Lember, Ole Helby Petersen, Walter Scherrer and Martijn van den Hurk (eds.), *Public Private Partnerships in Transport: Trends and Theory P3T3*, 2013 Discussion Papers. Part I Country Profiles, Brussels: COST, pp. 18–41.

Van Montfort, C.J. (2008), *Besturen van het onbekende: Goed bestuur bij publiek–private arrangementen*, Den Haag: Lemma.

Vlaamse Regering (2003), *Vlaams Decreet betreffende Publiek–Private Samenwerking*, Brussels.

Wallerstein, Immanuel (2004), *World-Systems Analysis: An Introduction*, Durham, NC: Duke University Press.

Weber, Fritz (2011), 'Verstaatlichung und Privatisierung in Österreich 1945–1986', *ZögU (Journal for Public and Nonprofit Services)*, 34 (2), 126–47.

Wettenhall, Roger (2003), 'Rhetoric and reality of Public–Private Partnership', *Public Organization Review*, 3 (1), 77–107.

Wieland, Leo (2013), 'Viel Beton, wenig Sinn. Haben die EU-Fördermittel Portugals Wirtschaft genutzt oder geschadet?', *Frankfurter Allgemeine Zeitung*, 20 June 2013, p. 19.

Willems, Tom and Wouter van Dooren (2011), 'Lost in diffusion? How collaborative arrangements lead to an accountability paradox', *International Review of Administrative Sciences*, 77, 505–30.

Yescombe, E.R. (2007), *Public–Private Partnerships: Principles of Policy and Finance*, Oxford: Butterworth-Heinemann.

Zervakis, Peter A. and Gustav Auernheimer (2009), 'Das politische System Griechenlands', in Wolfgang Ismayr (ed.), *Die politischen Systeme Westeuropas*, Wiesbaden: VS, pp. 819–68.

Ziekow, Jan (2011), 'Wandel der Staatlichkeit und wieder zurück? PPP im Kontext der deutschen Diskussion um die Rolle des Staates', in Jan Ziekow (ed.), *Wandel der Staatlichkeit und wieder zurück? Die Einbeziehung Privater in die Erfüllung öffentlicher Aufgaben (Public–Private Partnership) in/nach der Weltwirtschaftskrise*, Baden-Baden: Nomos, pp. 43–66.

Zimmer, Annette (2009), 'PPP im Krankenhausbereich: Das Universitätsklinikum Gießen-Marburg als Solitär', *Zeitschrift für Sozialreform*, 55 (3), 253–73.

Zimmermann-Steinhart, Petra and Tessa Kazmeier (2010), 'Frankreich – Der dezentralisierte Einheitsstaat', in Roland Sturm and Jürgen Dieringer (eds.), *Regional Governance in EU-Staaten*, Opladen: Budrich, pp. 173–90.

Zohlnhöfer, Reimut, Herbert Obinger and Frieder Wolf (2008), 'Partisan politics, globalization, and the determinants of privatization proceeds in advanced democracies (1990–2000)', *Governance: An International Journal of Policy, Administration, and Institutions*, 21 (1), 95–121.

Index

Agenda 2010 (Germany) 7
Agentschap voor Infrastructuur in het Onderwijs (AGIOn, Belgium) 102–103
Ahern, Bertie 85, 86, 88, 209, 211
ASFINAG (Austria) 137, 139, 141, 177
Asociación de Empresas Constructoras de Ámbito Nacional (SEOPAN, Spain) 22, 183, 186–9, 205, 235
Australia 70
autonomous communities (Spain) 158, 159, 180, 181, 184, 186, 187, 200, 213
Azienda Autonoma Nazionale delle Strade (ANAS SpA) 165
Aznar, José María 1, 142, 184, 209, 210

Bail Emphytéotique Hospitalier (BEH) 151, 152, 154
Bankia (Spain) 183
banking sector 11, 12, 14, 29, 33, 120, 169, 182, 183, 201, 203
Barroso, José Manuel 171, 178, 209
Berlusconi, Silvio *vii*, 1, 142, 160, 161, 162, 162, 166, 167, 168, 169, 208, 209, 211, 227
Bildt, Carl 63, 64, 65, 209, 211, 213
Blair, Tony 9, 67, 70, 77, 134, 135, 142, 209, 211, 215
Brown, Gordon *vii*, 9, 68, 70, 71, 77, 209, 211, 214, 222
Building Schools for the Future (BSF) 72, 102
Bundesrat 106, 114, 133

Cajas (Spain) 183
Cameron, David 1, 73, 77, 211
Catalonia 182, 187, 189
CDU/CSU (Christian Democrats, Germany) 31, 85, 114, 120, 121, 123, 124, 129, 131, 210, 223,
Centre d'expertise français pour l'observation des partenariats public-privé (CEF-O-PPP) 150, 151
Channel Tunnel 69
Channel Tunnel Rail Link 69
Chirac, Jacques 145, 149, 150, 153, 168, 210
Ciampi, Carlo Azeglio 157, 158, 160, 161, 167
classical Keynesianism 6, 131, 214, 215, 217, 218
clientelism 180, 181, 190, 192, 200, 201
Cohabitation (France) 144, 145, 146, 171
Comisiones Delegados del Gobierno (Inter-Ministerial Committees, Spain) 181
Community Support Framework (CSF, Greece) 194, 198
Comprehensive Spending Review (UK) 74
concessions 150, 151, 162, 164, 168, 169, 175, 177, 182, 183, 184, 185, 186, 187, 188, 189, 204
concession law 27, 28
Conservative Party (UK) 1, 13, 68, 69, 70, 73, 74, 75, 94, 204
Consociationalism 105, 108, 134, 141
Constitutional Council (Conseil Constitutionnel, France) 145, 146, 151, 152, 155, 169
construction sector 31–3, 35, 44, 47, 51, 52, 58, 75, 119, 121, 131, 182, 184, 199, 202, 206

Contrat de Partenariat (France) 152, 154, 155
Cortes Generales (Spain) 180
Court of Auditors 99
credit crunch 13, 14, 30, 33, 92, 148, 154,

D'Alema, Massimo (Italy) 157, 160, 161, 162, 163, 167, 211
Dáil Éireann 81, 82, 83
Danish Enterprise and Construction Authority 55, 57, 210
DBFM contracts 29, 52, 77, 78, 100, 101, 102, 103, 110, 111, 128,
Democrazia Cristiana (DC) 158, 160
devolution 67, 77, 158, 213

Eastern enlargement (EU) 94, 174, 185
Elstat (Greece) 193
Emilia Romana 158, 166
ESA 95 79, 100, 101, 112
Estradas de Portugal (EP) 175, 177, 205
European Central Bank (ECB) 14, 29, 41, 85, 91, 148, 203, 218
European Commission 2, 12, 15, 16, 17, 41, 116
European Investment Bank (EIB) 4, 17, 18, 21, 22, 33, 59, 88, 92, 108, 151, 164, 176, 186, 194, 203
European PPP Expertise Centre (EPEC) 4, 13, 14, 17, 18, 22, 27, 28, 29, 30, 52, 56, 97, 104, 153

Federal Council 106, 114, 115, 120, 133
Fianna Fáil (Ireland) 67, 81, 82, 83, 84, 85, 86, 88, 93, 209
financial sector 29, 31, 33, 34, 35, 44, 47, 51, 52, 84, 85, 93, 161, 169, 183, 184, 206, 207, 219
Flanders 29, 96–103
Flemish government 52, 99–103
Forza Italia 142, 159, 160, 162, 167, 209

global financial crisis 4, 7, 8, 11, 12, 16, 19, 22, 29, 30, 37, 41, 67, 84, 85, 90, 100, 103, 111, 112, 130, 154, 169, 175, 178, 183, 193, 198, 199, 201, 203, 206, 208
gross domestic product (GDP) 5, 11, 12, 16, 24, 25, 26, 38, 39, 40, 44, 45, 46, 47, 48, 49, 51, 52, 53, 66, 84, 85, 93, 135, 141, 156, 174, 176, 182, 184, 189, 193, 197, 201, 207, 219, 220
Guterres, António 175, 178, 211

Herkules (Germany) 119, 131, 132
Hollande, François 13, 14, 146, 153, 156
hung parliament (UK) 68, 93

Institut de la gestion déléguée (IGD) 150, 151
inter-departmental coordination (Denmark) 53
interest group organization pluralism 5, 34, 36, 47, 62, 93, 131, 142, 148, 174, 181, 200, 206
corporatism 5, 34, 36, 50, 53, 62, 65, 67, 82, 87, 93, 107, 112, 115, 131, 134, 135, 140, 142, 148, 173, 183, 218
Inter-Ministerial PPP Committee (Ireland, Greece) 89, 94, 181, 196, 198, 210
International Accounting Standards Board 37
International Financial Services Centre (IFSC) 84
International Monetary Fund (IMF) 41, 85, 91, 179, 180, 193, 219
Irish Business and Employers' Confederation (IBEC) 87

Jospin, Lionel 145, 149, 210,

Karamanlis, Kostas 1, 41, 192, 194, 198, 208, 210
Keynesianism (see also classical and privatised K.) 134, 215, 216, 217,
Kohl, Helmut 9, 116, 117, 123
Kok, Wim 108, 109, 112, 211

legal traditions 4, 5, 26, 27, 28, 29, 35, 47, 66
common law 5, 27, 68, 81, 92
case law 16, 27, 47
civil law/code civil 27, 47, 66, 195
Legge Obiettivo (Italy) 161, 162, 163, 167, 211
Liberal Democrats (UK) 73, 77, 95, 204
Lijphart, Arend 105, 108, 141
Local Government (Contracts) Act 1997 70
London Underground
Boris Johnson 68, 77
Ken Livingston 9, 68
Tube Lines 67, 68
long-term investment funds (LTIFs) 16

Major, John 1, 9, 69, 70, 77, 211, 214, 215,
Merloni laws (Italy) 158, 162, 164, 165, 167, 170, 211
Mission d'appui à la réalisation des partenariats public-privé (MAPPP) 22, 29, 146, 150, 151, 155, 210
Mitterrand, François 144, 145, 149

National Development Finance Agency (NDFA) 86, 88, 211
National Development Plan (Ireland) 84, 86, 88
National Health Service (NHS) 9, 70, 73, 76, 78, 79, 109, 125, 159
Nea Dimokratia (ND, Greece) 142, 189, 192–4, 198, 200, 202, 209, 210
New Labour/Labour Party (UK) 1, 7, 68, 70, 71, 72, 74, 93, 94, 112, 117, 123, 134, 135, 142, 168, 197, 202, 212, 214
New Public Management (NPM) 8, 9, 60, 107,
New Zealand 70
Non-Profit Distributing (NPD, Scotland) 77, 78, 79, 80

Office for Government Commerce (OGC, UK) 70
ÖPP Deutschland AG 122, 123, 126, 130, 131, 132, 210
Operational Task Force (OTF, UK) 71, 72, 77, 94, 211
Osborne, George 74, 75
Österreichische Volkspartei (ÖVP) 134, 135, 136, 141, 142, 143, 209, 210

Pällmann Commission (Germany) 117, 118
Parpública (Participações Públicas, Portugal) 176, 177, 178, 211
Partenariato pubblico-privato (Italy) 162
Partido Popular (PP, Spain) 178, 184
Partnerships UK (PUK) 22, 71, 77, 168, 211
PASOK (Greece) 189, 192, 193, 197, 198
PFI credits 9, 67, 74, 82, 92, 94
policy diffusion 5, 142, 212, 213
Post Office privatization (UK) 68
PPP Acceleration Law (Germany) 32, 120, 121, 194
PPP Policy Team 71, 94
privatized Keynesianism 5, 6, 12, 131, 214-220
privatization 9, 40, 43, 106
Prodi, Romano 157, 160, 161, 162, 165, 166, 167
PSOE (Spain) 183, 184, 209, 210
public sector comparator (PSC) 72, 109, 151, 176, 178, 185, 195, 200

Qualitative Comparative Analysis (QCA) 21, 26, 48, 49, 50, 52

Rajoy, Mario 182, 204
Rassemblement pour la République (RPR) 145, 210
red–green coalition (Germany) 1, 112, 114, 115, 117, 119, 120, 124, 136, 168
Reinfeldt, Fredrik 64, 65, 209
Rete Ferroviaria Italiana (RFI) 165
Ryrie Rules 1, 69, 70, 170

Sarkozy, Nicolas *vii*, 1, 13, 22, 146, 147, 149, 150, 156, 168, 169, 193, 202, 209, 210
Scharping, Rudolf 119
Schröder, Gerhard *vii*, 7, 120, 123, 134, 136, 141, 142, 143, 209, 210
Schüssel, Wolfgang 1, 114, 134, 135, 136, 138, 141, 143, 208, 209, 210, 213,
Scottish government 77, 78, 79
Scottish Futures Trust (SFT) 77, 78
Scottish National Party (SNP) 77, 78
SCUT model (Portugal) 175, 178, 205, 207
Simitis, Konstantinos 197, 198
social partnerships (Ireland) 81, 82, 84, 93, 134,
Soffin (Germany) 11
Social Democrats 53, 54, 55, 60, 62, 63, 64, 65, 106
SPD (Germany) 32, 115, 120, 121, 123, 124, 130, 134, 141, 142, 143, 202, 209, 210
SPÖ (Austria) 134, 136
Special Secretariat
  Greece 41, 194–8, 202, 208, 210
  Ireland 89, 94
Stability and Growth Pact 148, 149
State Authorities (PPP Arrangements) Act 2002 (Ireland) 86, 88
State guarantees 11, 14, 26, 28, 29, 30, 154, 169, 202
Supreme Court 68

Toll Collect (Germany) 21, 114, 118, 119, 123, 131, 132, 142, 143, 168
Trans European Network (TEN) 42, 156
Tremonti, Giulio 161, 168
Troika (ECB, EU, IMF) 41, 85, 91, 174, 193

Union pour un Movement Populaire (UMP) 13, 145, 156, 209, 210
Unità Tecnica Finanza di Progetto (UTFP) 161–4, 166–8, 211

Vanhanen, Matti 59, 60, 65, 209
Verhofstadt, Guy 98
Verkehrsinfrastrukturfinanzierungs-gesellschaft (VIFG, Germany) 118, 119
veto players *viii*, 4, 5, 30, 31, 35, 44, 47, 50, 51, 52, 68, 96, 108, 111, 115, 160, 172, 181, 199, 207, 208, 212, 213

Wallonia (Belgium) 97, 104, 105

Zapatero, José Luis Rodríguez 183, 184, 208, 209, 210